Philosophy Through Video Gai

How can *Wii Sports* teach us about metaphysics? Can playing *World of Warcraft* lead to greater self-consciousness? How can we learn about aesthetics, ethics, and divine attributes from *Zork*, *Grand Theft Auto*, and *Civilization*? A variety of increasingly sophisticated video games are rapidly overtaking books, films, and television as America's most popular form of media entertainment. It is estimated that by 2011 over 30 percent of US households will own a Wii console—about the same percentage that owned a television in 1953.

In *Philosophy Through Video Games*, Jon Cogburn and Mark Silcox—philosophers with game industry experience—investigate the aesthetic appeal of video games, their effect on our morals, the insights they give us into our understanding of perceptual knowledge, personal identity, artificial intelligence, and the very meaning of life itself, arguing that video games are popular precisely because they engage with longstanding philosophical problems. Topics covered include:

- The Problem of the External World
- Dualism and Personal Identity
- Artificial and Human Intelligence in the Philosophy of Mind
- The Idea of Interactive Art
- The Moral Effects of Video Games
- Games and God's Goodness

Games discussed include: *Madden Football, Wii Sports, Guitar Hero, World of Warcraft, Sims Online, Second Life, Baldur's Gate, Knights of the Old Republic, Elder Scrolls, Zork, EverQuest Doom, Halo 2, Grand Theft Auto, Civilization, Mortal Kombat, Rome: Total War, Black and White, Aidyn Chronicles.*

Jon Cogburn is Associate Professor of Philosophy at Louisiana State University.

Mark Silcox is Assistant Professor of Humanities and Philosophy at the University of Central Oklahoma.

Philosophy Through
Video Games

Jon Cogburn and Mark Silcox

Routledge
Taylor & Francis Group

NEW YORK AND LONDON

First published 2009
by Routledge
270 Madison Ave, New York, NY 10016

Simultaneously published in the UK
by Routledge
2 Park Square, Milton Park, Abingdon, Oxon OX14 4RN

*Routledge is an imprint of the Taylor & Francis Group,
an informa business*

© 2009 Taylor & Francis

Typeset in Sabon by
RefineCatch Limited, Bungay, Suffolk
Printed and bound in the United States of America on acid-free paper
by Edwards Brothers, Inc.

British Library Cataloguing in Publication Data
A catalogue record for this book is available from the British Library

Library of Congress Cataloging in Publication Data
A catalog record has been requested for this book

ISBN10: 0–415–98857–8 (hbk)
ISBN10: 0–415–98858–6 (pbk)
ISBN10: 0–203–87786–1 (ebk)

ISBN13: 978–0–415–98857–5 (hbk)
ISBN13: 978–0–415–98858–2 (pbk)
ISBN13: 978–0–203–87786–9 (ebk)

Contents

Preface   vi
Acknowledgments   x
Note on Book's Webpage   xiii

1 I, Player: The Puzzle of Personal Identity
   (MMORPGs and Virtual Communities)   1

2 The Game Inside the Mind, the Mind Inside
   the Game (The Nintendo Wii Gaming Console)   17

3 "Realistic Blood and Gore": Do Violent
   Games Make Violent Gamers? (First-Person Shooters)   50

4 Games and God's Goodness (World-Builder
   and Tycoon Games)   73

5 The Metaphysics of Interactive Art (Puzzle and
   Adventure Games)   91

6 Artificial and Human Intelligence (Single-Player RPGs)   109

7 Epilogue: Video Games and the Meaning of Life   135

Notes   156
Bibliography   182
Index   191

Preface

The most famous philosophers of the Western tradition have traditionally been depicted in art, literature, and popular culture as spacey dreamers with their heads in the clouds, lost in silent contemplation of massive tomes or falling down well shafts while staring at the stars. To anyone who takes this image of the philosophical life seriously, it must be hard to imagine how the revelatory insights that philosophy is supposed to provide could be achieved while playing a video game. Gazing up at the heavens and pondering life's deepest conundrums might provide its own distinctive set of rewards, but it certainly won't get you very far in *Doom*. Most such games require the sort of focused concentration on private, short-term goals that has traditionally been viewed as strictly incompatible with the types of gratification that are distinctive of philosophy.

So why suppose that one *can* achieve philosophical wisdom through the medium of video games? If we're right in thinking that people do, then the path must begin at some point a little *after* one has fought off the demons, won the virtual golf tournament, or at the very least, pressed the "pause" button. The work of a philosopher begins when the mind takes hold of whatever residual thoughts remain, once one has succeeded (or failed) at the highly specific tasks set by the game. Fortunately, in our experience at least, there is almost always at least some such residuum. Whether she is taking a break from something as simpleminded as *Pac-Man* or from a work of art as deep and involving as *BioShock*, the habitual gamer always eventually finds herself pondering some vivid piece of imagery, some quirk of gameplay, or some anomalous feature of the diegetic world that she has just been inhabiting. What would it be like to *be* Pac-Man? To live on Myst island? To rule one's very own world? These thoughts can flicker out of existence as quickly as they arrive. But for the philosophically inclined, they might also lead to deep confusion, sleep loss, a change of career, or an experience of conversion.

Although few gamers realize it, when they engage in these sort of reflections they are taking part in an ancient practice that runs through the whole history of Western culture. The systematic, self-conscious practice of philosophy in fact grew out of earlier historical pursuits that were far closer to game-play than they were to abstract reasoning. As Johan Huizinga points out in his magnificent book about "the play element in culture," *Homo Ludens*,[1] philosophical argumentation was first carried out by the sophists of ancient Greece through the medium of the *epidexis*, a form of public rhetorical performance. These displays of verbal acuity, to which certain of the Greek sophists such as Gorgias and Prodicus would sometimes charge an attendance fee, often centered around the examination of riddle-questions like "What is the same everywhere and nowhere?" or "All Cretans are liars; I am a Cretan. Am I lying now?"[2] Huizinga proposes that the origins of philosophy in gameplay are evident in many of its most distinctive values and practices: "May it not be that in all logic," he wonders, "and particularly in the syllogism, there is always a tacit understanding to take the terms and concepts for granted as one does the pieces on a chess-board" (*Ludens* 152–153)?

Given these historical facts, it is perhaps surprising that the great Western philosophers have had so little to say about the practice of game-playing. Of course, the idea that philosophy itself is a game—a frivolous distraction from the serious occupations of making money, saying one's prayers, or protecting Our People from the Bad Guys Over the Hill—is as old as philosophy itself.[3] More subtle and provocative analogies between philosophy and game-play have been suggested by Thomas Hobbes, who seemed to think that the rational decision to leave the state of nature and cast in one's lot with a civilized culture is a decision that closely resembles the strategic projections of game-play, and by Ludwig Wittgenstein, whose famous analogy between games and human languages has excited some contemporary philosophers while leaving others perplexed.[4]

But perhaps the most famous modern philosophical argument about games is John Stuart Mill's criticism of the view that "push-pin is as good as poetry." Mill was a hedonist—he thought, that is, that the only thing in the world with any intrinsic value is pleasure. But Mill was horrified by the thesis endorsed by other hedonistically inclined philosophers (especially his forerunner Jeremy Bentham) that the difference in value between simple-minded games such as push-pin[5] and great works of art can only be established by determining which provides the largest number of people with the greatest amount of pleasure in the real world. If more people have gotten their kicks from playing *Joust* than from looking at paintings by Manet, then according to Bentham's standard, this makes *Joust* more objectively valuable. Against this, Mill argued that a distinction needs to be drawn between what he called "lower" and "higher" pleasures. The latter species of pleasures, he thought, might have more genuine value even if a lot fewer people are in a position to enjoy them, because they would be chosen by what he called "competent judges,"—highly experienced people with access to a broad basis for comparison.[6]

Contemporary ethical theorists have tended to take rather a high-minded and dismissive attitude toward this dispute. Many of them have wondered (in a broadly Kantian vein) why any serious moralist (as opposed to, say, a French chef or a rock musician) would bother to concern herself with such grubby matters as trying to discern the "higher pleasures," when she could instead be composing rhapsodies about the importance of social justice, self-sacrifice, or eternal salvation. But there has been something of an upsurge of Millian sentiment in the philosophy of the past twenty years or so. Books with names like *Philosophy Goes to the Movies, Philosophy of Wine, The Philosophy of Erotic Love,* and even *The Philosophy of Horror*[7] have been hitting the bookshelves in large numbers, and drawing a surprisingly enthusiastic readership. Not all of the authors of these works have been committed to the truth of philosophical hedonism. But all of them do seem to believe that it is the business of philosophy to understand how we have fun, and to provide substantive reasons why, for example, most old French Burgundies are better than most young Australian Shirazes, or why *Curse of the Demon* is more worth watching than *Friday the 13th*.

The philosophically informed love of video games that we developed in our youth, and that continues to enrich our lives today, leads us to hope that we can perform something like the same service for some of the greatest works of art within this massively popular but still under-analyzed new medium. Both of us witnessed the development of video games as a form of entertainment and (eventually) of art at about the same pace that we developed our consuming interest in philosophy. We remember *PONG* hitting our local convenience stores around the time that we first began to experience rudimentary curiosity about where the universe might have come from. The PC revolution, and all of the wonderful text and graphical adventure games (*Zork, King's Quest, Ultima*) that came in its wake, arrived when we began to have doubts about the central tenets of our religious upbringing. The Nintendo 64 hit the stores while we were both slaving away at our doctoral dissertations, and the glorious, revelatory beauty of even the earliest three-dimensional games for this console cheered us both up through what are normally some of the bleakest days in the life of any career academic.

Of course, there is plenty in video games to interest the philosopher, independently of whether he or she thinks that any of them are truly valuable works of art. Their mere novelty as an entertainment medium, and the enormous amount of logical and psychological effort that goes into the production of even the simplest (and ugliest) of games, are phenomena that are by themselves certainly worthy of serious philosophical attention. Nonetheless, in addition to hoping that the reader will be persuaded by the metaphysical, epistemological, ethical, and aesthetic arguments herein, we also hope to show that the appeal of many video games is closer to that of great poetry than it is to the transparent and forgettable charms of push-pin.

In each of the following seven chapters, we begin by describing a puzzle that arises from reflection on some particular genre or species of video game.

Why do players identify so closely with the protagonists of multi-player Role Playing Games? Is it rational for them to do so? How should the surprising success of the Wii be expected to influence the future of game design, and why was it so unanticipated? What (if anything) might be morally wrong with playing violent video games? How close does the expert at world-building games like *Black and White, Rome: Total War,* and *Civilization* really come to "playing God?" What does the phenomenon of interactivity tell us more generally about the aesthetic experiences that are part of shared humanity and the good life? Why is the "artificial intelligence" in video games so bad? Any serious attempt to answer these apparently straightforward questions must end up drawing heavily upon the resources of Western Philosophy. In addition, we try to show how plausible solutions to at least some of these puzzles support legitimate and creative contributions to this ancient and justifiably venerated tradition.

Our approach to the philosophical discussion of video games reflects the type of training that both of us received in the North American philosophy departments where we were educated, and where we have both found professional homes. In most English speaking universities, so-called "analytic" philosophy has been the dominant school of thought for over a century. Analytic philosophers tend to take the view that the problems of philosophy are best discussed separately and on their own terms, rather than from the perspective of some overarching worldview, metaphysical theory, or ideology. The specifically philosophical issues that we have elected to focus upon here—the problem of the external world, the puzzle of personal identity, the nature of intelligence, and the questions of whether the depiction of violence is immoral, whether morality can be based on religious belief, and what makes an artwork what it is—are those that have seemed to us to arise most naturally from reflection on the most popular contemporary genres of video games. Thus, while this book may profitably be read from beginning to end, any chapter can also be read out of order by the reader who is specifically interested in its central topic. All of this being said, we ourselves have some reservations about the lack of a broader perspective in much contemporary philosophy. In our last chapter we will try to adopt such a perspective by considering in some detail what video games might have to teach us about the overall meaning of human life itself.

We hope that these discussions will strike a chord or two with fans of video games who have at some point or other been provoked to abstract speculation by the casting of a spell, the killing of a monster, or the exploration of a virtual world. Philosophical wisdom arises from the strangest, most unpredictable wellsprings. Writing this book has only served to strengthen our conviction that video games represent a rich and hitherto largely untapped philosophical resource.

Acknowledgments

If Emily Beck Cogburn had not proofread several drafts of each chapter, and each time given us incisive and detailed comments for rewriting, this book would have been twice as long and half as good. And it would have been one-fourth as good if our Routledge editor Kate Ahl had not also provided such thoughtful, detailed, and rigorous assistance during the entire project. We would also like to offer similar thanks to Routledge editorial assistants Mathew Kopel and Michael Andrews.

We thank the philosophers, teachers, and writers whose work we have found to be indispensable in thinking about video games: Adam Cadre, Noël Carroll, Andy Clark, Amy Coplan, Chris Crawford, Eva Dadlez, Surendranath Dasgupta, Richard Dawkins, Daniel Dennett, Ronald de Sousa, Sandra Dodd, Jacques Dubucs, Georg Feuerstein, Stanley Fish, Patrick Fitzgerald, William Gibson, Ian Hacking, Kathleen Higgins, Douglas Hofstadter, Nick Hornby, Douglas Kellner, Peter Ludlow, Bryan Magee, Greil Marcus, Graham Nelson, Alva Noë, Camille Paglia, Derek Parfit, Graham Priest, Andrew Plotkin, John Protevi, Hilary Putnam, Roger Scruton, Johanna Seibt, Mary Sirridge, Francis Sparshott, Robert Solomon, Stephen Stich, Neil Tennant, Evan Thompson, Francisco Varela, Michael Wheeler, Mark Wilson, Mark J. P. Wolf, and Crispin Wright. If the manuscript *had* turned out four times as long, the ideas of all of these thinkers would have been discussed much more extensively.

One of the things that make video games nice to philosophize about is that nearly everybody has opinions about them. The illuminating conversations we've had with friends and colleagues about the relevance of games to philosophy have been the most fun part of the writing process. People who deserve special thanks in this regard are: Karynne Abel, Michael Aristidou, Andrew Arlig, Jack Arnold, Chris Blakley, Mary Brodnax, Jeff Brody, Robbie Burleigh, Eric Caudill, Chris Cogburn, Thomas Mike Cogburn, Roy Cook, Brandon Cooke, Damon Crumley, Ian Crystal, John Curtis, Logan Dixon, David Donahoe, James Donellon, James Donovan, Troy Fassbender, Mark Ferguson, Chris Fillebrown, Salvatore Florio, Jason Glenn, Nicole Goldie, Christopher J. Hamilton, Jeremy Hanna, Neal Hebert, Charles Hollingsworth, Derrick Huff, John Ickes, Laurent Kieff, Shaun King, Ira

Knox, Stetson Kveum, Brendan Lalor, Sean Lane, Bob Lee, Courtney Lewis, Jim Lewis, David (Ty) Lightner, Roderick Long, Drew Martin, Jason Megill, Mario Mejia, Bill Melanson, James Mock, Brian Morton, Seth Murphy, Doug Orton, Scott Orton, Chet Pilley, Lauri Pixley, N. Mark Rauls, Chris Ray, Justin Rice, Randy Robinson, Jeffrey Roland, Robert Rose, Joe Salerno, Tracey Salewski, Tom Salewski, Heidi Silcox, Mary Silcox, Ed Slovik, James Spence, Craig Taylor, Frank Torres, Eric Ward, Margaret Wilson, Rob Wilson, Sean Whittington, Eryn Whitworth, Ian Van Cleaf, Jonathan Tall, Cathal Woods, Franklin Worrell, and Wei Zhao.

Rebecca Hurst and Logan Larson were our research assistants during the latter stages of the book's completion. Their thoughtful suggestions and intelligent observations about gaming saved us from committing a number of bloopers, and we greatly enjoyed our discussions of the book's philosophical content with both of them. We wish them many triumphs in their future academic careers.

Jon Cogburn would like to thank Louisiana State University for sabbatical leave (academic year 2007–8), which made it possible to finish the book in a timely manner. Given the severe financial and human exigencies faced by Louisiana as the result of Hurricanes Katrina and Rita, this was entirely unexpected. After all that has happened it has been overwhelming to be a part of Louisiana's strong commitment to offering an excellent (and free) college education to all residents. Cogburn would also like to thank the members of the original steering committee for LSU's Laboratory for Creative Arts and Technology (now the Human and Social World subgroup of LSU's Center for Computation and Technology): Jorge Arevena, Stephen Beck, Ralph Izard, John Lynn, and Susan Ryan. It was great, even if for a brief time, to be an integral part of a group so committed to the centrality of the human–computer interface to the academic study of information technology. It was, and still is, a beautiful dream.

Mark Silcox would like to thank all of his colleagues, students, and friends at the University of Central Oklahoma's College of Liberal Arts for the colossal leap of faith that they took in hiring him, and for providing a deeply civilized and intellectually engaging workplace environment. He is very grateful to his sister, Mary Silcox, and his father, Peter Silcox, for their sound advice and support during a period when his academic career seemed to be dangling headfirst over a gloomy precipice. He would also like to thank G. Christopher Klug for hiring him as a writer for both *Aidyn Chronicles: The First Mage* and *Earth and Beyond*, and for providing such a friendly and enlightening introduction to the world of professional game design.

Nephews, nieces, and offspring who have prevented us from completely embracing our cyborg future include: Austin Songhua Chu, Thomas Beck Cogburn, John, Meredith, and Paul Reimann, and Alex, Avery, Jon, and Trevor Wilson.

Finally, we dedicate this book to our mothers, Helen Cogburn and Antonia Silcox. Though we discovered the pleasures of video gaming by ourselves, it was because of our mothers' guidance, love, and conversation that both of us learned to love reading.

Note on Book's Webpage

We strongly encourage readers of this book to avail themselves of the web resources posted at http://www.projectbraintrust.com/ptvg/. For each chapter we have included a list of key words, arguments, links mentioned in the text, and discussion questions. We also include links to a moderated discussion board, web resources for writing philosophy papers, a glossary, and download sites for freeware games related to each chapter's discussion. The content of the site is not static, and will be expanded and improved based on discussion board consensus. We hope that these resources will prove helpful to teachers who want to use the book in courses on philosophy and game design as well as to readers who are tackling it by themselves.

1 I, Player: The Puzzle of Personal Identity (MMORPGs and Virtual Communities)

1.1 The Problem

Chris and Alayne Edwards owned adjacent plots of land. Alayne liked to work in her garden; Chris performed science experiments in the main room of his house. They got into the habit of paying visits back and forth to admire each others' handiwork, and had discussions about their hobbies and enthusiasms that lasted well into the night. During these conversations, something clicked, and friendship turned into courtship. They passed a memorable weekend together at a nearby resort owned by friends, spending the daylight hours exploring the luxurious grounds and the nighttime enjoying candlelit dinners in the open air.

Then, Chris made the bold move of catching a plane across the Atlantic to meet Alayne face to face for the very first time. To their genuine surprise, they had a great time, and soon decided to get married.[1]

Does this story hang together? Perhaps it will appear less paradoxical if we point out that the events described in the first paragraph all took place within the virtual community *Second Life*, while the flight across the Atlantic and subsequent marriage happened in what people like to think of as the "real" world.

Video game players tell less dramatic, but equally paradoxical stories to one another all the time. When recounting one's progress the previous night through the newest chapter of *Halo* or an unexplored stretch of Azeroth in *World of Warcraft*, one will often say things like "*I* killed a dozen members of the Covenant" or "*I* had a planning meeting with the other members of the Jewelcrafter's Guild." But does the personal pronoun in these sentences really refer to you, the person who sat in her basement eating pizza and clicking a PC mouse until dawn? On the one hand, it's hard to see how it could; after all, *you* certainly didn't kill anyone, and you probably haven't ever manufactured a piece of jewelry in your life. On the other hand, when Chris and Alayne told their friends "*I* have fallen in love with my next-door neighbor!" it certainly seems as though they were saying something true.

This is the newest version of an old philosophical puzzle. It turns out to be extraordinarily unclear exactly what is going on when a person says "I remember growing up," for example, or "I lost half my body weight," or "I'll get a good grade if I force myself to study." Our ability to use these sorts of expressions meaningfully seems to presuppose knowledge of a clear *criterion of identity*, a reliable way, that is, of telling: (1) when something still counts as the same object or person after having undergone changes over a period of time, and (2) what makes two different things or people different from one another.

People are especially tricky, since we all go through both psychological and physical changes throughout our entire lives. For example, a relative of one of this book's authors used to countenance voting for George Bush in 2000 by saying, "George Bush is not the same person he was before finding Jesus in his forties. He's grown up." Then, four years later, as a prelude to telling you why he might vote for Bush in 2004, the relative would say, "George Bush is not the same person he was before September 11. He's grown up."

Whatever their merit in the case of the 43rd President of the United States, such observations about someone's becoming a "different person" often do have a certain plausibility, especially when we assess whether people are morally responsible for past actions. However, these ways of speaking also contradict other well-entrenched linguistic practices. The 43rd President still talks on the phone with his father and calls him "Dad." If a completely different person was instantiated in his region of space-time, would it be at all rational for him (the new person) to continue this sort of a relationship with the elder Bush?

Note also that the locution "he's not himself" can correctly describe many states of consciousness, from mild grumpiness to full blown dementia. But how can one not be oneself? Doesn't logic itself dictate that everything is what it is, and not what it is not?

The strange use of the word "I" by participants in role-playing games, from tabletop *Dungeons and Dragons* (*D & D*) all the way to Massively Multiplayer Online Role Playing Games (MMORPGs) like *Everquest* and *World of Warcraft*, not only adds a new level of complexity to the whole discussion, but also ends up providing support for some fascinating philosophical theses concerning the nature of the self. In this chapter, we will first examine (and dismiss) the view that the contested class of statements in the first person are all simply false. Then we will delve more deeply into the nature of the self to solve our original puzzle about the relationship between the "I" of the player and the "I" of the player's avatar. We will arrive at the metaphysically surprising conclusion that the temporal and spatial boundaries of the self are fundamentally *vague*.

1.2 A Fictional Self?

We begin by examining more closely the relevant kinds of self-ascriptions that Role Playing Game (RPG) players are likely to make. A puzzling fact about these games is that the rules often allow the player's avatar (the entity that represents the player, usually by carrying out actions dictated by the player's manipulation of the game controllers) to do things that the player herself clearly *can't* do. In these circumstances, it seems as though the character/avatar's identity is partially constructed by the game master or computer or programming team. If the character does something the player is incapable of, it is extremely misleading for the player to ascribe the character's actions to herself. It is the apparent intractability of this problem that might tempt some philosophers to throw up their hands and just say that all such self-ascriptions are false.

1.2.1 Role-Playing

There is a sense in which role-playing games are as old as the impulse that we've all felt as children to say to one another "Let's pretend . . ." But the idea that such games are more fun with explicit, mathematized rules, and that they can be played just as effectively through conversation and die-rolling as they can through schoolyard play-acting, is a much more recent innovation.

Commercial RPGs first became popular during the mid-1970s, via the craze for tabletop games such as *Traveler, Paranoia, Top Secret*, and, most famously, *D & D*. One thing that distinguished these games from close cousins like *Clue, Monopoly*, and *Axis and Allies* was the unusual way that the player was represented within the game. Instead of being signified by a little plastic counter, a metal car, or fifty cardboard hexagons with tanks printed on them, the tabletop RPG player makes a long series of die rolls to "create a character." The result of each roll is taken to represent one of a group of basic character traits such as physical strength, intelligence, charm, dexterity, and so on. Further rolls and calculations are made to determine each character's more specialized skills, e.g., programming computers, making public speeches, climbing mountains, or taming animals. Each character's attributes get recorded on a sheet of paper at the outset of the game, and are referenced at later points to determine things like the outcomes of fights or negotiations with non-player characters. For example, a character's Dexterity score will determine how likely she is to successfully hit an unarmed person with her bare fist, should she decide to do so (the score determines how high the player's die roll has to be for a successful hit). Her Strength will determine how much damage her fist can do. Each character has a finite number of Hit Points, which are lost when the character is wounded and regained upon healing.

Such mechanisms of "character creation" are still present in most contemporary MMORPGs like *Everquest, Anarchy Online*, and *World of Warcraft*. When a player joins any of these games for the first time, she is expected to "customize" an in-game character in a variety of ways similar to those just described, as well as others that range from choosing a suitable name to picking a polygonal 3-D avatar's height, gender, skin color, and facial configuration.

But sophisticated players of tabletop role-playing games are able to go a step further. They can actually "play" their characters, in the sense that their success in the game can depend upon how good they are at pretending to be the people represented by the statistics that they have recorded on their "character sheets." Among especially serious players of *D & D* and other tabletop RPGs, it is often forbidden to speak in one's own voice during a game, rather than the voice of the character that the player is supposed to be. And even when this convention isn't strictly observed, a competent GM (i.e., "game master"—or "Dungeon Master," or "Administrator," or whatever the person is called who controls events in the game-world) will reward players for performing their parts plausibly, and penalize them for acting "out of character."

There is simply no parallel to this phenomenon in computer RPGs. It is practically impossible to imagine how one could even begin to program a computer to pass spontaneous judgment upon how well some human player imitates a dwarf, a wizard, a paladin, or whatever. Real, theatrical role-playing still does take place in contemporary MMORPGs though. In fact, the universe of *World of Warcraft* contains some designated "role-playing realms" in which players are encouraged to act "in character" through the game's instant messaging system. But there are no palpable in-game rewards like the finding of treasure or the earning of experience points made available to the player for being good at this. To achieve these goals, all the player can do is to have her character attempt the various tasks that the game actually puts before her, such as crawling through a cave or fighting off trolls, and then wait while the computer crunches numbers to find out if she succeeds or fails. This can often be a lot of fun, but it is also something quite different from actually pretending to be another person.

There is a powerful sense, then, in which pen-and-paper tabletop RPGs are more liberating works of interactive art than MMORPGs. But there is another sense in which they are far more constraining. A *D & D* player of average intelligence who tries to step into the role of a character who is a total genius will need constant hints and cues from the GM about how she should use her talents most effectively in the game-world. The same problem applies to many of the other primary or secondary character traits that are usually represented in these games with a simple quantitative score, such as Wisdom, Courage, and (perhaps most dramatically) Charisma.[2] In order to achieve any kind of realism, the GM must be imaginative and quick-witted enough to keep the players honest about how their characters would behave, and to make compensatory adjustments whenever there is an inconsistency between what can reasonably be expected of the player and what one would expect of her character. Sometimes these adjustments will come in the form of mere suggestions to do things differently. Sometimes they are enforced by having non-player characters (also known as NPCs, the human and non-human agents controlled by the game master) respond to the player's actions in various ways. And sometimes the GM must prohibit certain sorts of behavior outright. When a wealthy Paladin who is supposed to be in the 98th percentile for charm goes around the *D & D* game-world spitting on the ground and cursing at shopkeepers, something has clearly gone wrong in a way that it never could in a video game. For, assuming that a game like *World of Warcraft* allowed spitting as a possible action, all the Paladins could simply be *programmed* not to do it.

RPGs present us with plenty of contexts in which players say "*I do X*" even though the action they describe is utterly beyond their capacities. Of course, when the claim in question is something like, "*I charm the dragon,*" this is so for the uninteresting reason that the player herself lives in a world that does not contain any dragons. But when the claim is something more like "*I charm the shopkeeper,*" a problem of interpretation arises just because the person speaking may not be especially gifted with bargaining savvy. In these cases, the GM and programmer must help the character manifest a virtue that some human beings in the real world have, but that the player herself systematically lacks. But then there is a sense in which the player can't even really *play* the character at all. The character's rational behavior is mostly a function of the game master or computer that is playing the character *for* her. Under these specific circumstances, it seems especially misleading for the player to say, "*I charmed the shopkeeper.*"

We cannot stress strongly enough the omnipresence of this disconnect between character and player in RPGs. Smart players play dumb characters and vice versa. Charismatic players play charmless characters and vice versa. Lawful good players play chaotic evil characters and vice versa.

Indeed, the problem is so prevalent that one of the primary skills of a decent GM is seamlessly and non-intrusively guiding and shaping all of the players' behavior to help craft an entertaining yet believable narrative.[3] Given the all-pervasive role of the game master (or the programming team) here, must it not be false for the player to think that she is speaking about *herself* in any coherent sense whatsoever, when she describes the actions of her character?

1.2.2 Naïve Fictionalism

The simplest solution to this problem would be to adopt a position of naïve fictionalism toward the claims that are made by participants in RPGs when they are speaking "in character." This approach amounts to saying that the claims in question are simply *false*.[4] When a *D & D* player tells the GM "*I search the dungeon for treasure,*" or when a participant in *Second Life* says "Last night I redecorated my house," their assertions fall into the same semantic category as more straightforwardly implausible remarks like "Ben Franklin was President of the United States" or "My sister is a pumpkin."

An unsophisticated fictionalist interpretation of the gamer's use of "I" has considerable intuitive appeal. There are two major problems with it, though. The first is relatively obvious: when gamers make these sorts of claims, informed, rational people don't normally *treat* them as though they were false. It would be weird, after all, for the GM of a tabletop game to respond to a player's assertion that she's searching the dungeon by saying "No, you're not—you're here in the dining room of my apartment!"

The second, trickier problem arises when a player says something in character that clearly would be true even if it were said in a more everyday context. Take, for example, the following assertion: "I noticed for the first time yesterday that it's difficult for a person to tip over a cow,"[5] and imagine it being made by a player of *Asheron's Call*, a popular early MMORPG from the 1990s in which it was possible (though tricky) for player characters to tip over virtual cows in the diegetic realm (i.e., the fictitious video game world that is typically represented on a 2-D monitor). Even if it were clear from the context that the person was talking about an event in the game, she also in this case happens to be saying something that is *clearly* true, both about her own epistemic state and about a property of real-life cows. To say (as the naïve fictionalist must) that the claim is false merely because of the slightly peculiar context in which the word "I" is being used would be explanatory overkill.

Clearly, then, we must look for a better approach to solving our original puzzle about the RPG player's use of "I" than that of the naïve fictionalist. Our problem would be solved if we could avail ourselves of a less naïve philosophical understanding of the nature of fiction itself,[6] which is surely necessary in any case. Whatever else might set apart fictional narratives from other forms of art and human communication, the view that it is simply their *falsehood* is catastrophically simple-minded.

However, rather than trying to work out such a theory we will focus here upon issues about the metaphysical status of the self that arise specifically in the context of video games. We will show that certain philosophical concerns strongly motivate a philosophy of the self that allows us to differentiate true first-person avowals ("I met Alayne last night" being true in the real world even if only their avatars had met) from ambiguous ones ("I have an eighteen Charisma" being true in the game world and false in reality), while leaving a vague area in between ("I am brave" used to refer to uncharacteristic honesty exhibited on a person's own MySpace page).

1.3 The Temporally Vague Self

Here we examine the attempts of some major philosophers in the Western tradition to construct a general, metaphysically plausible criterion of identity for objects and persons over time. We will look at René Descartes' views on these topics, since his contributions to the subject in the seventeenth century have been by far the most influential in the history of Western philosophy. Then, we'll examine some reasons offered by the skeptical eighteenth-century Scottish philosopher David Hume for doubting that there could be any criterion of identity whatsoever for the human self. Our main conclusion will be that the self is temporally vague. In Section 2.4, we will go on to examine Andy Clark's "extended mind hypothesis" in order to argue that the self is also spatially vague. We will show how this vagueness renders coherent and plausible some of the ways players of video games use the word "I."

1.3.1 Our Cartesian Heritage: Criteria for Identity

Questions about the nature of human selfhood have usually been discussed by philosophers as instances of a more basic and abstract issue in metaphysics: the problem of persistence through change. How can we make sense of the superficially paradoxical fact that an object can undergo changes over a period of time while remaining (in some metaphysically significant way) exactly the "same thing?" All human beings change as they grow into adulthood, casting off old molecules, beliefs, commitments, and projects as they continuously take on new ones. At the same time, most of us keep the same proper names, and are easily re-identifiable by other human beings who know us as "the same person" each time they meet us throughout all of these processes of transformation. Furthermore, it is pretty clear that if we couldn't rely on both of these things taking place, we wouldn't be able to understand the conventions for using words like "I" and "you" in RPGs at all, let alone anywhere else.

1.3.1.1 The Parmenidean Challenge

The earliest philosophers of the ancient world found the phenomenon of persistence through change quite puzzling. Surely, they reasoned, it is simply a *contradiction* to say about anything that it is "the same, yet different" today from how it was yesterday. The Greek thinker Parmenides proposed a radical solution to this puzzle; in a strange metaphysical poem written in the sixth century BCE, he argued that all change that takes place over time is an illusion. The universe, for Parmenides, is really just a single undifferentiated thing, "like the bulk of a well-rounded ball,"[7] and our attempts to think of any part of it as undergoing change are uniformly paradoxical. His argument for this startling conclusion is rather obscure. There are two "roads" that human thought can take, he argues:

> one, that "it is and cannot be"
> is the path of persuasion (for truth accompanies it):
> another, that "it is not and must not be"—
> this I say to you is a trail devoid of all knowledge.

("Way" 132)

The point most scholars think Parmenides is making here is that it is simply nonsensical to think of "that which is" in any way that involves negation (e.g., the universe didn't always exist, black is not grey, Steve is not Mary, and so forth). From this starting point, Parmenides makes the following further inference:

> [B]eing, it is ungenerated and indestructible
> whole, of one kind, and unwavering, and complete.
> Nor was it, nor will it be, since now it is, all together,
> one, continuous. For what generation will you seek of it?
> How, whence, did it grow? That it came from what is not I shall not
> allow you to say or think.
>
> ("Way" 134)

Here Parmenides seems to be arguing that if we say that anything changes in any way whatsoever, we commit ourselves to the view that it *is* now in a way that it *was not* before. Thus, however much "custom" tempts us to talk about parts of the world coming into existence or ceasing to be, all such thought involves an incoherent commitment to the idea that the universe *both is and is not*. To believe this about anything would be a violation of the Law of Non-Contradiction, a philosophical principle which states that nothing can ever have logically incompatible properties.

We mention this weird ancient argument, not because we expect the reader to find it persuasive, but rather because it demonstrates at least one very basic difficulty associated with finding a general criterion of identity for objects over time. Common sense suggests that a cake is still a cake after you have removed one slice, but not when all that is left are crumbs, and that a log is still a log when you have just put it in the fire, but not when it has burned up into ashes. But matters get more difficult when one tries to come up with an uncontroversial and exceptionless way of filling in the blanks in the following much more general formula: a *thing* remains the (kind of) *thing* it is when it changes in way *x*, but not in way *y*. How much gradual change can occur over time before an object is no longer considered to be the same? When one reflects upon how little prospect there seems to be of solving this ancient philosophical puzzle, one begins to understand why Parmenides might have gotten frustrated enough to actually deny that any change ever takes place.

1.3.1.2 Descartes' Experiment

Perhaps the most famous and influential attempt to discern a criterion of identity for all objects was made by René Descartes in his *Meditations on First Philosophy*. Descartes describes a modest experiment that he performs with a piece of wax taken from a honeycomb. To start off with, he says, the wax in his possession is hard, firm to the touch, has a faint scent of flowers and a taste of honey and sounds hollow when it is tapped. But when he holds the wax over an open flame, it changes quite radically: "Look: the residual taste is eliminated, the smell goes away, the color changes, the shape is lost, the size increases; it becomes liquid and hot . . . and if you strike it, it no longer makes a sound."[8] Has the piece of wax changed in *every* respect, so that there is no clear justification on the basis of how it appears for calling it the same object at all? Not quite, claims Descartes. There is one property that the wax has retained through all of the physical and chemical trans-formations it has undergone as the result of being heated. That property is *extension*, the characteristic of occupying a determinate part of space. The official "Cartesian" position (to use the term that is applied to philosophical positions that originated in Descartes' writings) is therefore that extension is the sole *essential property* shared by all material objects—the one feature, that is, that they continue to possess regardless of however else they may change. All material objects are different from one another, then, just insofar as they take up different parts of space.

Unfortunately, Descartes' argument is not convincing, for a couple of reasons. First, contemporary physics actually undermines his view in a variety of ways. Quantum mechanics treats the spatial location of fundamental particles as indeterminate, and in addition actually countenances *massless* particles (e.g., gluons, gravitons, and photons). It seems clear that Descartes' pre-Newtonian notion of extension could not apply to such peculiar entities. And second, some "objects" that we would hesitate to classify as material also have extension in space, for example, holograms, rainbows, and mirages.

In the present context, what is interesting about Descartes' approach is that he thought that he could show that human minds have identity over time in much the same way as material bodies. "Surely, my awareness of my own self is not merely much truer and more certain than my awareness of the wax, but also much more distinct and evident . . . when I see, or think I see (here I am not distinguishing the two) it is simply not possible that I who am now thinking am not something" (*Meditations*, p. 22). The essential property that distinguishes mind from matter, and one "self" from another, according to Descartes, is *thought itself*. A person can undergo any other sort of change—loss of body parts, loss of sanity, or even (perhaps) some-thing more weirdly science-fictional, like a brain transplant—but as long as the same proprietary sequence of thoughts continues to accompany each of these transformations, they all may be regarded as happening to the *same person*. However strange, varied, unpredictable or irrational a person's thoughts are, as long as there is thinking still going on, for Descartes, it is always the same "you" that is doing the thinking.

1.3.2 Our Humean Heritage, Part One: The Vague Self

Philosophy also contains a very different tradition of thought about per-sonal identity, according to which the notion of a temporally continuous self that retains its identity through physical, environmental, and even some psychological change is an illusion. The eighteenth-century Scottish philosopher David Hume was the most influential Western defender of this view. In a chapter from his *Treatise of Human Nature* called "Of Personal Identity," Hume sets up his own views in opposition to thinkers like Descartes, who "imagine that we are every moment intimately conscious of what we call our self; that we feel its existence and its continuance in existence; and are certain, beyond the evidence of a demonstration, both of its perfect identity and simplicity."[9]

To obtain some intuitive support for his skeptical attitude toward the Cartesian view of the self, Hume performs his own rather perplexing thought experiment. "For my part," he says, "when I enter most intimately into what I call *myself*, I always stumble upon some particular perception or other, of heat or cold, light or shade, love or hatred, pain or pleasure. I can never catch myself at any time without a perception. . . . If anyone, upon serious and unprejudiced reflection, thinks he has a different notion of *himself*, I must confess I can reason no longer with him" ("Personal" 132).

Give it a try. If you are like most of Hume's readership, you will find it incredibly difficult to pick out anything like a specific sensation, thought, or memory image that is simply *of yourself*, as opposed to being, say, an impression of your body at a particular time and place, or of the objects or stimuli that are or were part of your immediate surroundings.

What is the significance of this fact, which seems to show that we have access to no direct empirical information whatsoever about what the self *is*, as opposed to what it is usually accompanied by? A strict empiricist (somebody who believes that all of our beliefs must be based directly upon the evidence of the senses) might propose that Hume's experiment shows there is *no self at all*, and that we must regard all of our talk about it as fictional in the same way as we do talk about the Greek gods, woodland spirits, or outmoded scientific concepts like the luminiferous ether. An admission that the self does not exist would be a pretty radical departure from common sense, though, and even the normally skeptical Hume is cautious about going quite this far. Instead, he proposes that while each perception, impression, or memory that we have is in fact a "distinct existence," we have an unavoidable tendency to "suppose the whole train of perceptions to be *united* by identity" ("Personal" 168). The self is not, then, some special kind of entity that undergoes or persists through all of the changes in our perceptions, emotions, and memories; rather, it is simply a concept that we use to refer to the sum of all those things taken together.

The contemporary British philosopher Derek Parfit makes roughly the same point in a helpfully clear way.

> "[T]he word 'I' can be used," Parfit says, "to imply the greatest degree of psychological connectedness. When the connection has been reduced, when there is any marked change of character or style of life, or any

marked loss of memory . . . [we] would say 'it was not I who did that, but an earlier self' . . . what matters in the continued existence of the person are, for the most part, relations of degree."[10]

We can extract the following argument from the suggestions made by both of these philosophers about what the self *must* be, given what it *isn't*. The first three premises are fairly self-explanatory.

The Similarity Argument

1   The self must exist; it is clearly something more than a merely fictional object.
2   There must, then, be some criterion for determining whether or not *the same self* continues to exist over any given period of time.
3   None of the experiences that a human being undergoes constitutes a direct awareness of the self's existence.

In the absence of any such experience, the Humean concludes, there is no deeper fact of the matter that explains what makes people the same over time. Instead, all we have to guide us are the various (frequently inconsistent) types of similarity that people use to judge other people to be the same or different from how they were earlier on in time.

4   Since there is no deeper explanation of personal identity over time, the only facts of the matter concerning personal identity are the various (physical, psychological, etc.) relationships that people actually appeal to in judging problematic cases of identity.

From this perspective, you are the same person you were six years ago to the extent that a number of things hold, for example, (a) your body has the appropriate spatio-temporal connection to that person, (b) your mind has the appropriate continuity of experience, (c) your character is similar in relevant ways, and (d) you are engaging in the same projects or kinds of projects.

In philosophical thought experiments, (a) and (b) are often shown to come apart.[11] Suppose your mentality were somehow transplanted into another body. Which body is now you, the old one or the new one? And it is entirely unclear what the "appropriate spatio-temporal connection is." Suppose over years while you were sleeping your body was slowly replaced with silicon. Is the resulting cyborg still you? Suppose your character changes radically for the worse, as the father of one of the authors' childhood friends did when his brain cancer became advanced. Was the confused, violently abusive man the same person as the earlier loving father? All of these concerns lead us to the conclusion of our argument.

5   It follows from Premises One through Four that the self is vague.

As we will show, this conclusion provides a compelling solution to our puzzle about gamers' use of the pronoun "I."

When philosophers say that some property is vague, they mean that it allows series of indeterminate cases.[12] The colors red and orange are vague because between paradigm instances of each there is a series of colors such that any two next to each other are indistinguishable, while the whole series (starting with orange) gets increasingly red. Look at your PC monitor while you are playing some particularly vivid game like *Bejeweled* or *World of Warcraft*. Now turn down the brightness control on your screen. If you do this just a little at first, an orange polygon on the screen will still look orange. But eventually, if you keep doing this, you will realize the color is no longer orange, but grey. When did that happen? Any point in time that you pick will be arbitrary, since someone else could pick an indistinguishable color one touch of the dial away. There would be no way to argue that your pick is better.

Now consider the progression from a healthy person to someone in the last phases of Alzheimer's. From minute to minute the person is the same, but by the end the person you knew is no longer there. This is the same sort of phenomenon as the imperceptibly gradual change from orange to grey described in the preceding paragraph.

Less depressingly, from this perspective the claim that teachers frequently make that a liberal education leads to greater "self-realization" can under these circumstances be taken literally. It makes perfect sense (as any teacher of adolescents or young children will tell you) to talk about a person becoming "more like himself." The case of a person slowly becoming a cyborg through slow sequential replacement of bodily parts is right on the borderline; it is not at all clear what one should say about him.

The conclusion that the self is vague is troubling in some ways. How disconnected does a set of states have to be from some earlier set before we say that it counts as belonging to a *different* self? What should we say about a person who goes into a year-long, dreamless coma? Or the victim of Multiple Personality Disorder whose personalities have access to different or incompatible sets of childhood memories? Or the possibility that we might one day be able to transplant a human brain from one human body into another? If Hume and Parfit are correct that there is no deeper self other than the factors that normally lead us to make judgments of similarity, we can expect to hear nothing very much more enlightening in answer to all of these sorts of questions than "it depends."

However reluctant one might be to adopt this model of human identity, we think that it provides the best prospect for solving our original puzzle of what is meant by the gamer's "I," when she uses it to refer to her character in an RPG. To make this case we will have to add to the Humean notion of a temporally vague self a notion of a spatially extended self on the model proposed by the contemporary philosophers Andy Clark and David Chalmers. The examples we considered above concerned what makes something the same thing over time; we took for granted what makes something the same person in space. It is an immediate consequence of Clark's and Chalmers' work that the self is also vague in space. Moreover, for Clark especially, computing machines serve as paradigmatic means by which the vague self extends outward from the body into its environment.

1.4 The Spatially Vague Self

A large part of what the brain does involves helping the body to organize and manipulate the environment in order to simplify computational tasks. For some tasks, the brain can do the computational work alone, but for many it can't. We can do some math problems with pen and paper, but not just with our brains. Part of what it is to be a human being is to structure one's living and work environments in ways that aid us in our everyday lives.

In their enormously influential 1998 paper, "The Extended Mind,"[13] Andy Clark and David Chalmers describe three different ways that a person might conceivably play a game of *Tetris*: (1) visualizing the pieces rotating in mid-air, (2) using a computer mouse to manipulate representations of them on a monitor, and (3) accessing a cyborg brain-implant to perform the rotation operation as quickly as the computer does. They argue that all three techniques involve the same kinds of cognitive processes. They also point out that it would seem perfectly natural to most people to say about case (1) that everything involved in the playing of the game was going on "inside" of the player's mind, even though as a matter of fact (and as anyone who has ever been obsessed with *Tetris* eventually discovers) it is much easier to play the game in the manner of case (2).

From these observations, the argument to what philosophers call "the extended mind thesis" is very quick. The mind paradigmatically performs computational tasks such as figuring out the date of one's dental appointment and balancing one's checkbook. If Clark and Chalmers are correct, the brain often does not do this kind of thing very well by itself. Rather, the brain frequently helps the body to externalize the task so that one can exploit the environment to help, for example, by writing on a calendar or clicking buttons on a calculator. The computational processes are thus performed by both the brain and the body, working in tandem with the external environment. In these circumstances, it begins to seem completely arbitrary to identify the mind with *just* the brain rather than with the brain, the body, and the environment *taken together*.

But if this is true, then (to return to the main topic of the present chapter) the *self* cannot be just the brain or the body, but must shade into the environment as well. By this we do not mean to presuppose that the human mind is just the same thing as the self. There are plenty of other properties relevant to human selfhood that aren't clearly or exclusively psychological in nature—one's good looks, perhaps, or one's physical skills, or the ability that some philosophers believe we have to make utterly free decisions that are not predetermined by any features whatsoever of either the body or the mind. It is even possible (though perhaps rather tricky) to imagine a single mind taking part in the continuous existence of two different selves through the weird brain-transplant scenarios of which academic philosophers are so fond,[14] or through the sort of hive, group, or pack mind hypothesized by Douglas Hofstadter and wonderfully portrayed in the writings of science fiction author Vernor Vinge.[15]

Nonetheless, there is a strong analogy between the "extended mind" hypothesis and the view of personal identity that we saw defended earlier by Parfit and Hume. For Clark and Chalmers, the human mind is an enormously powerful, but rather ragtag collection of psychological affects coupled with external props to our cognitive processes such as calendars, notebooks, and the *Tetris* player's desktop mouse. For the same reason that it makes sense to view external objects in our immediate environment as proper parts of our thoughts, why not think of external entities like characters that we play in *D & D* or *World of Warcraft* as parts of our very selves?

Conceived of in this way, the self may be viewed (to use a different gaming metaphor) as being like a giant jigsaw puzzle made up of a broadly diverse array of pieces, some of which look the same or form part of the same pattern, while others might only have in common with their fellows the fact that they fit neatly together at the edges. Unlike a regular jigsaw, however, the self's outer edges are constantly expanding as we acquire new experiences. Whenever one uses the word "I," it is always partly indeterminate which section or how much of the puzzle one is referring to. Perhaps it is a whole year-long narrative of continuous experiences, or perhaps something as transitory as an evening spent in front of the PC, killing orcs and interacting with fellow gamers across the globe.

1.5 Conclusions

It is probably not possible to give an utterly knock-down, persuasive deductive argument proving that our broadly Humean way of thinking about the constitution of the human self is better than any of the possible alternative views. The most we can hope to do is to show how well it accommodates gamers' everyday intuitions about their own speech and practices.

Different sorts of online and tabletop role-playing games actually provoke very different types of psychological involvement from their players, depending on the rules that each one uses, and also the different social conventions that they reinforce. At one end of the scale, there are traditional high fantasy games like *D & D* and *World of Warcraft*. In these sorts of games, the roles that the player takes on are wildly fantastical, the traits of her character are determined by die rolls or an online "character generation" engine, and the motivation that keeps most people playing can be described without too much oversimplification as being fundamentally escapist in nature.

At the other end of the scale there are social-networking websites like *MySpace, Facebook*, and *Match.com*. The user of *MySpace* creates a persona for herself with perhaps even more care, attention to detail, and manifest artificiality than the more conventional gamer who wants to imagine herself as an axe-wielding dwarf. The *MySpace* user's interaction with other users is normally carried out through media that have different rules of etiquette than everyday conversation (e.g., emails, chatrooms, or IM interfaces) and her motivations for establishing a "network" through these means are usually different from the motives that govern the rest of her social interactions. Some of these websites even have a primitive method of scoring—many users of *Facebook*, for example, engage in open competition with one another to see who can get the most official "friends." But most users of these services don't really think of them as "games" at all. Rather, one's *Facebook* or *MySpace* avatar is more conventionally viewed as a way of augmenting one's own personality, or extending one's own social reach past traditional, geographical, or cultural boundaries.

Between these two extremes, one finds curiously hybrid games like *The Sims Online* and *Second Life*. Here, players select new names and appearances for themselves just like participants in fantasy RPGs. But the practices that they engage in online bear a striking similarity to the pastimes that flesh-and-blood people enjoy in the real world; they tend gardens, go to concerts and parties, flirt, make out, discuss politics, or just hang around inside their own homes for an evening. What is more (to get back to our example of Chris and Alayne and their encounters in *Second Life*), when online characters undergo major changes in their "lives," these are often carefully orchestrated to correspond to similarly radical changes in the lives of their players. It was no mere private quirk or strange conceit that led Chris and Alayne to have their online characters get married inside of the game's diegetic realm around the same time that they did it in the "real" world.

When the *World of Warcraft* player says "I killed nine goblins last night," is she really using the word "I" in exactly the same way as the player of *Second Life* who says "I watered my garden last night" or the *Facebook* user who says "I made three new friends yesterday?" For the naïve fictionalist, the answer to this question must be a depressingly unexplanatory "yes." All three of the players just described are making claims about themselves that are equally false, and for exactly the same reason. But the Humean about personal identity who accepts something like the Clark/Chalmers "extended mind" hypothesis can say something much more interesting and intuitive here. What each of these speakers is doing with the word "I" is referring *truthfully* to different parts of the puzzle that constitutes her own self. Perhaps the escapist *D & D* player's "I" picks out a part of herself that is more marginal and less essential than the *Second Life* player's, whose avatar in the game might be something that she identifies with, and would be as unhappy to lose as Hemingway was when he lost a trunk full of manuscripts.[16] And perhaps both of them are speaking in a different register from the *MySpace* user who believes (however eccentrically) that her online inter-actions are no less personal or intimate than those that she participates in when away from a computer.

Once one has gotten used to the philosophical thesis of the vague self, it becomes easier to see how, through video games and online communities, we are now developing ways to spatio-temporally extend ourselves that until recently would have seemed implausible in a science fiction novel. And in the non-diegetic realm one may come to realize that talk of "losing oneself" in another person or experience is not metaphorical, but rather a literal description of how our extended selves interact, overlap, and combine with one another.

2 The Game Inside the Mind, the Mind Inside the Game (The Nintendo Wii Gaming Console)

2.1 The Problem

Throughout 2006, tens of millions of gamers waited for the newest versions of the Microsoft Xbox and the Sony Playstation. Early demonstrations of both consoles had revealed game-play that bordered on photorealism, the culmination of hundreds of millions of dollars invested by research universities and corporations toward improving graphical capacities. At the time, nobody saw Nintendo's promised new *kinesthetic* interface (those parts of a machine's physical apparatus that the user physically manipulates to accomplish tasks) as relevant to improving the realism of modern video games. Instead, nearly everyone involved had been working toward constructing *sensory* interfaces (the visual, auditory, tactile, olfactory, and gustatory aspects of the computing machine that are relevant to the user's performance of her tasks) that made games look and sound like movies. It is no exaggeration to say that most gamers expected the release of the Xbox 360 and Playstation 3 to be defining moments in gaming history. But this was not to be.

Instead, the new console with a much *worse* sensory interface than its competitors captured the imagination of the world. Compared to the Sony Playstation 3 and Microsoft Xbox 360, the Nintendo Wii's graphics are primitive, and most of the games that have been made for it (so far) are consistently childish in content. Yet demand for the Wii was so great that as late as August 2007 (over eight months after its initial release) used consoles were being purchased on Amazon.com for $150 over the retail price. By this date the Wii had outsold the Playstation 3 by three to one and was on track to outsell the new Xbox (which was released much earlier) by early 2008.[1] Perhaps even more impressively, the console has found an enthusiastic audience among generations who have traditionally been well outside the video game industry's core demographic (i.e., those above fifty-five and those below twelve years of age), especially since the release of the *Wii Fit* exercise system in December of 2007.[2] And just as strange as the unexpected demand was the fact that Wii gameplay seemed to many gamers to be much more *realistic* than that of its competitors.

For desktop computers, the kinesthetic interface is the keyboard and mouse. For the planes flown by the US Air Force and Navy, it includes an eye-tracking system inside the pilots' helmets. For the Playstation and the Xbox, it is a controller with a set of buttons and small joysticks manipulated by the player's fingers. Consider the humble Xbox controller depicted below in Figure 2.1.

Since only the fingers are involved, players typically sit still on couches or chairs while manipulating it see (Figure 2.2). While there are no important differences between the Playstation and Xbox controllers, the Wii controller looks quite different (see Figure 2.3). But mere inspection of the controller does not reveal the revolutionary difference between the Wii's kinesthetic interface and those of its competitors. Compare the picture of the two drowsy couch potatoes in Figure 2.2 to that of the brave pugilist in Figure 2.4. Instead of sitting on the couch, the player is standing and moving around. Moreover, it is immediately clear to anyone who has used this console that he is playing *Wii Boxing*, and that his in-game avatar has his guard up.

Such an interface is possible because the Wii console includes a motion sensor that is placed on or below the monitor to track the movement of the two controllers. Players control their avatars with bodily movements similar

Figure 2.1

Figure 2.2

to the in-game movements of their avatars. Consider the shot of someone playing *Wii Golf* in Figure 2.5. Again, one needs only to view the player to be able to tell what game he is playing.

Of course, the experience of playing Wii versions of competitive sports like golf and boxing bears only the tiniest passing resemblance to the "original" versions of these activities. The Wii boxer does not need to engage in any footwork at all, and the exhaustion that he experiences during gameplay is of a quite different flavor from that of a real-life boxer who has taken a few shots to the head. The difference between putting and hitting a tee shot in *Wii Golf* consists in a very small adjustment of wrist speed and acceleration, rather than the radical differences in exertion and movement that distinguish them in real life. Other inventive but very crude simulations of real-life activities that have already been used in Wii games include holding the controller sideways to simulate holding the reins of a horse (in *Wii Play*), leaning from side to side on a balance board to simulate skiing (in *Wii Fit*), and waving the controller across one's body to simulate knife slashes (in *Resident Evil 4*).

At first blush, it might seem bizarre to suggest that including these sorts of tasks can make a game more "realistic" in the same way that the vivid and highly individualized images of hockey players' faces in *NHL 08* are more

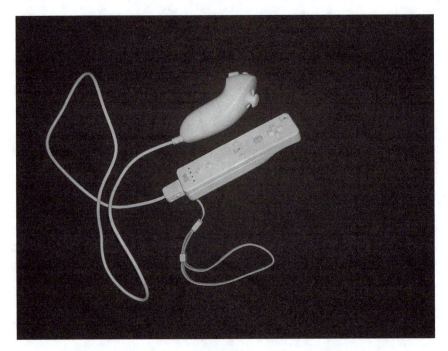

Figure 2.3

"realistic" than they were in *NHL 98*. But perhaps before this issue is pre-judged, it is worth making a critical examination of some common philosophical assumptions about just what perceptual realism is supposed to amount to in the first place. Philosophers have theorized quite extensively about how human perception works, how it influences our beliefs and desires, and (most importantly) about the extent to which we can rely upon our perceptual apparatus to provide us with a realistic depiction of the external world. Reflection upon the strengths and weaknesses of some of these theories can help us understand why nearly everyone mistakenly expected that demand for competitors' consoles would be so much higher than for the Wii, and also why Wii play does seem more realistic to many gamers.

In this chapter, we will argue that very few people predicted the success of the Wii because nearly everybody's view of the human–computer interface presupposed the truth of *phenomenalism*. According to this philosophical theory, people do not directly perceive the actual world, but instead experience a realm that is a function of their own private sensory manifolds. For the phenomenalist, this is an inevitable part of the way perception works— so much so that, on this view, no sense whatsoever could be made of the idea that any person could ever escape the *Matrix*-like prison of her very own sensory manifold and see things as they really are.

Figure 2.4

By contrast, *enactivist* theories of perception hold that human beings *do* directly perceive the world. According to enactivism, this direct perception is a function of the way we physically manipulate ourselves and our environments. Unlike phenomenalism, enactivism provides a compelling explanation of why Wii game-play is more realistic.

We begin here by assaying the philosophical case for phenomenalism, as well as some of the standard problems with this theory. Then we show how the enactivist rebuts traditional arguments for phenomenalism. In the course of our discussion we will find that, not only does enactivism explain the success of the Wii, but the success of the Wii provides some unique and helpful empirical evidence for the truth of enactivism. Our critique of phenomenalism and our defense of enactivism in the philosophy of perception have non-trivial implications for what can be expected from the next generation of video games.

Figure 2.5

2.2 Our Russellian Heritage, Part One: Phenomenalism

In the late 1990s, moviegoers were presented with a battery of films the dramatic effectiveness of which depended heavily upon the ancient philosophical distinction between appearance and reality. *The Thirteenth Floor,* *eXistenZ*, and *The Matrix* were all released in 1999, and each of them presented the viewer with a world in which reality differed radically from the way it appeared to the characters in the story. The appearance/reality theme was explored extensively in video games and science fiction long before the film industry used it; perhaps the first and best example remains the magnificent text adventure game from 1985, Infocom's *A Mind Forever Voyaging*, in which the main character wakes up one morning to learn, not only that his whole life up to that point has been a computer simulation, but also that he himself is the computer doing the simulating. It is unlikely to have been an accident, though, that these films came out just as video games' sensory interface reached a level of realism sufficient to fool the very inattentive. Nearly every serious gamer in the late 1990s experienced a loved one saying "What movie is that?" during a game of *Doom* or *Madden Football*. Of course, usually only someone walking past the monitor on the way to the kitchen could be fooled. Nonetheless, everyone realized that games were going to get closer and closer to what some designers of the period referred to as the "holy grail" of complete photorealism. And the plots of movies like *The Matrix* relied upon that very idea.

Historical precursors of the distinction between a "world of appearance" and the real world can be found in print as early as the *Baghavad Gita* and Plato's *Republic*.[3] In the Western philosophical tradition, the most influential articulation of the idea can be found in the writings of René Descartes.[4] In *Meditations on First Philosophy*, Descartes asks the reader to consider a general hypothesis about the reliability of our everyday beliefs about the world. He deliberately entertains the possibility that "not God, who is supremely good and the source of truth, but rather some malicious demon of the utmost power and cunning has employed all his energies in order to deceive me. I shall think that the sky, the air, the earth, colors, shapes, sounds and all external things are merely the delusions of dreams which he has devised to ensnare my judgment" (*Meditations* 15).

The Matrix presents the limiting case of this daring hypothesis that we could all be mistaken about the nature of reality, since every occupant of the Matrix is being fooled by the machinations of nefarious beings. Descartes, by way of contrast, ends up concluding that our senses don't normally deceive us, since God's benevolence and love for his creatures rules out the existence of such powerful and villainous deceivers.

Some philosophers, however, have argued that the radical difference between appearance and reality is simply a part of the human condition. In *The Problems of Philosophy*, Bertrand Russell develops his account of the distinction with reference to the humble table in his Cambridge office. "To the eye it is oblong, brown and shiny, to the touch it is smooth and cool and hard; when I tap it, it gives out a wooden sound. Anyone else who sees and feels and hears the table will agree with this description, so that it might seem that no difficulty would arise."[5] Yet after considering the table more deeply, Russell goes on to conclude that "it becomes evident that the real table, if there is one, is not the same as what we immediately experience by sight or touch or hearing." (*Problems* 11) As we will see, Russell did not need to invoke the possibility of a robot conspiracy or malicious supernatural beings in his arguments for this chasm between appearance and reality.

Consider the state of affairs depicted in Figure 2.6, meant to illustrate the way that most people naturally think of what is involved when a person (call him Bill) perceives Russell's table.

The circle represents the parts of the world that don't include Bill. Here, he is depicted as perceiving the rest of reality as it really is. But if Russell is

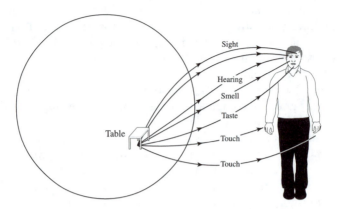

Figure 2.6

correct, this picture is wrong. For the Russellian, Bill doesn't really perceive the real properties of the table, and hence doesn't perceive the table itself.

According to Russell, Bill only directly perceives *sense data* ("the things that are immediately known in sensation: such things as colors, sounds, smells, hardness, roughness, and so on" (*Problems* 12)), the perception of which is *caused* by the table. The experience of perceiving sense data is called "sensation" by Russell. If one adds to this Russell's view that real objects *cause* us to have sensations of sense data, then the correct picture of Bill's perceptual circumstances would be that which is depicted in Figure 2.7.

On Russell's phenomenalist view, it would be easy for sinister machines or a malevolent god to fool us. Since all we directly perceive is sense data, the god simply needs to create *false* sense data. Also, since on this view perception of sense data is our primary contact with reality, it seems reasonable that in the

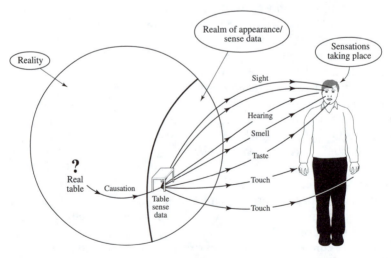

Figure 2.7

quest for greater realism in game design, companies like Microsoft and Sony would concentrate on the development of photorealistic graphics. But why think this is the best way to view our interactions with the real world, let alone with the fictional worlds presented to us by video games?

2.2.1 Arguments for Sense Data

Russell continues his detailed discussion of the properties of his office table in the following manner:

> . . . as soon as we try to be more precise our troubles begin. Although I believe that the table is "really" of the same colour all over, the parts that reflect the light look much brighter than the other parts, and some parts look white because of reflected light. I know that, if I move, the parts that reflect the light will be different, so that the apparent distribution of colours on the table will change. It follows that if several people are looking at the table at the same moment, no two of them will see exactly the same distribution of colours, because no two can see it from exactly the same point of view, and any change in the point of view makes some change in the way the light is reflected.
>
> (*Problems* 2)

He goes on to discuss all of the different sensory modalities through which the table can be experienced, arguing that his point about possible changes in how the table can present itself to us applies to each. Generalized to all objects, this point can be rendered as the first premise of the following argument.

2.2.1.1 Russell's Problems of Philosophy Argument

1 The properties we perceive, such as shape, smell, sound, and texture, change as we change our positions and techniques of observation.

Russell never explicitly states the next premise, but it is clearly needed for his eventual conclusion.

2 Real properties of objects are stable, in that they typically don't change merely as a result of either changes within people as they observe these objects, or changes in techniques of observation (i.e., from looking with the naked eye to looking through some instrument like a microscope).[6]

Russell concludes that, "the real table, if there is one, is not the same as what we immediately experience by sight and touch and hearing" (*Problems* 3). If we read what he says about the table as a generalized argument for the existence of sense data, we can present Russell's conclusion as:

3 Therefore the properties we perceive are not real properties of objects.

On this basis, Russell has license to define sense data as the properties we *actually perceive*, in contrast to the real properties of the table (which, for Russell, *cause* sense data but which we don't actually perceive).

The argument just presented is far from being the only defense of phenomenalism in the philosophical canon. Another concerns the perceptual capacities of different creatures. Anybody willing to spend half an hour thumbing through a college zoology textbook is bound to be stunned by the variety of ways that different creatures perceive the world.[7] Bats use echolocation, a biological mechanism that works like a ship's sonar. For dogs, smell is localized in the same way sight is for human beings. Birds perceive magnetic currents in order to know where to migrate. The capacities of these creatures seem incredibly strange to us humans, confined as we are to our own sensory apparatuses.[8] This sense of strangeness lends plausibility to the following argument:

2.2.1.2 The Argument from Different Minds

1 Other creatures (e.g., bats, dogs, and birds) perceive the world completely differently from how we do.
2 It follows that neither we nor these other creatures are perceiving the world as it actually is, but at best, the world as it is presented to us by our own sensory manifolds.
3 This shows that what we and these other creatures directly perceive is sense data, rather than the real properties of objects.

As with Russell's Argument, this gains plausibility from the thought that reality is the way it is independently of all of the different ways it can be perceived to be.[9]

2.2.2 Phenomenalism and the Player as Homunculus

Players perceive a game's diegetic realm by looking at the monitor and touching the game controls; they think about what to do; they then manipulate the interface to change the diegetic realm. According to some philosophical accounts, human beings live in a very similar feedback loop with respect to reality itself.

How seriously one takes this analogy between human beings getting around in the world and players moving their avatars around in games depends upon the extent to which viewing entities in a diegetic realm represented upon a monitor really is like viewing the real objects in one's immediate physical environment. Thus, one's (even implicitly or subconsciously held) philosophical views about perception will determine to a large extent one's approach to designing video games.

On the surface, phenomenalism seems to suggest that there is a very strong similarity between the perceptual feedback loop constitutive of the human condition and the gamer's feedback loop. This becomes more clear once we think a little more carefully about how the phenomenalist is required to think of the "interface" between a normal human perceiver and the sense data that are the objects of her perceptions. Most versions of phenomenalism eventually make reference to some sort of "eye of the mind," by which they mean whatever it is within each of us that is *experiencing* sense data.

The phenomenalist's eye of the mind is strongly analogous to how we normally think of a person watching game-play. Just as the player takes in the movement of colors on the video monitor, the eye of the mind perceives the sense data presented to it. Thus, if phenomenalism were true, it would seem that realism in game design would be achieved by improving a game system's sensory interface as much as possible. Paradoxically, though, this deeper analogy reveals an Achilles' heel for phenomenalism itself.

To see why this is so, we need to return to the original question that we raised in connection with the success of the Wii, viz. what makes one video game more realistic than another? There is obviously a sense in which quasi-photographic video games like *Tiger Woods PGA Tour '08* and *Top Spin* are more realistic than cartoonish games like *Outlaw Golf, Mario Tennis,* or even *Wii Sports* itself. But we think that there are also (perhaps rather surprisingly) some compelling reasons why it is a mistake to say that the image presented through one video game's visual interface looks better than the image presented through another's because it looks more like the real world.

2.2.2.1 A Deeper Analogy: Phenomenalism and Realism

So what makes one game system's interface (that of the Wii, say) more realistic than another's? To assess this, we need to examine how different philosophies of perception explain what makes one human experience more realistic than another. The immediate answer one wants to give is that one experience is more realistic than another if that experience more faithfully *represents the way things are.* So, for example, when someone who is short-sighted looks at a game monitor without her glasses, she doesn't see Mario. When she puts her glasses on, she does see him. Since Mario *really is* on the screen, the perception with glasses better represents the way things are.

Unfortunately, the initially plausible characterization of greater realism in terms of faithful representation falls apart with very little prodding. For when the aforementioned person looks at the monitor through her glasses, there are a lot of properties she still doesn't see. She does not see what kind of light is reflecting off it in the part of the spectrum not visible to human eyes. She does not see the motions of the individual molecules composing the monitor. Of course, there are machines that allow us to perceive all of this stuff—electron microscopes, photomultiplier tubes, etc—but when using these sorts of instruments, one no longer perceives Mario! So which is more realistic, the perception of the monitor as seen through glasses or the perception that one might be able to get through an electron microscope?

Perhaps this problem is really not so dire. One perceives the properties of the *very small* parts of the monitor more realistically with an electron microscope because an electron microscope more faithfully represents them as they are. Perhaps if we relativize realism to the appropriate domain (e.g., relative to the very small, an electron microscope is more realistic than the human eye; relative to more "middle-sized" objects, the eye is as realistic as it needs to be), then we will be on our way toward a good theory of what, in general, a good "representation" of the world is supposed to amount to.

Phenomenalism has additional problems, though. Remember that for the phenomenalist we never directly perceive the real properties of the world. Therefore, it would be extraordinarily misleading for the phenomenalist to say that a more realistic perception is one that faithfully represents these properties as they really are. For the phenomenalist, there is no fact of the matter about what something *really* looks (or sounds, tastes, feels, and smells) like. There is just a bunch of looks (and sounds, tastes, feels, and smells) which vary from species to species, creature to creature, and experience to experience. How, then, can one say in the first place that *any* perceptual experience whatsoever is more realistic than any other?

The conclusion that nobody's perceptions are any more realistic than anybody else's might seem at first glance to provide some welcome support for the ethical view that everybody is entitled to her own opinion. Perhaps everybody is, but this doesn't mean that every opinion is equally true or warranted by evidence. The stronger view that truth is relative to a person or group of people, in the sense that whatever the majority of the people in that group believe is true merely in virtue of them believing it, is called relativism. Relativism is notoriously difficult to defend from disturbing counterexamples. The most pressing problem is that many forms of relativism are self-refuting. If one embraces a strong form of relativism, one ends being simultaneously committed to the views that *nothing* is true for everybody and also that relativism is true for everybody (since relativism itself is surely *something*).[10]

A.J. Ayer, perhaps the most renowned English-speaking phenomenalist from the previous century, devised an ingenious solution to the problem of how to account for one group of sense data being more realistic than another group. He realized that if phenomenalism is true, then it cannot be the case that greater realism is a function of any perception's more accurately resembling the way things really are. But for Ayer, the route to radical relativism can be blocked. All that the phenomenalist has to believe is that the most realistic perception is the one that is most similar to one or more *privileged* perceptions.

For Ayer, a "privileged perception" is one that has the greatest predictive value.[11] To see how this works, consider looking at a game CD from two different angles. From the first, you perceive the roundness of the disk. From the second, the disk looks more elliptical. When, in a non-philosophical frame of mind, we say that the first perception more accurately tracks the "real shape" of the disk, there is a sense in which we are saying something true. If we experience the round-shaped sense datum first, then we will more accurately predict the kinds of sense data we will get if either we move or the disk gets moved. We expect a round disk to fit into a round CD drive, but also to look elliptical from certain angles. If we saw the disk from one of these angles first and mistakenly thought that we were viewing an elliptical object, our ability to make these sorts of predictions about future sense data arising from that object would be greatly impeded.

Ayer's insight about the ways in which sense data both can and cannot be said to accurately represent the external world provides us with a key to understanding how the visual interface works in contemporary video games. For just as the phenomenalist cannot make realism a matter of comparing perceptions with reality, certain technological limitations (to be described below) make it the case that greater realism in a gaming system's visual interface cannot be a matter of similarities between the player's visual perceptions and real things. Rather, the game designer is forced to strive for greater fidelity to certain very specific sorts of privileged representations.

When one looks at a computer screen, one is looking at a representation, and looking at representations is radically different from looking at actual objects. In his recent book, *Action in Perception*,[12] Alva Noë discusses the differences between watching an actual sporting event and a representation of one on television. "When you watch a live sporting event on television," he points out, "you are able to track what's happening, but you do so in a perspectivally non-veridical way. Perhaps you adopt the standpoint of one or more cameras. Crucially, you don't correctly or veridically experience the event's spatial relation to yourself" (*Action* 168). In other words, when the camera is focused on the home team's goal post, the viewer can't suddenly decide to focus on the people to the right and 15 feet behind the goal post. For the viewer at a live event this would be as easy as a quick tilt of the head or a refocusing of the eyes.

When we look at things in the world, our eyes determine a focal point in space. We can focus left-to-right and up-to-down, and also closer-to-farther-away. The latter of these abilities is in part a function of the muscles in the eye affecting how the light behaves prior to hitting the back of the eyeball, and part of it is a function of where we point each eye's retina. When we look at things closer to us in space, we cross our eyes more than when we look at things that are further away.

Now imagine what would have to be the case for the visual interface of a video game console to mimic this process. First, one would need eye-tracking technology that captured both the position of the player's retinas and state of her muscles. Then, for every possible point of view of the player's avatar, the program would have to be able to present an unimaginably large number of different foci, depending upon the position of the player's retinas and the state of her musculature at a given time. All of this information would be necessary just to determine what the player is looking at. Then, the gaming console would have to store images of each possible focal point for each focus. Independently of the formidable task of building much better eye trackers, the computational load of having the console store all of the possible focal points is probably just too much.

The first attempt at simulating near-to-far focusing in a successful game franchise was made by the designers of the *Deer Hunter* series; in these games the player is able to see things far away in greater detail by looking through a rifle scope than he can just by looking at the screen. The view through the scope is represented by a circle on the screen, the inside of which contains a larger, clearer representation of something that was portrayed as smaller and blurrier prior to bringing up the scope. More recently, *Call of Duty 4* has employed blurring to represent distance, albeit in a highly stylized and unrealistic way. But even these rather radical innovations in interface design fall well short of the kind of thing we've been trying to envision. The player of *Deer Hunter* is not permitted to adjust the focusing distance of the scope on the fly as one could while setting up a real rifle. And the player of *Call of Duty 4* can always bring the blurry parts of the screen into focus *as* blurry parts of a screen, something that cannot be done within her own visual field. In real life, things in the less distinct parts of the visual field come into focus when one focuses on them.

When we look at a representation of the world such as a painting or a movie screen, two kinds of focusing are going on. First of all, the representation *itself* has a focus. The camera zooms in on a face, or the artist paints a bowl of fruit, leaving everything else in the background blurry. Second, the viewer's own eyes focus on different parts of the representing medium's surface. I can examine Cezanne's still life apple, but when I try unsuccessfully to bring into focus the blurry table on which the apple sits, I end up noticing properties of the medium itself, such as the brush strokes and cracks in the paint. Crucially, when looking at real objects in the world, the viewer's eyes shift focus with respect to the *objects themselves*, and are not limited by the perspective of the medium. With a real bowl of fruit in front of me, I can focus on the apple itself, noticing its blotches of red and green, and then zoom in on the stem, enjoying the minute crenellated patterns of gorgeous shades of brown.

This is just one reason why, when designing video games, it is not possible to really mimic the way the world looks, for the player's eye does not have control over the first kind of focusing. When focusing on the represented content, the player is locked into the focal point determined by the designer. If the player departs from this, she ends up focusing on the surface of the monitor itself. Thus, EA Sports' *Madden Football* does not visually approximate an actual football game seen in the flesh. At real games viewers can focus on anything they choose. *Madden Football* determines a focal point for you, just like a TV broadcast of a real football game.

2.2.2.2 A Deeper Disanalogy: The Player and the Homunculus

So the images produced on a two-dimensional screen by a video game are importantly different from the representations of the world that our senses provide us with. The next question that we need to ask is, how do those latter sorts of representations themselves work? Is the phenomenalist correct in thinking that there is something *inside* of us that works like a video screen that displays the information about the world that our senses have gathered for us to the inner "eye of the mind?" Alva Noë refers to the view that looking at the world is like looking at a picture as the "snapshot conception of vision," and defines it as the belief that vision, like a photograph, is "sharply focused, uniformly [and fully] detailed, and high-resolution" (*Action* 35). Noë provides some very plausible reasons for why this cannot be how vision works at all.

We can all perform a simple experiment that shows the snapshot conception to be wrong. Look straight ahead at a point on the wall in front of you. Randomly select a colored piece of paper and then wave it about six inches from your ear. You will notice the movement, but you won't be able to tell the color. If you slowly move the paper into the center of your visual field, you still won't be able to determine what the color is until it is within 20–30 degrees of the line of sight you have established with the wall. As Noë comments, "This proves that we don't experience the periphery of our visual field in anything like the clarity, detail, or focus with which we can take in what we are directly looking at" (*Action* 49). The effect Noë describes is even more extreme if one does the same thing with a playing card. As the card moves toward the central region the viewer experiences first its movement, then its color, then whether the card is a face card or not, and finally the card's identity. Our lack of ability to perceive detail in our peripheral vision is due to the fact that the retina has more (color detecting) cones and fewer (movement detecting) rods at the center, and more rods and fewer cones at the periphery.

Noë's point forces an interesting question upon the phenomenalist. Is the sensory manifold described by phenomenalists supposed to be like a photograph? In particular, do the sense data presented to the "eye of the mind" have a focal point selected?

One thing the Russellian cannot say is that the eye of the mind brings sense data into focus in the same way that the physical eye brings the world into focus. If the eye of the mind were thus tasked it would follow that two viewers could perceive the same sense data and have different experiences determined by different focal points selected by each viewer's inner mental eye. But then the Russellian would have to draw the highly improbable conclusion that there is a *second* eye of the mind viewing what we might call "second-order sense data," the existence of which is itself dependent upon the initial unfocused sense data.

This line of thinking provides a clear example of what philosophers have called the "homunculus fallacy."[13] The problem with Russell's view is that it ends up envisaging some sort of tiny sub-person inside of the mind of each human being (the word "homunculus" means "little man") that receives information in something like the same way that we ordinarily sized people are supposed to through our sense organs. The Russellian invokes sense data and an internal mental "perceiver" to explain how the physical eye and brain perceive objects in the real world. But now, on the assumption that the sense data presented to the mind are not focused, the posited mental perceiver itself needs to focus on the sense data. A complete picture of how Bill gets perceptual information would now need to include another version of Bill (Bill's homunculus) viewing second-order sense data caused by the first-order sense data (see Figure 2.8).

Apart from the intrinsic weirdness of viewing the operations of the mind in this way, this picture is also fundamentally unstable. For since Russell's original argument for the existence of sense data is perfectly general, it would apply yet again to the phenomena represented in Figure 2.8, so that our picture would have to include still another homunculus directly perceiving third-order sense data. It looks as though the Russellian will eventually need to posit an infinite number of progressively tinier homunculi to explain Bill's initial perception of the table![14]

How then does the phenomenalist navigate between the Scylla of homuncularism and the Charybdis of the snapshot conception of visual perception? The Scylla is the result of holding that sense data are not focused and that the eye of the mind focuses on parts of it, analogously to the way the human eye or a camera focuses on objects in the world. The Charybdis is the result of holding that the sense data are focused and the eye of the mind deter-

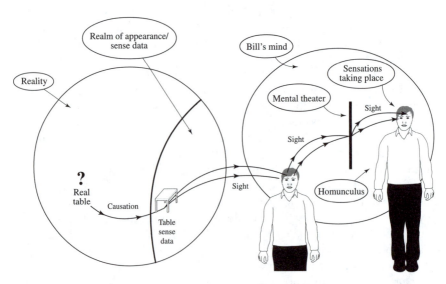

Figure 2.8

mines a focal point. The only way to navigate between the two is to hold that the sense data presented to the mind are already focused and that the eye of the mind does not itself determine a focal point.

But now the mental perceiver of sense data is of necessity utterly unlike human beings perceiving things in the world, for the mental eye does not itself bring things into focus, but can view representations already focused. And also, we would want to ask, if it is not the mental eye, then *what* is doing the focusing? This is a weird question, because for a lot of philosophers the intuitive plausibility of phenomenalism derives from the fact that the eye of the mind is supposed to be something recognizably like an eye looking at representations. But human, animal, and bird vision would be so blurry as to be useless if the eyes did not constantly move in saccades (quick movements) and microsaccades (continuous vibrations over a smaller area). And the ability to focus is an integral part of what real eyes do.

This way of avoiding homucularism and the snapshot conception of vision makes it unclear exactly what the eye of the mind is doing. However, it must be admitted that this is not a knockdown argument. Weirdness alone is not sufficient reason for abandoning a philosophical theory.

2.3 Our Russellian Heritage, Part Two: The External World

Earlier we mentioned the rash of entertainingly paranoid films from the late 1990s about characters trapped within an entirely virtual world. Part of what makes these films more than mere escapist entertainment is that they provoke the same thought that has occurred to many gamers who have found themselves deeply emotionally invested in the world created by a particular game. The thought is this: what if, when I leave the theatre or turn off my Xbox, I'm really still inside of a game-world? This spooky question turns into a philosophical problem when one starts to wonder whether there is any way we could test out the hypothesis that we are not still trapped in such a virtual world.

Philosophers refer to this conundrum as the Problem of the External World. There are actually two logically independent ways of formulating the problem. The *empirical* problem of the external world exists for everybody. This is just the task of deriving a scientifically adequate account of why it is that people come to have the experiences they have and believe the things that they do about the existence of a world beyond their own perceptions. Solving this problem is at least a large part of the agenda of contemporary cognitive science. In contrast, the *philosophical* problem of the external world is the task of explaining how we can have knowledge of anything other than sense data if we only directly perceive sense data.

The philosophical version of the problem was famously viewed by Martin Heidegger as an embarrassment to philosophy.[15] In his classic eighteenth-century discussions of the problem, *Principles of Human Knowledge* and *Three Dialogues Between Hylas and Philonous*, the British philosopher (and

Anglican Bishop) George Berkeley describes the philosophical version of the problem as insoluble.[16] He defends a very eccentric philosophical position about the external world that is nowadays known as idealism. A Berkeleyan idealist believes that all that exists are mental entities (i.e., thoughts, feelings, sensations, desires, and emotions), the minds that apprehend them, and God, who is the original source of all of these phenomena that present themselves to the human mind, which he originally created. Berkeleyan idealists are paradigmatic examples of phenomenalists, but in addition they believe that there is no external physical reality whatsoever causing the sense data that presents itself to the eye of the mind.

On Berkeley's view, the evil computers in *The Matrix* could not really fool us about the nature of reality by altering our sense data to make us see things that aren't there. For the Berkeleyan idealist, sense data are *all that is there*; there is nothing "more real" behind them that we could be missing out on. This is a strange view. Normally we think that physical objects such as chairs and tables have independent existence outside of our minds. But idealism requires us to believe that things like chairs and tables are really nothing more than clusters of thoughts, feelings, sensations, desires, and emotions that subsist only within the minds of thinking subjects like ourselves (and God). Berkeley's view of our perceptual orientation is depicted in Figure 2.9.

Note that the "reality" part of the picture is now completely gone. Only the realm of appearance remains.

Russell was understandably wary of the possibility that his own philosophical picture of how we get knowledge about the external world might be

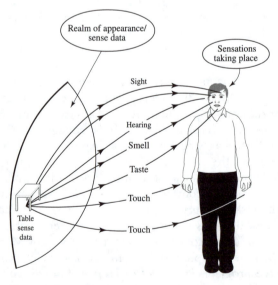

Figure 2.9

in danger of collapsing into Berkeley's brand of wildly unintuitive idealism. He therefore sought to show that, contra Berkeley, objects in the external world *cause* our sense data, rather than sense data being all that there is. We don't perceive the real table, just sense data somehow caused by the table. But we are not (according to Russell) simply deluded when we ask what the sense data can tell us about the nature of the real table.

Consider the status of "unobservable" entities in the sciences, such as electrons. The Russellian takes electrons to exist as the things that cause measuring devices in scientists' laboratories to register their existence. The view that the unobservable theoretical entities of science exist is called "scientific realism." Even though this view makes a bit of a mystery of the real world, it doesn't at first glance seem all that far from common sense. After all (to pursue the video game analogy a bit further), it is not as though the fact that we only ever see images on the screen prevents more sophisticated gamers from speculating about the structure of the underlying programming code. The scientific realist wants us to think of entities that are not directly observable as playing a role that is analogous to these invisible lines of code. They are what makes the perceptible parts of the world apparent to us.

Nonetheless, we will try to demonstrate here that Russell's solution to the philosophical problem of the external world runs afoul of empirical data concerning perception. We will argue that, even given the considerable intuitive plausibility of Russell's account of the relationship between sense data and scientific knowledge, a non-phenomenalist view of the matter turns out to be preferable.

We originally presented Russell's main argument for phenomenalism in the following way.

2.3.1 Russell's Problems of Philosophy Argument (again)

1   The properties we perceive such as shape, smell, sound, and texture change as we change our positions and change techniques of observation.
2   Real properties of objects are stable, in that they typically don't change merely as a result of either people changing as they observe the objects, or our techniques of observation changing.
3   Therefore the properties we perceive are not real properties of objects.

Russell goes on to suggest that when we actually perceive an object, our minds engage in some kind of inferential behavior. The mind takes in the various sense data it perceives, and from this, manages to draw conclusions about what kinds of objects it is confronted with. So we see something that appears to be made of wood with legs and deduce from this that it must be a table.

If this is the correct model of how a human being's "visual interface" lets her obtain justified beliefs about the external world, then insofar as we mean to talk about the "real color" of an object we are talking about the "sort of color which it will seem to have to a normal spectator from an ordinary point of view under usual conditions of light" (*Problems* 10). Likewise with shape, "the 'real' shape is not what we see; it is something inferred from what we see. And what we see is constantly changing in shape as we move about the room; so that here again the senses seem not to give us the truth about the table itself, but only about the appearance of the table." (*Problems* 11) Given this, we can add the following to Russell's argument.

4   With color and shape it is clear that we indirectly infer the real, stable properties of an object by making inferences from the sense data we directly perceive when viewing the object.
5   From these examples, it is plausible to think that all real properties of objects are such that we get our knowledge of them by making inferences from the sense data we directly perceive when viewing the object.

But, how could these inferences possibly take place, given that we do not perceive the world itself while it is busy causing our sensations? Russell holds that because objects in the external world cause our perceptions, we can know about relations between those objects. We take his argument for this claim to be the following.

2.3.2 Russell's Argument about Knowledge of Relations

1   If two events are different in some way, then their causes must be different.
2   Sensations of sense data are effects caused by physical objects.
3   Thus, if two sensations are different in some way, then the physical objects which cause them must be different.
4   Thus, our immediate knowledge of differences among sense data allows us to make inferences about the differences among physical objects (those that cause the sense data).
5   Since relations express a kind of difference, when we know that a relation (such as "is darker than") holds between two sense data (say two shades of red), we know that differences must hold between the physical objects that cause the sense data.

So far there is perhaps not that much to object to here. Russell wants something stronger than the preceding conclusion, though. He wants to conclude that when we see two instances of the same relation between sense data we can infer that there are two instances of *the very same relation* between the physical objects. He writes that "[i]f one object looks blue and another red, we may reasonably presume that there is some corresponding difference between the physical objects: if two objects both look blue, we may presume a corresponding similarity" (*Problems* 34). He supposes of any two pairs of adjacent red and blue sense data, that there will be a difference in the two sets of objects that cause them, and that this difference will be the same in each case. Moreover, he assumes that all causes of perceptions of blue will be similar, just as all perceptions of blue are similar.

To get the conclusion he wants, Russell must add to the above argument the premise that:

6   If two effects are similar, then their causes must be similar.

Only with this claim assumed to be true can he conclude that our knowledge of the relations between our own sense data deserves to be regarded as the sort of knowledge about the external world that the sciences have always promised us.

But Premise Six is false. Consider the following relatively well-known facts about the early history of video game design. Throughout the 1980s and early 1990s the most advanced video games were designed by constructing objects out of a finite set of uniformly colored polygons—red circles, yellow triangles, purple octagons, and so on. Polygons of exactly the same shape, size, and color could quite easily show up as parts of radically different objects—e.g., in some outfit worn by Mario, or in the flames from a distant explosion in Mario's environment—in spite of significant differences in the underlying programming that caused them to appear on the screen in each of these different contexts. If differences such as these can underlie perceptible similarities even within the very restricted realm of a single old-school video game, then surely even more radical causal variation must be possible in the world at large.

Our use of this video game analogy might well come across as something of a cheat. Surely, the shapes on the screen can still be counted as the "same" objects, even if the code behind them is different. After all, whatever causes two polygons to appear side by side on a screen within the programming of a game is not the only factor that leads us to see one as a yellow square and the other as a red triangle. In a more basic sense, what causes our perception is the relationship between the mechanism of the human eye and the wavelengths of light that impinge upon it. And we were all taught in high school physics class that perceived colors are simply nothing over and above wavelengths of light reflected by objects in the world outside of us.

Unfortunately for the Russellian, though, high school is a kingdom of lies. In a related context, Alva Noë discusses metameric pairs[17] (*Action* 151), which are objects that are the same color even though their spectral power distributions (what Noe calls "surface spectral reflectance"; hereafter SSR) are quite different from each other. The spectral power distribution of an object measures the amount of light reflected or absorbed by the object at all visible wavelengths. If the color of an object were a one-to-one function of the reflected wavelengths, then objects that appeared to be the same color would have similar spectral power distributions. But they don't. Some objects are metameric pairs in some lighting conditions but not in others. This gives rise to what has been called the "jacket and pants problem,"[18] where a pair of pants and jacket match beautifully under the otherwise unforgiving fluorescent light of the clothing store, but clash with one another in sunlight or the warmer ambience achieved by tungsten bulbs.[19] Likewise, in what Noë calls "the push–pull effect," context radically affects the way we perceive color, such that objects with the same SSRs are perceived as being radically different colors depending upon context. For example, grayish paper on a yellow background looks violet, while the same paper on a violet background does not. This phenomenon is the *converse* of metameric pairs, and just as ubiquitous a part of vision.[20]

These facts about vision spell trouble for the phenomenalist. But they are far from being esoteric—in fact, they need to be taken into account by any competent artist or designer.[21] When trying to depict a realistic game-world using some contemporary game design engine, one must be aware (for example) that green grass in bright sunlight actually looks yellow when one is staring straight at it, or else the game will end up looking like an "angry fruit salad" (a common term of derision among people who do this kind of work).[22]

We have now seen that classical phenomenalism runs into trouble not only when it comes to avoiding the homunculus fallacy, but also when it comes to providing convincing reasons for why we should believe in an external world. Perhaps a more sophisticated version of phenomenalism could overcome these difficulties. We have surely done enough by now, though, to motivate the search for a wholly different account of what it is for the human mind to perceive objects in the world and think about the information it obtains thereby. The theory we will look at next is called enactivism, and has been most clearly articulated and persuasively defended by Alva Noë. As we will quickly come to see, the enactivist not only provides a better account of how our senses inform us about the outside world. He is also able to provide us with a much more plausible explanation for why games that strive for realism in other dimensions than the purely visual (e.g., those designed for the Wii) are likely to be the wave of the future.

2.4 Our Heideggerian Heritage, Part One: Noë's Enactive Theory of Perception

Perhaps the most natural and intuitively appealing argument for phenomenalism that we presented earlier on was the Argument from Different Minds. Here it is again.

1 Other creatures (e.g., bats, dogs, and birds) perceive the world completely differently from how we do.
2 It follows that neither we nor these other creatures are perceiving the

world as it actually is, but at best, the world as it is presented to us by our own sensory manifolds.

3   This shows that what we and these other creatures directly perceive is sense data, rather than the real properties of objects.

Noë attacks this argument head on, discussing the apparently radical differences between human perception and, for example, the strange color perception that pigeons must have as a result of the five distinct kinds of cones in their eyes. Noë asserts that this difference alone is no reason for holding that the properties don't exist independently of the viewers (*Action* 145). Perhaps the pigeon and the human are seeing different properties that are really there, and would continue to be there even if there were no humans or pigeons. Why can't it be the case that the pigeon's visual system allows it to focus on real aspects of the things that it sees, aspects that are just not perceived by creatures with the human visual system?

Is this plausible? Siding with the non-phenomenalist in this case requires at least a sketch of an account of how the same underlying reality can be so multi-faceted as to present incommensurable sensory properties to different creatures perceiving it. But Noë has powerful allies in this endeavor.

Near the beginning of his magnum opus, *Being and Time*, the German philosopher Martin Heidegger famously contends that, when we perceive some everyday object such as a hammer, it is in fact not the properties that arise from its "objective presence" that we first become aware of cognitively. In fact, the normal situation is that we first and foremost cognize the things we can *do* with the hammer. Under normal circumstances we apprehend it as something that can drive in nails, straighten boards, or (if we are somewhat desperate) open tins of soup *before* we notice the particular shade of silver that it is, or even the type of material it is made out of. According to Heidegger, these latter sorts of properties, which are the concern of the perceptual psychologist and occupy a privileged position in the phenomenalist's account of our knowledge of the external world, normally only enter our conscious awareness when something happens to impede our performance of the sorts of tasks that the hammer is *for*—e.g., if the handle is too hot to hold, or the head is too light to pound in a recalcitrant nail.

This phenomenon is made especially vivid by the experience of playing certain sorts of fast-paced video games; however rich and absorbing the background environments of first-person shooters like *Gears of War* or driving games like *Gran Turismo* might be, the player often finds herself thinking of everything she sees either as something to shoot at or as something to avoid crashing into. Perhaps a somewhat less adrenaline-fueled version of this process is *always* what is going on when we perceive the world—perhaps, in Heidegger's terms, it is the world's "readiness-to-hand," rather than its "objective presence" that we register via our sensory apparatus (*Being* 69–70).

Heidegger's discussion of these matters is highly abstruse, and it must surely strike some readers as unintuitive to suggest that we somehow "see" (say) a car's usefulness at getting us to grandma's house before we register the fact that it is purple. But the Heideggerian view has been taken seriously by some schools of empirical psychologists.[23] For the modern enactivist, perception both depends upon and is constituted by the perceiver's ability to move himself in goal-directed ways. According to this view perception *just is* registering possibilities of action afforded by the environment. It is not the case that we first see something (e.g., flatness) and then cognize the perception in terms of opportunities for action it presents us with. Rather, to see something just is to detect it as "affordable" for characteristically human actions. The enactivist is therefore able to provide a solution to the empirical problem of the external world by describing how our movement and the input to our nerves simultaneously create both possibilities of action and beliefs about the real-world objects that surround us.

Noë's approach to the philosophy of perception also disarms Russell's *Problems of Philosophy* Argument from Section 1.2.1. Noë's enactivist position turns out to be inconsistent with both Premise One and Premise Two of Russell's argument. In Noë's view, all objects in the external world really have two different types of properties, both of which can be objects of perception. He distinguishes the properties that we perceive as existing entirely independent of our observation (F-properties) from those we perceive as constituting the way that objects appear given one's spatial relation to them (P-properties) (*Action* 83). Noë argues that reflection on the nature of our own perception supports the claim that, *contra* Russell, we directly perceive both of these kinds of properties.

Here is an example to demonstrate how Noë wants us to think of the distinction between these two sorts of properties. One of the recurring skits on the sketch comedy television show *Kids in the Hall* involves a character staring in an angry yet simultaneously giddy manner at passersby, closing one eye, while holding a thumb and forefinger in front of the other and saying, "I crush your head!" as he pinches the two fingers together. Sometimes, when discovered, he points his thumb pad forward, Fonzie-style, and moves it over his open eye until the visage of the offending person is obscured, shouting out things like "You disappear!" Part of what makes this routine so funny is the way the camera assumes the head crusher's perspective, so the viewer sometimes sees a giant thumb and forefinger pinching down on some hapless pedestrian's head. As Figure 2.10 shows, the camera's perspective can simultaneously make it look both like the victim's head is being crushed and like it is only being occluded by a pair of fingers.

This image is humorous because we can perceive it as occupying both a perspectival and a factual dimension. Perspectivally, we can tell the fingers just look bigger because they are closer, and that any head crushing is nothing more than occlusion of the line of sight. Our ability to perceive the perspectival properties allows us to not quake in fear for the victim. Yet

Figure 2.10

when we look at it from a factual perspective it can look like just a little bit like we are seeing a real world where a poor person's head is being crushed.

The enactivist's view of perception is distinct from that of the phenomenalist because it involves the insight that perception always involves registering these two aspects of the world (*Action* 169). The main philosophical lesson that we can learn from Noë's account of how P-properties fit into our overall picture of the natural world is that there just *isn't any* mysterious "inner realm" where a person-like homunculus observes sense data as though they were images on a video screen. Or, as Noë himself puts it, "If there is a mind/world divide (in a Cartesian sense, a divide between the mental interior and the non-mental outside), then P-properties are firmly on the world side of the divide. They depend on relations to perceivers, yes. But perceivers (at least their bodies) are also on the world side of the divide" (*Action* 83). If the existence of P-properties can be explained by objective science, then there will be no need to invoke sense data to explain the properties we perceive. In the case of an object's shape, the laws of perspective make explaining P-properties in terms of objective, external properties a straightforward task. For example, the compact disk on its side looks like an ellipse because if you were to occlude it (and just it) with a flat, two-dimensional object at any distance between your eye and the disk, you would use an ellipse. The closer the occlusion is to your eye, the smaller an ellipse you have to use. With the mathematics of such planes of occlusion one can explain very well the perspectival dimensions involving shape.

Noë's claim that we perceive both the P-properties that change as our perspective changes and (when not subject to delusion-inspiring illusions) the real non-changing properties of objects in the world is controversial, but does not seem to represent too much of a violation of common sense. When we see a tomato, for example, we see that it has the property of redness (F-property), the same color possessed by the fire engine. At the same time, though, we see all of the minute differences in shading (P-properties) that change as lighting conditions shift (*Action* 142), as we move the tomato, and as we move in relation to the tomato. And normal human viewers can easily and immediately distinguish between a green wall that is actually green (F-property) and a white wall that looks green because it is placed under a green light (P-property).[24]

The account of perceptual knowledge presented here is called "enactivist" because it treats perception (just as Heidegger did) as being primarily a source of practical knowledge (intellectual skill that manifests itself in behavior), rather than propositional knowledge (knowledge that some set of declarative statements is true). The practical abilities that allow for perception in humans all involve stimulation of our nerves changing as a function either of our own movement in relation to the perceived object or of the object's movement in relation to us.

If an integral part of the perceptual process is bodily interaction with the environment, then we have a very good explanation of why the peculiar sort of kinesthetic realism provided by the Wii has been so appealing to gamers in spite of the primitiveness of its graphics relative to those offered by the Xbox 360 and the Playstation 3. Noë's view implies that our ability to perceive serves its principal evolutionary function, not by providing us with raw factual information about either the inner or outer worlds, but rather as an integral part of our engagement in survival-relevant physical behavior. As we mentioned in Section 1.1 of the present chapter, even the best games designed so far for the Wii provide only a shadowy simulacrum of what it is really like to ride a horse, throw a football, or (one presumes) flee from rampaging zombies. But if Noë's views are correct, then games that put us through the motions of simulating such behavior will be bound to make immersion in the game-world seem more complete than it ever could when experienced entirely from the perspective of the sofa.

2.5 Empirical Considerations in Favor of the Enactive Theory

The philosophy of perception lies at the crossroads of philosophical and empirical investigation. Here we present some further empirical evidence that is highly relevant both to the debate between phenomenalism and enactivism and to the issue of what constitutes realism in the design of video games.

First, we consider certain extravagant claims made about so-called "visualization" by new age gurus and some sports psychologists. As we will show, the deep-seated desire of human beings to believe claims like this account for a great deal of phenomenalism's perennial attraction. Second, we will discuss the phenomenon of muscle memory and suggest that the commonsensical attribution to muscles of a literal capacity to "remember" their experiences is scientifically valid. Finally, we will attend to the strange phenomenon of people who wear light reversing eyeglasses. In all three cases, the reality of things is exactly what one would expect if enactivism about perception were true.

2.5.1 A Good Walk Spoiled

According to an endlessly repeated urban legend, an American prisoner of war in Vietnam who spent his time in captivity thinking about golf discovered that upon his release his game was radically improved. The story is recounted in detail in a number of places, including the book *A 2nd Helping of Chicken Soup for the Soul*.[25]

This is too good to be true. Snopes.com has exhaustively researched the story and determined that there is no POW golfer.[26] Moreover, the new and growing academic sports psychology research on this issue (for example in the *Journal of Applied Sport Psychology*) reveals no cases remotely analogous to the POW golfer. New Age visualization doesn't accomplish a fraction of what its gurus claim for it. Anyone who has mastered a video game that involves completing tasks with time limitations knows that no amount of *faux*-meditation[27] is going to substitute for the humongous time and energy sink of developing the relevant sensorimotor skills. And if you've mastered a particularly tricky repertoire of these skills, such as playing *Guitar Hero* or performing brain surgery, you remember vividly the hour upon hour of relevant practice it took you to get to the top.

To the minimal extent that visualization does help, it only helps those intensely engaged in actual training.[28] It is for exactly these reasons that, unlike the practice of sitting in a room and thinking about golf, we can expect games like *Wii Golf* (or perhaps their more kinesthetically realistic descendents) to actually improve people's golf games.

Whenever something possesses as much truthiness ("The quality of stating concepts one wishes or believes to be true, rather than the facts"[29]) as the

Vietnam POW golfer myth, the philosophically inclined must ask, "Why?" In this case, the tragic aspects of life lead us to want to believe that just thinking about things will make them better. Strangely, in its new age guise, phenomenalism[30] is attractive to the legions of people taken in by the golfer myth for the very same reason. Unlike Berkeley (who believed in a robust form of objectivity ensured by God's thinking the universe) many people hold that to the extent that our perceptions of the world are all in our minds, we can exert much greater power over the world just by thinking in certain ways. And the fact that nothing remotely like this is true[31] thus provides some evidence for enactivism over at least popular non-theistic versions of phenomenalism.

2.5.2 *We Want to Pump You Up*

The concept of "muscle memory" has had obvious common sense appeal since long before the invention of game systems like the Wii that make use of a realistic kinesthetic interface. Anyone who has self-consciously mastered a complex sensorimotor skill knows that there is *something it is like* to be able to use that skill. Part of what it feels like is that the relevant muscles in some sense know what they are doing. And sometimes you can perform a task better if you *don't* think about it, and rather just let the muscles do their thing.

Furthermore, anyone who has played *Guitar Hero* (which, along with *Dance Dance Revolution* and first person arcade shooters such as *Silent Scope*, was one of the few pre-Wii games with an inventive kinesthetic interface) has probably gone through periods of not being able to play as much as formerly. After such a period, when you pick up the guitar controller again, it doesn't do what you want it to do right away. But for most players, it doesn't take that long to get the mojo back. The jump from bad-because-out-of-practice to competent is much easier than the jump from bad-because-still-learning to competent, even if the two kinds of badness make it equally hard (initially) to get a good score in the game. It is as if your muscles remember what to do, and it just takes a little warming up before you can lose yourself in the glory of Rock.

Here is one area where we've been told over and over again that common sense is wrong, insofar as your muscles don't really "remember" anything. Consider for example the online literature by the company Simlog, which produces state of the art training tools for people who operate heavy machinery. Simlog's products involve proprietary software and interface hardware that simulate complicated tasks such as the operation of a crane. The hardware is an essential part of adequately training people on these dangerous machines, since so much of the training is developing the proper sensorimotor profiles. One would expect the designers of these technologies at Simlog to embrace the idea the muscles really can "learn" and "remember." But on their website we get the following remarks: "Of course, during the 'drill-and-practice,' your muscles aren't really memorizing anything (since all memories are stored in your brain). Instead, what you see with your eyes is interpreted by your brain in the form of nerve signals to your muscles to make your body move."[32] The idea that memory is only in your brain is presented by the company as being scientifically informed common sense. But is it?

J.L. Andersen and P. Aagaard[33] have discovered that muscles really do *remember*, in a near-literal sense of the word. These researchers measured composition of motor proteins in muscle fiber for people at four stages: (1) sedentary men prior to engaging in a gym regimen, (2) the same men after engaging in a three-month gym regimen of resistance training, (3) the same men again, after a three-month layoff period, and (4) the same group after re-engaging in the resistance training. Not surprisingly, the subjects were able to increase their weightlifting abilities faster from (3) to (4) than they were in their initial jump from (1) to (2). This is just like the *Guitar Hero* guitarist who has not played for a long time finding out that, although he's initially horrible, it doesn't take that long for him to rock out again.

Andersen and Aagaard discovered the physiological basis for this phenomenon. As expected, after the initial training period, subjects had much higher levels of the protein MHC IIA in their muscle fiber (an average increase of 42% to 49% of MHC motor proteins). They also had much lower levels of MHC IIX (from 9% to 2%). Muscles higher in MHC IIA are able to lift more and muscles higher in MHC IIX respond well to training. But here is the strange part: after the three month period of deconditioning (phase (3)), as the average subject's MHC IIA levels went back down to his slothful pre-training level, his MHC IIX levels went up to 17%! The much higher MHC IIX levels characteristic of phase (3) over phase (1) provide a chemical basis for the easier training. So even though subjects could not lift any more than they could initially, it was easier for them to get back this ability, because their muscles *really did remember*.

This aspect of sensorimotor remembering is therefore not "all in the brain"; it is in the parts of the body doing the work. When the weight trainer says that her muscles remember what to do, this is true because the muscles themselves are primed to be able to repeat the relevant tasks with much less training. Moreover, it is not unlikely that more fine grained motor skills such as manipulating a game controller work the same way. The reason the *Guitar Hero* player can retrain so quickly is in part because the chemical and geometric makeup of the relevant muscle fibers store the memory of having done the relevant task through the kind of latencies uncovered by Andersen and Aagaard. All of this is what one would expect if enactivism is true. If perception is a matter of doing and being able to do then one would expect that mental states like remembering needn't all come together at one place in the mind or the brain.[34]

At this point, the hardened phenomenalist will likely argue that it follows from the very concept of remembering that muscle memory somehow does not count. This is not a debate we can hope to engage in here. We will close the discussion, however, by again noting that one of the most interesting lines of thought in the contemporary philosophy of mind comes from Andy Clark and David Chalmers' forceful arguments for the extended mind thesis (see the discussion in Chapter one). If their position that the mind does not stop with the brain, or the body, but actually expands to include parts of one's physical environment is correct, then the attempt to define away muscle memory begins to look pretty implausible.[35]

Clark has said that his "eureka" moment as a philosopher of mind involved reflection on Alzheimer's patients who remain functional by arranging their houses in certain ways. By offloading their memories into the environment, they are able to cope with the degeneration of their brains for longer than they otherwise could. According to the extended mind thesis, the highly functional Alzheimer's patient who needs a notebook to record recent memories or a careful arrangement of fridge magnets for longer-term memories is more like the rest of us than we might think. Consider the following perfectly normal human behaviors: doing a long math problem on a blackboard, painting a picture and responding aesthetically to it as you work, or swapping a standard console game controller out for a big plastic wheel to play driving games like *Need for Speed* and *Gran Turismo*. Clark and Chalmers argue that, if we assume the mind is where the problem-solving, artistic creation, or game-beating strategy take place, and if there is no practical difference between the person who does it in her head and the person who does it with external props such as pen and paper, canvas, or driving wheel, then the mind must actually include the external props. Compared to this strange suggestion, the idea that our mind includes our muscles should seem at least relatively commonsensical.

2.5.3 *I Want to Ride My Bicycle*

Anyone forced by a cruel genetic heritage to remove recalcitrant ear hairs with a pair of tweezers knows that getting your reflection in a mirror to follow your commands is tough going. But until Ivo Kohler's ground breaking experiments, nobody had any idea how difficult it could be.

Subjects in this series of experiments were made to continuously wear left-to-right inverting lenses over their eyes, so that researchers could study their adaptation times. The inverting glasses were constructed so that light that would normally hit a position so many degrees to the right of the visual field would instead hit it at the same number of degrees to the left.

A natural prediction to make about this scenario is that people would find it more difficult to do regular things. Removing someone else's ear hairs would now be as difficult as removing your own in the mirror. Strangely, this prediction only gets it one-third correct. After an initial period of wearing the reversing lenses, people did report seeing things such as their left arm doing what their brain told their right arm to do, and text appearing as it does in a mirror. If one tried to remove a friend's ear hair in this state, much hilarity would ensue.

But the period of adaptation *preceding* this phase was far uglier and more terrifying than anyone conducting the experiment foresaw.

> During visual fixations, every movement of my head gives rise to the most unexpected and peculiar transformations of objects in the visual field. The most familiar forms seem to dissolve and reintegrate in ways never before seen. At times, parts of figures run together, the spaces between disappearing from view; at other times they run apart, as if intent on deceiving the observer. Countless times I was fooled by these extreme distortions and taken by surprise when a wall, for instance, suddenly appeared to slant down to the road, when a truck I was following with my eyes started to bend, when the road began to arch like a wave, when houses and trees seemed to topple down, and so forth. I felt as if I were living in a topsy-turvy world of houses crashing down on you, of heaving roads, and of jellylike people.[36]

The subjects of Kohler's experiment did not just see a mirror image world, initially. Instead, they were immersed in an existentialist's worst nightmare! Nothing made visual sense and everything was nauseating to behold.

Luckily, vomit-inducing surrealism was merely a phase that the subjects passed through. As they moved about in this nightmare-reality, order slowly began to reassert itself, and in phase two they reported living in the mirrored world that researchers expected. They extended their right arms, but saw their left arms extending. Print appeared as if the book was held up to the mirror. They could pickout their friends. With eyes closed, they could pick their own noses. But they could not pick their friends' noses (at least not with any skill). But then, after more days there was another transition, and the perceptual field began to appear the way it initially was! When a subject willed his right arm to pick something up, the right arm moved flawlessly and he actually perceived his right arm moving. At this point he could ride a bicycle just as he did prior to wearing the spectacles. Unfortunately, though, when the spectacles were removed, even though there was nothing interfering any longer with the light that hit the surfaces of their eyes, the subjects again had to go through the phases of horrific existentialism and simple reversal before returning to normal.

Noë argues persuasively that these superficially surprising results are in fact just what the enactivist would predict. If perception not only assists but is *constituted by* features of one's overall sensorimotor capabilities, then we have a great explanation of all three phases. The subjects' initial nausea was due to the fact that perspectival shape properties were all reversed. But once the subjects learned to move and manipulate things in this reversed world, it began to make sense as a world. And then finally, once these sensorimotor profiles are relearned in the reverse world, the subject notices no difference from the time prior to wearing the spectacles. But if enactivism is correct, this is because there *is* no difference. Perception itself just is a function of such mastery.

Video games present some possible ways in which this test could be extended. One could reverse the monitor and see what happens with experienced gamers. Note that, on a truly reversed monitor, when the player manipulated the game controller to go left the avatar would move right.[37] We predict that this total reversal, when wedded to traditional kinesthetic interfaces like that of the Wii, would lead the player to the hilarity stage, where graphical effects, monsters and environmental backdrops would all look backwards, and game controller routines would have to be relearned before the game felt right. But we also suspect that, as the level of kinesthetic realism improves in the games of the coming decades, this sort of reversal experiment might cause expert players to go through an initial phase of existentialist horror similar to the experiences had by Kohler's subjects at the start of his experiment. Indeed, such reversal tests could help to gauge a game's overall kinesthetic realism: the greater the level of existential madness following the reversal of the game-world, the more realistic the interface.

2.6 Conclusions

D.Z. Suzuki's version of an old Zen saying is, "Before Zen, men are men and mountains are mountains; during Zen study, things become confused; after enlightenment, men are men and mountains are mountains, only one's feet are a little off the ground."[38] While this chapter no doubt fails to provide the health benefits of a life of meditation in the Hindu or Buddhist tradition, overcoming phenomenalism is an intellectual version of the Zen journey toward enlightenment.

With everything we have on the table at this point, it becomes easier to answer our original questions. Question One: why did people mistakenly expect that demand for competitor consoles would be so much higher than for the Wii? Answer: the player-as-phenomenalist-homunculus paradigm of video game design was as entrenched as phenomenalism itself. Question Two: why does Wii play seem so much more realistic to players, even though its visual interface is so much worse? Answer: enactivism is true. Perception is not an isolated mental phenomenon, as the phenomenalist believes, but rather a function of one's overall sensorimotor profile.

For video games with a fairly traditional kinesthetic interface, realism is achieved by having the sensory interface more closely approximate the privileged representations of reality that are presented to us in photography, movies, and television. But *total* realism—the sort of sensation a player might get of feeling that she is "really there," in the midst of the game's action—will never be achieved through this sort of interface until games can track players' focus in a way that mimics how our eyes can bring any object in the visual field into focus. By way of contrast, greater kinesthetic realism will be achieved by developing game controllers and styles of game-play that more closely mimic the ways that people manipulate objects in non-game environments. By devising game controllers that better mapped the relevant sensorimotor skills, the Wii's designers launched us into the next phase of the gradual but (so gamers hope) inevitable transition toward truly realistic and immersive video games.

3 "Realistic Blood and Gore": Do Violent Games Make Violent Gamers? (First-Person Shooters)

3.1 The Problem

From the third century BCE to the fourth century CE, one of the most popular forms of entertainment in the civilized world was gladiatorial combat.[1] Citizens of ancient Rome watched prisoners of war, slaves, and criminals fight one another with deadly weapons, often with the predictable outcome of maiming or death. Sometimes, for variety, the audience was treated to the spectacle of bloody fights between exotic, imported animals. If the games were sponsored by a particularly wealthy politician, then historical battles might be recreated. Under the emperor Nero there was a brief vogue for stage plays, in which people who had been condemned to death were cast in key roles. When the convicts' characters died in these plays the performers were duly executed in full view of the audience as a part of the performance.

Such exhibitions were officially banned by the Emperor Constantine in 325 CE, but had a brief revival in Christian Rome shortly after his edict. In various permutations, similar spectacles have been with us to this day. To the non-fan, the sport of American football can seem to consist of nothing more than gigantic, highly trained masochists crashing repeatedly into one another, and professional hockey regularly includes dangerous fistfights for which normal citizens would be arrested. The deleterious short and long-term health effects of both of these sports (not to mention boxing and the increasingly popular "cage fighting") are comparable to those that were suffered by Roman gladiators. Likewise, our television news broadcasts, documentaries, and films contain graphic portrayals of crime at home and military engagements abroad that are watched by millions voluntarily, for reasons that bear (at best) a dubious connection to the desire to be politically informed. Still, we modern people can surely console ourselves that our tastes are not *quite* as gruesome as those of the ancient Romans.

Or can we? Consider the video games of the *Grand Theft Auto* series, where the player takes on the role of a career criminal: stealing cars, cruising for prostitutes, and shooting people in public streets. Or take *Soldier of Fortune*, whose designers used a special rendering system so that the player can target specific human body parts with simulated gunfire. Or *Half Life 2*, the first few hours of which are gunfights in the sewer system of a future world where the only thing that differentiates the player from his human quarry is the fact that the latter all wear masks. Unlike the gladiators, we are not actually exposed to the threat of death or dismemberment. But also unlike the Roman spectators at gladiatorial contests, we who play these games are doing something more than merely watching. The players of first-person shooter (FPS) games act out a part in the simulated deaths of other human beings, and usually not just one or two, but dozens and dozens within an average hour of game-play. Might not even the most bloodthirsty onlooker at one of Nero's entertainments balk at the opportunity to take on a more active role in the slaughter?

Of course, the key word in the above description of FPS games is "simulated." The player knows that she is not causing real agony, mutilation, and death. The closest one ever comes to doing any real harm to man or beast is when one "kills" another real player's avatar in online multiplayer FPS games such as *Counterstrike, Unreal Tournament*, or *The Ship*. And players of these games do not usually come to identify with their avatars in the ways that are characteristic of more immersive games such as *Second Life*. Surely (one might think) this difference in degrees of realism makes all the ethical difference between our tastes in entertainment and those of the Romans. For surely the moral wrongness of violence derives from the fact that people actually get hurt by it; if nobody is being injured in any way, then, it follows that the makers, sellers, and players of these games have nothing to feel guilty about.

In fact, one might make the following suggestion: playing FPS games is not only blameless but therapeutic. Ever since the massive popularity of *Doom* in the early 1990s, a segment of the population that is demonstrably more prone to committing violent crimes than any other (males between the ages of eighteen and forty-five)[2] have been the most avid consumers of a type of entertainment that allows them to vent their aggressive feelings without punching, hitting, or shouting at anything other than a game controller or a PC monitor. Perhaps ethical criticisms of FPS games, like the complaints one sometimes hears about violent sports, represent nothing more than a failure to acknowledge the dark side of human motivation and the need to channel our hostile affects away from one another and in the direction of more harmless pursuits.

The ethical debate about violence in entertainment and the arts is surprisingly an old one. Both of the greatest philosophers of the ancient world, Plato and Aristotle, had strong views on the subject. Plato thought that violent entertainment was morally destructive to impressionable consumers. Aristotle suggested that, if placed in the right context, certain displays of violence in art can actually have a morally edifying effect on their audience. A comparison of these two philosophers' ethical approaches to the depiction of violence thus presents us with a philosophically troubling dilemma; we are faced with a pair of views that both seem more or less equally plausible, yet have a strong appearance of being logically incompatible.

In this chapter, we examine arguments for and against the moral wrongness of violence in art. While the upshot of our discussion is broadly pro-Aristotelian, we will also suggest that when it comes to the question of whether we are morally harmed by playing games like *Doom* and *Grand Theft Auto*, one must attend to tricky questions about the nature of the violence depicted, the precise kind of enjoyment derived from the games, and the different ways in which a human being can be morally harmed.

3.2 Our Platonic Heritage: The Emulation Argument

Most gamers are familiar with the little stickers on game packaging that describe their level of "mature content." These ratings range from "Early Childhood" to "Adults Only," and include descriptions of the kind of potentially offensive content in each game (e.g., "Violence," "Crude Humor," "Use of Tobacco," etc.) They are applied to games by a group called the Entertainment Software Ratings Board (ESRB). The ESRB was formed in 1994 by major companies in the game industry as the result of pressure from the US Congress. Since commercial video games (unlike pornographic films, in the age of digital video) are extremely expensive to make, this rating code has the effect of destroying the economic viability of "Adults Only" games by limiting where and when they can be sold. Because of this, and given the specifically political pressure that led the industry to impose the rating system in the first place, many consider the current system to be an instance of censorship.[3]

The main reason why censorship of video games took off in the 1990s and not earlier[4] was a crucial improvement in the technology of game design during that period, viz., the production of games for 16-bit gaming consoles. Suddenly, visual images and in-game sound were startlingly more realistic than they had ever been before (though the games from this era look comically artificial to anyone who has played near-photorealistic shooters like *Max Payne, Crysis*, and the recent versions of *Battlefield* and *Call of Duty*). The most infamously violent game of this period was *Mortal Kombat*, a two-dimensional fighting game that features huge eruptions of gore, elaborate spectacles of dismemberment, and the opportunity to cause a "fatality" (via decapitation, impalement on long metal spikes, or other equally gruesome means) at a point in the game after one had already beaten one's opponent.

One of the strangest features of the ESRB rating system is that it treats games as being worse if they are especially *realistic* in their portrayal of violence. In the original rating system first formulated in 1994, two phrases that were sometimes included on labels as a warning to parents and sensitive souls were "Realistic Blood and Gore" and "Realistic Violence." And as of 2007, the ESRB was still warning players of the presence of "Real

Gambling." From the perspective of the philosophical aesthetician, this is bizarre. In most other art and entertainment media, particular works are conventionally viewed as aesthetically *superior* to the extent that they evince realism. Few things are normally more off-putting than psychologically implausible characters in a novel, errors of perspective in a landscape painting, or out-of-period costumes in a historical film. But the thesis that realistic art is morally dangerous precisely because of its realism is in fact a very old opinion. It receives its first lengthy and energetic defense in the writings of Plato.[5]

Plato's *Republic* is presented to the reader as the record of a discussion between the famous philosopher Socrates and some local aristocrats, public figures, and hangers-on in ancient Athens, including Plato's own brother, a young Athenian citizen named Glaucon. Much of the book consists of a long description by Socrates of what life would be like in a perfectly just society. The task of describing such a society is undertaken by Socrates (who was Plato's real-life teacher and friend) not for the conventional reason that has motivated many other thinkers to construct imaginary utopias, viz., the hope that others will try to bring the fictional societies that they describe into existence in the real world. Instead, Socrates suggests that the structure of a city is in some way analogous to the structure of an individual human soul. If one could discover what justice would be in the former, he reasons, then one could also figure out how the personal virtue of justice would manifest itself in the latter. "Perhaps [Socrates says] . . . there is more justice in the larger thing, and it will be easier to learn what it is. So, if you're willing, let us first find out what sort of thing justice is in a city, and afterwards look for it in an individual, observing the ways in which the smaller is similar to the larger" (*Republic* 43).

Having set the terms of the debate in this way, Socrates goes on to propose that certain types of art must be banned in the ideal republic. He prohibits forms of music that, as he puts it, represent "the soft modes, suitable for drinking parties" (*Republic* 74). When a gifted actor or reciter of poetry visits his hypothetical city, Socrates suggests that the rulers should "pour myrrh on his head, crown him with wreaths, and send him away to another city" (*Republic* 73). But Plato reserves his most aggressive and withering criticism for the poetry of Homer.

Plato's attack on Homer's portrayal of Achilles in the *Iliad* bears a provocative similarity to the concerns raised by contemporary politicians and parents that led to the establishment of the ESRB. Homer's epic poems were by far the most widely read works of literature in Plato's own time, as well as the inspiration for much Greek religious practice. Homer announces in the first line of the *Iliad* that the epic's general theme is going to be "the wrath of Achilles," and its plot revolves around the Greek hero's petulant unwillingness to fight alongside his Greek compatriots in the Trojan war, until at last the death of his best friend Patroclus enrages him, at which point he goes on a rampant killing spree. Plato morally disapproves of Achilles' actions, and describes as grounds for his disapproval Achilles' willingness to accept bribes, rebel against a river god, make a spectacle out of murdering the Trojan hero Hector, and massacre Trojan prisoners of war (*Republic* 67).

Plato's main explicit concern is that depictions of this sort of character as a hero will encourage any young man charged with guarding the just city to emulate Achilles' behavior, making him "ready to excuse himself when he's bad" (*Republic* 68). Plato is less concerned, then, with the mere depiction of violence than he is with Homer's apparent attempts to elicit sympathy for people who perform certain kinds of violent acts. Plato's argument for the censorship or removal of works of art like the *Iliad* may therefore be summarized as follows.

3.2.1 The Emulation Argument

1   It is against society's interest to have citizens with unpredictably violent personalities.
2   Works of art that depict characters with violent personalities implicitly encourage their audiences to imitate the characters in question.
3   Thus, works of art that depict violent acts or images are morally harmful.
4   The state is therefore entitled to prevent the production and consumption of this sort of art.

To anyone who has been raised in a society with free speech protections like those enshrined in the First Amendment of the United States Constitution, this argument might come across as highly dubious. Even if the premises were themselves totally plausible, the jump from claims about *society's* problems and interests to a conclusion about what *the state* is entitled to do is a positively sinister argumentative move to make in many political contexts. For example, one can admit that the food many of us enjoy is unhealthy without holding that diet should be controlled by an authoritarian political regime. Perhaps we would all be better off if we only ate what our doctors advised us to, but not at that price.

From the perspective of contemporary discussions of violence in video games, however, there is something even more interesting going on in this ancient argument. Plato appears to have been more or less entirely unconcerned with the effect that the mere *depiction* of violence itself might have on a person's character. His complaint against Homer is not that Achilles is violent, but that it is the wrong *kind* of violence (e.g., killing the enemy is good, but killing prisoners is not). Plato's view reflects the way that many still think about violence in the media. The depiction of graphic violence in war movies such as *Saving Private Ryan* is subjected to moral criticism much less often than the forms of violence that are glorified in some "gangsta" rap songs or in movies such as *The Wild Bunch* or *Kill Bill*. Most consumers find games like those in the *Grand Theft Auto* series (where a player must direct his character to incessantly commit criminal acts to win) vastly more off-putting than historical FPS games such as *Battlefield 1942*, in which the player's character is fighting in a just war.

The fact that it is the player's avatar himself (the ultimate "good guy" in most cases) directly committing violence in video games is the main difference between video games and any form of entertainment that was available in Plato's time. Plato himself probably would have been appalled. Since what he feared above all else was that characters like Achilles would be emulated by the young, he probably would have been utterly horrified by an art form in which the emulation of violent characters was part of the audience's very experience of the work itself.[6]

3.3 Our Aristotelian Heritage: The Katharsis Argument

In Sophocles' *Oedipus the King*, the eponymous main character accidentally marries his own mother. When he finds out the identity of his bride, he walks offstage and gouges his eyes out, then returns to let the audience see his handiwork, via a wooden mask painted liberally with gore. The effect of this spectacle on its Greek audience in the fifth century BCE must have been at least as shocking as any of the gruesome "fatalities" in *Mortal Kombat* or the jarring bullet-to-the-head graphics in *Soldier of Fortune*. But Aristotle seems to have thought that this sort of graphic shock was something that could play an ethically *positive* role for the citizens of Ancient Greece.

3.3.1 *The Argument*

Aristotle thought that *Oedipus* represented the finest extant example of tragic drama. In his *Poetics*, he claims that part of the explanation of the play's success as an artwork was the depiction of the horrible events that befall Oedipus. It was principally though these jarring effects, he thought, that the play attains the goal that is shared by all good examples of tragic drama, i.e. the "achieve[ment] through pity and fear [of] a *katharsis* of such emotions."[7]

This remark is one of the most famous statements in all of philosophy, but it is also one of the most mysterious, thanks to Aristotle's use of the obscure term *katharsis* to describe the effect that successful artworks of a certain kind are supposed to have upon their audiences. The word *"katharsis"* rarely shows up in the surviving literature of ancient Greece, making it difficult to decide exactly what Aristotle was saying about the value of tragic literature.

Most scholars believe that *"katharsis"* is best translated into English as something like "purge," or "purification."[8] If these hypotheses are correct, then what Aristotle must have been referring to was something like the psychological version of taking a laxative, or the secular version of what some Roman Catholics claim to be doing when they give up certain sorts of food for Lent. But this is puzzling; most theatre enthusiasts pay for tickets and attend plays voluntarily, but neither Lent nor laxatives are very much fun for those who partake of them. So perhaps Aristotle was trying to describe the aims of tragic drama, not in terms of what the audience of a particular play might have found specifically attractive about an evening at the theatre, but instead in terms of the value of this sort of spectacle for the community as a whole. To put the suggestion in more modern-sounding terms, Aristotle's idea seems to be that the actors' imitation of horrific acts that evoke fear and pity from an audience will provide that audience with a healthy, harmless outlet for emotions that have to be suppressed during the course of everyday life.

One hears the same kind of claim regularly being made in defense of some of the video games that have received especially harsh moral criticism. Fans of FPS games often talk about their therapeutic value for purging hostile sentiments. This way of defending violent games is certainly dubious insofar as it depends upon the presupposition that the people who get pleasure out of blowing up aliens in *Gears of War*, or shooting at headless, bomb-throwing monsters in *Serious Sam* would be more likely to be causing similar kinds of carnage in the real world if they didn't have the pleasures of gaming to fall back on. Relatively few games simulate the sorts of violent situations that the average gamer would have any chance of encountering in real life. There is a lot of difference, after all, between wanting to punch one's irritating coworker after a bad day at the office and running down the street with a machine gun killing everything in one's path. And those games that do provide this sort of opportunity (*Hooligans*, for example, in which the player takes on the persona of a European soccer thug) cater to a very marginal audience and are often found offensive by otherwise thick-skinned gamers.

Still, there may be something right about this approach to defending games with violent content. People who love gaming are happier when they are able to do it regularly; arguably, happy people make better, safer citizens. The best way to present the argument we are trying to make, then, will be to retain the ambiguity of Aristotle's original terminology, rather than trying to provide any detailed paraphrase of what he means in more modern-sounding psychological terms. We'll just take it for granted for the time being that, whatever the word "*katharsis*" means, it must be something beneficial.

3.3.1.1 The Katharsis Argument

1   The audiences of some types of artworks can be led to experience a beneficial *katharsis* of emotions that would otherwise be dangerous to society.
2   The presence of violent acts or images in these artworks can contribute to bringing about this sort of response in their audiences.

3   It is therefore morally beneficial for some types of artworks to depict violent acts or images.

However one chooses to describe the preventative benefits of art (whether it is "escape" that they provide us with, or "therapy," or even a "purge"), we think that this quasi-Aristotelian argument has a strong air of plausibility.

3.3.2 Aesthetic Distance

Of course, the crucial phrase in Premise Three of the *Katharsis* Argument is "some types of artworks." The next thing we need to ask, then, is whether FPS games can plausibly be placed in the same category as Sophoclean tragedies. Are FPS games works of art that provide the *right sort of* psychological release? In connection with this question, another one of Aristotle's observations about the stage dramas of his own day proves especially relevant. Aristotle suggests that there are actually two different ways to stage the blinding of Oedipus; it can either be done "through spectacle" or through mere verbal narrative. Aristotle makes it clear that he think that the former method is "monstrous" and "less artistic" (*Poetics* 25). He defends this position by making the curious remark that "one ought to seek in tragedy, not every pleasure, but that which is appropriate" (*Poetics* 25). His point here seems to be that overly graphic spectacles of violence might overwhelm the audience in a way that prevents them from getting what is valuable from the experience of art. More generally, genuine aesthetic experience seems to require a certain level of *detachment* on the part of its audience.

A number of more recent philosophers have defended the idea that some sort of emotional detachment is a necessary condition for appreciating art.[9] It is probably this general attitude that causes some to believe that pornography, carnival rides, and bottles of expensive wine don't really qualify as artworks. It is also probably what lurks behind the intuition shared by many habitual readers that because novels require more imaginative work on the part of the consumer, they might be a "higher" art form than narrative films, where much more is "given."[10]

But if painting a mask red to represent the gore from Oedipus' blinding is "monstrous," then what are we to make of games where the skillful player can simulate the brutal deaths of a dozen separate humans or humanoid aliens in less than a minute? Perhaps some of these deaths, as depicted in FPS games with sophisticated storylines like *Max Payne* or *Gears of War*, can plausibly be viewed as essential to the structure of the narrative. But even in these games, most of the fights that the player engages in are little more than tests of her skill at manipulating the diegetic machine gun, flamethrower, or chainsaw with the game controller. And if mastering these sorts of skills is part of the fun of game-play, then the player must surely lack the requisite sort of detachment that Aristotle appears to demand as a precondition for achieving *katharsis*. When it comes to Wii games like *Resident*

Evil 4, in which the player's movements closely mimic what in real life (one presumes) would be required to vanquish a horde of zombies with a shotgun, the ethical outlook seems especially grim from an Aristotelian perspective.[11]

3.4 Empirical Considerations

At this point it is entirely unclear whether the Platonist or Aristotelian should win the day. Some of this ambiguity surely stems from the fact that the questions raised thus far cannot be entirely settled from the perspective of the philosopher's armchair. The Platonist critic would argue that FPS games are bad because children might emulate them. The Aristotelian might argue that at least some such games will have the opposite effect: because they provide the player with an outlet for aggressive emotions, he will as a result be less likely to act violently, and consequently develop a better character. These claims both involve empirical issues, and as such, should be addressed by the social sciences.

3.4.1 The Platonist's Empirical Case

Recent research by psychologists has demonstrated that there is an impressively strong correlation between the playing of violent video games and increases in a person's aggressive thoughts and behaviors. Craig A. Anderson, an experimental psychologist who teaches at Stanford, reports that "violent video game effect sizes are larger than the effect of second hand tobacco smoke on lung cancer, the effect of lead exposure to I.Q. scores in children, and calcium intake on bone mass."[12] It turns out to matter very little whether the violence depicted in games is "realistic" (to use the ESRB's terminology) like what one sees in *Max Payne,* or other-worldly and fantastical, like the sort depicted in *Gears of War.* Even more surprisingly, it doesn't seem to matter whether the game is designed to reward or to punish the player for killing characters within the game. Either way, players of such games show a marked increase in hostile affects, both during play and afterwards.

A number of psychologists who have examined these results have suggested that it is precisely the interactive nature of the games in question that causes them to produce such startling effects on the ideas and attitudes of players.[13] The apparent correlation between violent video games and aggression might lead one to think that the Platonist's position on the ethical status of violence in games is in fact the most plausible. The data that psychologists have collected appears to indicate that, whereas Plato was relying mostly on mere speculation in applying the Emulation Argument to Homer's poems, those who support the agenda of the ESRB might now have a solid empirical justification for their beliefs about the potential social dangers of FPSs.

3.4.2 The Aristotelian Response

The case is really not this clear, though. Research since Anderson's study has shown a connection between the most violent forms of game-play and increased activity in the player's frontal lobes, the parts of the brain responsible for information processing and deliberative decision making.[14] Interestingly, the most violent people in our society characteristically have systematically depressed activity in their frontal lobes, leading them to be far more likely to act on the aggressive impulses that people with fully functioning frontal lobes repress and sublimate. Studies have shown that people with Anti-Personality Disorder, which is common among the most violent criminals, have on average 11% less frontal brain matter (and consequently much less activity).[15] This is an astonishingly large correlation, and should at least suggest the possibility that playing violent video games might causally inhibit the types of severe violence that result in prison sentences.

There is a further extremely important consideration about violence in contemporary societies that has yet to be broached. According to the Department of Justice, levels of violence radically decreased in the United States among men in the age groups that play the most video games during precisely the same period that violent video games became popular.[16] The declines in violence even included relatively minor forms of physical aggression, such as fights in school.

Unlike the behavior documented in these Department of Justice statistics, the actual aggressive behavior observed by psychologists during video game studies is almost negligible from an ethical point of view. In the study of violent video games by Anderson and Dill that is quoted most often, the indicators of increased violent thought and behavior were answers given on a questionnaire by *the players themselves*! In Anderson and Dill's article, descriptions of this data blatantly equivocate between the self-reporting of delinquency and actual delinquency. Such equivocations have unfortunately, but predictably, trickled down into the secondary literature.[17] It is thus vitally important to understand that the study did not correlate playing of violent video games with general delinquency; rather, it correlated playing of such games by college students with self reporting of morally delinquent thoughts and behaviors. No evidence whatsoever is presented to reliably connect such self reporting of college age video gamers with *actual* delinquent behavior. Furthermore, some of the ways that subjects were asked to describe themselves on the questionnaire included "I can't help getting into arguments with people who disagree with me" and "I don't think I am a very tolerant person."[18] One cannot help but think that a philosopher like Aristotle might conclude that such relatively minor forms of aggression (e.g., the initiation of lively philosophical arguments) could well be morally harmless, especially when accompanied by the sort of self-awareness that these students clearly exhibited.

In another oft-quoted study described in the same article, players of

Wolfenstein 3D were given the opportunity to "punish their opponent by delivering a noxious blast of white noise" (*Aggressive* 776). We are as bothered by noise pollution as the next person, but this behavior (in a psychology laboratory, at that) hardly seems like the kind of thing that is going to bring modern civilization to its knees. At best, it presents *prima facie* good reasons for parents properly concerned about socializing young children to be wary about the effects that such games are having on their children's development of good public manners.

Even the issue of possible negative effects on children is much more complicated than opponents of violent video games allow. In fact, *all* kinds of screen time are harmful to children of three years old and under, independently of the amount of violence portrayed. The American Association of Pediatrics recommends that children under the age of two years should not be exposed to any television whatsoever! Such exposure has been strongly linked to obesity, decreased school achievement, and (most shockingly, given the strength of the correlation) autism in the United States since people first began using televisions as substitute babysitters.[19] In contrast, there are *no* studies linking video game play to the kinds of violence reported in crime statistics. Thus, even given the available psychological data showing a strong correlation between video game violence and certain minor forms of aggression inside the psychology lab, a position of Aristotelian tolerance toward FPS games and their like has not been undermined.

3.5 Tentative Conclusions and Clarifications

Given that so much of the debate between the Platonist and Aristotelian involves empirical research, our pro-Aristotelian conclusions in the previous section must be very tentative. But current empirical research does at least suggest that playing violent video games does not produce the kinds of violence that the state has a clear interest in preventing. Likewise, it is at least empirically possible that they have actually *decreased* the overall levels of intolerable violence.

3.5.1 Our Millean Heritage: Liberty

One further thing it is essential to recognize is that no purely empirical result in psychology by itself deductively implies anything at all about what we should or shouldn't do about the presence of violent games in our society or about anything else for that matter. To paraphrase a famous motto from David Hume, it is simply impossible to derive any claim about what *ought to be* from any set of claims about what simply *is*. Hume remarked that

> [in] every system of morality, which I have hitherto met with, I have always remark'd, that the author proceeds for some time in the ordinary way of reasoning . . . when of a sudden I am surpriz'd to find, that

instead of the usual copulations of propositions, *is*, and *is not*, I meet
with no proposition that is not connected with an *ought*, or an *ought
not*. This change is imperceptible; but it is, however, of the last consequence. For as this ought, or ought not, expresses some new relation
or affirmation, 'tis necessary that it should be observ'd or explain'd; and
at a same time that a reason should be given, for what seems altogether
inconceivable, how this new relation can be a deduction from others,
which are entirely different from it.[20]

The type of logical error that Hume is talking about here is certainly not
only made by "systematic" moral philosophers. The psychologists who have
discovered a correlation between violent gaming and aggressive thoughts
and behaviors and gone on to claim that "something must be done" to
change the patterns of consumption in modern society have abandoned their
role as empirical scientists. Anderson, for example, ends a long paper—the
bulk of which merely reports some of the experiments that detected the
correlations described earlier on between gaming and violent affects—by
proclaiming that "the media-violence machine" should be made to turn "in
a Prosocial direction."[21] To be fair, it is hard to tell exactly what the suggestion being made here really amounts to. Perhaps Anderson is suggesting that
the government intervene in video game production. Perhaps, though, he is
just expressing a wish that designers try to produce less violent games of
their own volition—presumably out of the sort of spontaneously profit-
sacrificing social benevolence that academics so often seem disappointed not
to see more of in the capitalist marketplace.

But anyone who advocates making violent games less accessible to players
for the sake of building a better society must answer to the charge of *paternalism*. A paternalist is someone who believes that adults should not be
allowed to choose how to live their own lives, but instead should have their
decisions made for them by some figure of authority such as the government.

In spite of its ubiquity in some areas such as medical policy and the "War on
Drugs," this sort of external intervention in peoples' everyday decision making retains something of a bad reputation in modern, liberal-democratic societies. Paternalism has also been unpopular with many philosophers, for
reasons that are stated most clearly by John Stuart Mill in his 1859 book *On
Liberty*, a hugely influential and eloquent defense of the need for social insti-
tutions that protect freedom of speech, thought, and action. As Mill puts it,

[h]e who lets the world, or his own portion of it, choose his plan of life
for him, has no need of any other faculty than the ape-like one of imitation. He who chooses his plan for himself, employs all of his facul-
ties. . . . Human nature is not a machine to be built after a model, and
set to do exactly the work prescribed for it, but a tree, which requires to
grow and develop itself on all sides, according to the tendency of inward
forces which make it a living thing.[22]

Mill's point about the psychological damage that can be done to human beings when their decisions are controlled by outside agencies has been reiterated countless times throughout modern culture. It has been a persistent theme not only for philosophers, but also for novelists such as George Orwell, in *1984*, and Aldous Huxley, in *Brave New World*,[23] in movies like *The Matrix* and *Equilibrium*, and within the plots of games such as *Half Life 2* or *Messiah*, where features of the game-world closely reflect the sorts of grim, authoritarian dystopias that so many twentieth-century artists have imagined to be in our civilization's future.

The form of censorship imposed by political threat with the ESRB is old hat to politicians, who employed it perhaps most effectively during the McCarthyist 1950s to attack the comic book industry. Recent scholarship[24] has shown how the resulting "comic book code" not only obliterated sales and ruined the livelihoods of many American artists, but also kept the art form in a state of permanent juvenile retardation from which it has only recently recovered (arguably thanks to some very strong anti-censorship court rulings involving pornographic comics in the 1980s).[25] And given Americans' high tolerance for violence and low tolerance for explicit sexuality, it is no surprise in the reign of the ESRB that high budget and quality explicitly violent games are being mass produced, while explicitly sexual games are not.[26] If (as is surely the case) thinking deeply about works of art is one of the ways that people make sense of their own lives, then it follows that Milleans should be particularly incensed whenever the producers of a nation's popular arts are forced to work at a level deemed appropriate (by our moral guardians) for children. For the ability to make sense of one's life is surely a precondition for rationally choosing how to live as an adult.

These psychological observations do not by themselves decide the issue, though, however plausible they might initially seem. After all, it was Mill himself who argued that an individual's right to make his own decisions stops precisely at the end of his neighbor's nose. "As soon as any part of a person's conduct affects prejudicially the interests of others," he asserts, "society has jurisdiction over it" (*Liberty* 83). This is a pretty vague pronouncement, and surely overstates the extent to which others can meddle in my affairs; if a white person is made uncomfortable by the presence of black people on a bus, their presence there certainly does affect her "interests," but this certainly doesn't give "society" the right to make people with darker skin ride at the back. But to be a victim of violence is to have one's interests acted against in a much more intrusive and less avoidable way, and even the most radically libertarian political philosophers should agree that the government of a well-ordered society will intervene in people's personal lives in order to protect them from serious physical harm.

Perhaps the defender of FPS games might protest that it is one thing for the government to stop people from performing violent acts and another to restrict their access to video games the enjoyment of which does not actually involve doing harm to other people. But this argument begins to look less plausible in light of the psychological studies we discussed earlier on, inconclusive though they are. If there really were (as further such studies might eventually establish) a strong correlation between the playing of these games and socially harmful forms of violence, then the quasi-censorship of the ESRB might arguably be consistent with Millean principles. However, given our society's acceptance of certain behaviors that unarguably often do lead to overwhelming harm (e.g., driving cars), even the availability of such evidence would not persuade every rational party to the discussion that violent video games should either be censored or banned outright.

3.6 Ethical Norms, Diegetic and Real

Encouraging violence is not the only way video games might harm society. Some kinds of games could also promote other anti-social behaviors. There have been hundreds of FPS games designed and published over the past couple of decades, and they take place in a broad variety of different environments, from the science-fictional realms of *Doom*, *Gears of War*, and *Halo* to the World War II environments of *Call of Duty* and *Wolfenstein 3D*, and from the quasi-realistic comic-book world of *Thirteen*, to the cartoonish versions of the Old West depicted in *Outlaws!* and *Red Dead Revolver*. In some such games (e.g., the "Christian" shooter *Catechumen* and the almost indescribably weird *Destroy all Humans!*), the player is required to inhabit freakishly idiosyncratic worlds that almost defy classification. But there are (perhaps rather surprisingly) some common environmental features that are shared by pretty much all of the game-worlds belonging to this genre. And some of them strike us as being far from morally neutral. In what follows, we will discuss some of the curiously persistent features of these gameworlds in order to suggest some more subtle ways in which we think that First Person Shooters might damage the characters of those who (over-)play them.

3.6.1 Xenophobia

Many people are shockingly ignorant about the world they inhabit. At the time of this writing, one third of American teenagers do not know that the Bill of Rights guarantees freedom of speech and religion, and less than half know that the Civil War took place in the latter half of the nineteenth century.[27] The ignorance of the average gamer poses a great challenge for designers of historically themed video games that involve re-enacting historical battles (e.g., the *Battlefield* and *Call of Duty* franchises). Some of these games rise to the challenge. The designers of *Battlefield Vietnam* clearly took into account the appalling ignorance of most of the American populace about the Vietnam War. As each set piece battle loads into the player's computer, period music plays and a screen is displayed that explains not only the battle, but also relevant historical and sociological facts about the Vietnam War.

When one leaves the realm of FPS games, one finds that an astonishing amount of history and culture can be taught by video games. Creative Assembly's *Total War* series is masterful in this way. From the very outset, the *Realpolitik* of the late Roman Republic's foundering client-state plutocracy guides every facet of *Rome: Total War* game-play.

Most video games do not come close to the level of excellence achieved by Creative Assembly. This fact alone is potentially quite ethically problematic. More troubling, however, is that when the video game player fights recognizably human enemies (rather than space aliens, demons, or zombies), the villains frequently belong to whatever ethnic group or government is making headlines at the time of the game's release for being hostile to the perceived interests of the United States. Thus *Ghost Recon*, a game produced in 2001, uses Russian ultranationalists as its villains, while *Splinter Cell: Chaos Theory*, which came out in 2005, uses the North Koreans. Games with Nazis as villains are perennially popular, but the ways in which they depict the German military vary widely, from the stark and convincing realism of *Day of Defeat* to the overstated and rather silly comic book effects of *Return to Castle Wolfenstein*, in which the SS runs a sideline in the reanimation of corpses and the "genetic engineering" of monsters with dripping fangs.

Most such games seem to be relatively free of crassly offensive ethnic stereotypes, especially when compared as a genre with either Hollywood movies (e.g., *The Sheik, The Godfather, Soul Plane*) or bestselling novels (e.g., Tom Clancy's Cold War novels, Michael Crichton's *Rising Sun*). And as far as we are aware, there are no games that reward behavior such as assassinating democratically elected leaders who offend United Fruit or British Petroleum, supporting murderous despots in the Southern Hemisphere, or torturing prisoners of war. Nonetheless, someone playing *Ghost Recon 2* who had no knowledge of Korean history might be more likely to acquire groundless and dangerous cultural prejudices about Koreans or Asians (viewing them, for example, as intrinsically warlike and threatening to the United States) via its depictions of attitudes and behavior.

Strangely, while *Battlefield Vietnam* goes to great lengths to help the viewer gain historical and sociological insight into the re-enacted battles, the game for which *Battlefield Vietnam* is an expansion pack (*Battlefield 1942*) does not. And while players of *Battlefield Vietnam* become aware that for many Vietnamese the war was a war of independence against Western colonialism, players of *Battlefield 1942* get no comparable insight into the nihilistic soul of Nazi ideology (nor the concentration camps it gave rise to), nor to how the economic conditions of the Great Depression enabled such hatred to fester and take over a struggling democracy. Clearly, the designers of *Battlefield 1942* assume that the players of that game are conversant with the relevant history. But this is not a sensible assumption. The same research cited earlier shows that twenty percent of American teenagers do not know that the United States fought Germany and Japan in World War II, and one quarter could not identify Hitler. For such ignorant souls, *Battlefield 1942* is a completely different game, and one cannot help but wonder what it teaches them.

As Plato's Socrates suggested in the *Republic*, the context within which violence is presented in any narrative artwork makes a big difference to how we should ethically evaluate it. Socrates does not object to the fact that Achilles is portrayed in Homer as doing very violent things, nor does he object that the poet's descriptions of blood and gore are too "realistic." Rather, he worries that the moral context of the violence (e.g., killing unarmed prisoners rather than in battle, fighting out of rage rather than out of necessity) in the *Iliad* will lead readers and listeners to admire Achilles' worst traits of character. But the ESRB does not take such differences into account. In the present day, where there are very credible reasons[28] to think that viewing the television series *24* has made it much easier for American soldiers to follow Bush administration mandates to abuse and torture prisoners (mandates which, it must be said, violated United States law, treaties constitutionally ratified by the United States Senate, the United States Military Code of Conduct, and United States Military policies on detainee treatment), Plato's original point could not possibly have more contemporary relevance.[29]

3.6.2 Xenaphilia

In "Women in Video Games. From Barbie to Xena,"[30] George Popescu provides an insightful typology of the roles of female characters in video games. "Barbie" characters are essentially passive. Some Barbies are just "eye candy" and play no significant role in the game's storyline. Examples include the bikini-clad women who wave the flags in the race driving game *Need for Speed Underground* or who sun themselves on golf courses in some golf games. Some Barbies do play a part in the storyline, but only as victims whose assault or abduction is the basis of the male character's quest. Consider the depiction of characters such as Pauline in the original *Donkey Kong*, Marian in *Double Dragon*, or the much more highly sexualized woman who is abducted in the opening scenes of *Baldur's Gate: Dark Alliance*.

"Lucy" characters are the sorts of "good wives" that populated 1950s American situation comedies such as *Leave it to Beaver*. *The Sims'* diegetic world is full of Lucies. Popescu writes that an examination of all of the choices a player of *The Sims* is offered in configuring his *Sims* family, "suggests that underneath this diversity there are classical sex and gender stereotypes. The first example that pops up when you want to configure a character is a white man with a white shirt, a pocket pro-tector, and gray pants, suggesting that this is the social norm of the game and the other characters only deviate from it" (*Gender* 4–5). Moreover, the options are limited to "sixteen bodies for women, five for children, and eighteen for men to choose from. No body is disabled or fat, the majority being slim" (*Gender* 5). In addition, only recent versions of the game allow same sex couples, and even the new versions do not allow same sex marriages.

Finally, "Xena" characters (named for the eponymous heroine of the TV series *Xena: Warrior Princess*) are warriors who function as the player's avatars. Perhaps the first influential examples of this sort of characters were in the *Mortal Kombat* universe. The most famous video game Xena remains Lara Croft, the hero of the massively popular *Tomb Raider* franchise. Part of the secret of this game's appeal to both men and women was the presentation of an active heroine with a compelling backstory doing things that had hitherto almost always only been done by male characters.

It is important to recognize, however, that even characters like Lara Croft are Barbies to some extent. Lara Croft herself is a patently unrealistic figure. It is doubtful that the relative sizes of her waist, breasts, and musculature could even be achieved even with surgery, in large part because the waist would require an anorexic thinness incompatible with her Xena-like muscular powers. With her scanty wardrobe and disproportionately large breasts, it seems clear that she was designed with an eye to sex-appeal just as much as the flag-wavers in racing games.

In the little that has been published by feminist scholars about video games, the character of Lara Croft looms large, in part precisely because of the uneasy relationship that exists between her exaggerated sex-relevant physical characteristics and her active, often quite dramatically sophisticated role in gameplay. The enormous diversity of the contemporary feminist tradition in philosophy and cultural criticism seems to us to present at least three quite different perspectives upon the significance and value of relatively complex, non-stereotypical female game characters like Lara Croft (and Cate Archer of *No One Lives Forever*, and Mona Sax of *Max Payne 2*) to the status of women in contemporary society.

The first possible approach is suggested by Carol J. Clover's[31] influential discussion of the "final girl" in mainstream Hollywood horror films such as *Silence of the Lambs, Halloween*, and the *Friday the Thirteenth* series. Clover argues that the perspective of the camera in these films initially leads the viewer to identify with the male killer,[32] but that it then shifts towards occupying the perspective of one of the female characters (usually the last survivor, hence the sobriquet "final girl") who ends up defeating the male killer. Clover regards these films as fundamentally anti-feminist in nature, on the grounds that the final girl only comes out victorious in virtue of her behaving just like male characters in traditional action and horror movies. It is in this light that Clover sees the weapon brandished by the final girl as a (symbolic) penis.[33] She argues that male viewers identify with the final girl solely in virtue of such "masculine" properties, and hence that there is a sense in which she is no longer perceived as female at all, but rather as a transvestite adolescent male.

Clover's opinions about violence in contemporary film are highly controversial,[34] but her insights concerning how male viewers identify with the final girl seem oddly prophetic when we consider video games. Her argument provides a neat explanation of why male players are often so enthusiastic to play female characters, a phenomenon now pervasive not only in games modeled after *Tomb Raider*, but also in RPGs and virtual communities such as *Second Life*.[35] However, Clover's analysis of these sorts of characters embodies certain presuppositions that are found to be disturbingly regressive by other contemporary feminists. The principal reason Clover characterizes the final girl as an "adolescent male in drag" is just because the final girl embodies many traditional gender stereotypes associated with men (e.g., decisiveness, aggressiveness, rationality) as opposed to gender stereotypes associated with women (e.g., passivity, empathy). But should characters like Lara Croft really be decried just because they inhabit the active place that used to be the sole proprietorship of male characters?[36]

It seems possible, then, that a feminist interpretation of "Xena"-type characters could at least begin by *applauding* the fact that female avatars are becoming less scarce in video games. However, there is still a great deal of debate about what one should make of the commonly exaggerated sexual dimorphism in video games. The term "sexual dimorphism" refers to the systematic differences in sex-relevant physiological properties between different sexes of a species, such as the male peacock's fan of feathers or the extra-long bills of the female Huia bird. Even the most casual video game player is bound to notice that female characters in games tend to have an unrealistic combination of large breasts, exaggerated hip to waist ratio, and soft facial features, whereas male characters tend to have an unrealistic combination of upper body mass, narrow hips, and chiseled features.[37]

One approach to this phenomenon (which could be identified with so-called "second wave" feminism)[38] would be to analyze these exaggerated instances of dimorphism in terms of that way that the projected "male gaze" systematically objectifies women. Given the significant physiological evidence that men tend to be more visually responsive in determining who they find sexually desirable,[39] it could be argued that the exaggerated sexual dimorphism in video games is radically *unequal*, on the grounds that the exaggerated sex-relevant physical traits in the male characters do not serve the purpose (for women) of objectifying men, whereas the exaggerated sex-relevant physical traits of the female characters do reliably serve this purpose for male players.

For "second wave" feminists sympathetic to this line of argument, the Lara Croft character is schizophrenic and problematic. While the fact that she is a player avatar in a genre traditionally dominated by men is to be applauded, the increased sexual dimorphism takes back with one hand what has just been given. Her unrealistically large breasts and large hip to waist ratio encourage the viewer to objectify her (and women generally). And since the sexual objectification of a person always partly involves not viewing him or her *as* a person, (i.e., a rational agent with beliefs and desires that must be respected) games like *Tomb Raider* can be viewed as ethically culpable impediments to the types of societal progress that every feminist (and presumably every sensible person) should want games to encourage. Moreover, some might argue that the very physical traits that are exaggerated work to inculcate arbitrary Western standards of beauty that on a deeper analysis are repressive to women, since they not only equate a woman's overall worth with her visual presentation to men, but also end up fetishizing weakness.[40]

All this being said some contemporary theorists (often called "third wave" and sometimes "post" feminists)[41] reject the presuppositions about sex that are central to arguments like the one just provided. Third wave feminists characteristically argue that one's autonomy is not automatically undermined by being seen as visually appealing in sexually dimorphic ways by the opposite sex. If—as the evidence from contemporary cognitive science and evolutionary biology suggests[42]—human standards of physical beauty and attractiveness are determined as much by evolutionary hard-wiring as they are by shifting cultural norms, then any criticism of attraction based upon dimorphism starts to look ominously like a criticism of sex itself. This sort of observation has caused many feminists of the past twenty years or so either to reject the idea that all physical attraction based upon sexual dimorphism between human beings involves objectification, or else to conclude (following existentialist philosophers like Jean-Paul Sartre)[43] that treating human beings at least partly as objects is simply a universal and unavoidable feature of our mental lives.

From this perspective, the exaggerated physical incongruities of characters like Lara Croft might well be seen as not only ethically harmless in and of themselves, but potentially beneficial insofar as they encourage people to not view human feminine dimorphic properties (larger breasts and a larger hip-to-waist ratio than the average human male) as being essentially tied to gender properties such as passivity and unreason. Third wave feminists are likely to argue that such decoupling of sexuality from gender ideology is actually empowering, since it shows that women need not be de-sexualized to be decisive, rational human beings.

3.6.3 Normalizing the Outrageous

Suppose that, for some of the reasons given above, we chose to abandon a position of Platonistic suspicion toward games like *Battlefield Vietnam* or *Tomb Raider*. Before we allowed ourselves to become too optimistic about the social utility of these sorts of games, there is a separate set of potential problems that have to be addressed. In addition to Plato's concern with the effect video games might have directly upon the player's actions, one should also worry about the assumptions that they convey about what is normal in the world. E.M. Dadlez describes this concern in an especially illuminating way by pointing out that "the motive for referring to certain fictions as harmful need not involve the sometimes unreasonable claim that people are inclined to imitate the behavior of fictional characters." Rather, one's disapproval of any work of fiction can just as justifiably arise from the mere recognition that "an emotional response to fiction is necessarily accompanied by the belief that the fictional event being portrayed is an event of the kind that could occur."[44]

In the case of most FPS games, what is noticeable is actually the *non-occurrence* of "events" involving any female character playing a constructive part in the action. In fact, it seems plain that the overwhelming majority of FPS games habituate players to the idea that the world could be purged of *any* constructive female presence whatsoever. This must surely be counted as a potential source of social harm.

Even games that make some genuine attempt at the egalitarian representation of women characters often just reinforce stereotypes. Consider the character of Mona Sax from *Max Payne 2*. The designers of this game make a genuine effort to represent her as a brave, competent agent on the model of the game's protagonist, and many of the game's best scenes consist of long fights in which the player switches back and forth between her point of view and Max's as they help each other to get out of tight situations. Nonetheless, she is repeatedly heard to describe herself without irony throughout the game as a "damsel in distress." And at the end, she turns on Max (having been paid off by one of the game's minor villains) only to find that she can't assassinate him in cold blood because she has "feelings" for him. It's as if the designers just could not bring themselves to have a major female avatar in an FPS that failed to instantiate some exaggerated piece of locker-room gender ideology.

What's more, even if there is merit in the suggestion that "Xena"-type characters might help antecedently prejudiced consumers get used to the idea of women playing active roles, it is surely just as possible that these gamers are also being conditioned to think that all women should look like Lara Croft. Whether games have such an effect is a difficult issue that requires empirical testing. At this point, we should note that the suggestion being made here is *not* refuted by biological data showing massive convergence about judgments of physical beauty across cultures.[45] The worry is not that playing games like *Tomb Raider* will lead people to make these judgments differently, but rather that they will cause less beautiful people to be treated with disinterest, condescension, and prejudice.

We are not arguing that statistical overrepresentation of unrealistically attractive people in the arts is in itself immoral. Given human psychological make-up, this would be like complaining about gravity. But when this is *all you get*, there is a problem of precisely the sort Dadlez raises. The graphical sophistication of contemporary video games has advanced to the point of allowing ambitious designers to exhibit an often amazingly careful concern with visual realism. But this concern with realism has yet to extend to the creation of female characters.

3.7 Concluding Homily

It seems to us that much of the alarmist rhetoric about the content of video games that has been in circulation since the start of the 16-bit era in game design might actually serve to distract gamers, parents and legislators from legitimate concerns with the effects that *overplay* might have on an individual's moral character. While debates about government intervention are rightfully concerned with propensity to violence and other forms of delinquency, in even minimally functioning societies the vast majority of people are not particularly violent or delinquent. The moral conundrums and choices that confront most of us, and the daily decisions which define our characters, almost never involve the kind of activities that the public debate over video games has so far focused upon.

But one can be non-violent and non-delinquent while still making a complete hash of being a human being. Most of us desperately want to be able to look back on our lives from our deathbeds and honestly find meaning and worth. And we can do this to the extent that we have spent our time here cultivating sensitivity, compassion, understanding, and wisdom, and also to the extent that we have used these to create objects of genuine worth and meaningful relationships with other people. From this perspective, even given their often considerable originality and artistic merit, there does seem to be something almost irredeemably coarsening about violent and sexist video games.

It may be objected that part of what makes some tragic or horrifying works of art great is their call to make us empathize with and understand the bad guy, for purposes akin to those of an Aristotelian *katharsis*. This sort of analysis seems perfectly appropriate whether one is examining timeless, unquestionable masterpieces such as Shakespeare's *Macbeth* or even relatively ephemeral works of pop culture such as Nick Cave's version of "Stagger Lee" or NWA's gangsta-rap album *Straight Out of Compton*, all of which require their audiences to take on the perspective of very bad people. However, even assuming that something like Aristotelian *katharsis* is at work, something has gone deeply wrong when violent or sexist artworks stop seeming transgressive and instead come to take on the appearance of normalcy. Just as *Battlefield 1942* would be quite a different game for someone who did not know the basic historical facts about World War II, surely *Grand Theft Auto* must be quite a different game for someone who (for whatever reasons) does not find it shocking and transgressive.[46] It no longer seems like moral panic to be concerned that a person whose cultural input consisted largely in pathologically violent movies, video games, and music might end up being severely hindered in his pursuit of the good life.

So speaks common sense. Unfortunately, it would be difficult to empirically test the effects of overconsumption of morally problematic art on people's lives. To correlate behavior with harm, one has to compare groups that engage in the behavior with groups that don't, controlling for other possible factors that might cause the harm. For example, it would be pointless to compare college students who do not play violent video games and prison inmates who do in order to determine whether playing video games leads to criminal behavior. But this is precisely the difficulty we mentioned earlier in connection with efforts to measure the extent to which playing violent video games leads to socially harmful behavior. How does one control for other factors? It is not at all clear what leads people to have more or less coarsened sensibilities. There are just so many ways to get life wrong.

The yoga scholar Georg Feuerstein writes about how, "much of our feeling, thinking and behavior has already been 'froze' around a few narrow themes—sex, status, work as drudgery, passive spectatorship, etc. . . ."[47] The ways one could fill in the "etc." here are legion, and as a result it is very difficult to get good empirical data on the extent to which excessive play of violent video games correlates with, much less causes, the kind of spiritual and aesthetic torpor that seems to be so prevalent amongst present day consumers of mass culture.

A few conclusions are in order, though. First, in spite of our severe reservations about how their results are presented, the kind of work that empirical researchers such as Anderson and Dill are doing is important to the task. To the extent that moral and aesthetic coarseness in behavior is correlated with morally and aesthetically coarse beliefs, it makes sense to track the prevalence of such beliefs amongst player of different kinds of video games in different population groups. Research similar to this already exists. For example, the psychologist S. B. Boeringer has shown that membership in a college fraternity or on an all-male athletic team radically increases the likelihood of blaming women for being the victims of sexual assault.[48] Furthermore, a separate study provides evidence for the contention that fraternity members are twice as likely as other college students to commit rape, and male athletes are ten times as likely to.[49] In this case, then, the morally contemptible blame-the-victim attitude seems to be highly predictive of behavior.

If there is a main conclusion to be reached here, it is again Aristotelian: too much of anything is bad.[50] From this perspective, in spite of the irrationality and "comics book code" style retardation of game content that has resulted from it, the moral panic over violent video games can be seen to have served some good purpose. The public outcry about violence in games has undoubtedly helped consumers think of extra-violent games such as *Hooligans*, *Postal*, and *Grand Theft Auto* as being fundamentally abnormal and transgressive. In this cultural environment, one can safely admire the brilliance of some such games (and *Grand Theft Auto* is undeniably in many ways a brilliantly imaginative and highly realistic work of game design)[51] without substantial risk to the development of one's moral character.

4 Games and God's Goodness (World-Builder and Tycoon Games)

4.1 The Problem

In classic world-builder games like *Civilization, Tropico, SimCity*, and *Age of Empires*, players direct the evolution of an entire culture through technological and scientific breakthroughs as well as military and cultural expansion. Usually, the player takes on the persona of some small-scale dictator (e.g., the inhabitant of the "throne room" in *Civilization II* or "El Presidente" in *Tropico*) whose status increases as her civilization expands. But, in fact, the player's power over the diegetic realm she directs is vastly greater than that of any real-life dictator. Unlike real-world leaders, the player is not surrounded by toadies telling her what she wants to hear. Instead, the interface provides her infallibly accurate information about much of the diegetic realm she rules. In addition, the player of world-builder games can maintain her authority without the internal power struggles that plague real-world dictators.[1]

It is for these reasons that the designers and fans of world-builder games are not exaggerating unreasonably or (at least in any simple sense) exhibiting impiety when they refer to world-builder games as "god games". The avatar's power over the world of the game is superhuman. And astute players and programmers of these types of games have wrestled with the moral quandaries that such power raises. How should someone with this kind of power rule?

In Chapter 3, we concentrated on the effect that certain games could have on the moral character of the player. Here, we are more concerned with the ethical systems implicit in god games. What would it mean for there to be a morality to these games? Should the player only be allowed to win if he does "good" things for the civilization over which he has power? And, if so, who or what determines which acts count as good? As we will show, the philosophical task of answering these questions about the ethical content of god games is threefold: (1) to discern the connection (if any) between God and morality, (2) to derive meaningful criteria to differentiate right from wrong, and (3) to describe how video games, properly informed by the answers to (1) and (2), might be designed.

Each section of the present chapter contains a discussion of how these problems impact the games built around them,[2] necessarily including an examination of several different popular philosophical accounts of the relationship between ethics and theology. Our central observation will be that there are provocative analogies to be drawn between certain problems that arise in the design of world-builder games and philosophical issues that arise for ethical theories that attempt to derive our moral obligations from claims about the nature and attributes of a divine being. We will suggest that for similar reasons, both philosophers and game designers would benefit from avoiding the view that ethics is dependent upon any particular religion or theology. We will also try to provide some reasons for thinking that, just as game designers have looked for ideas in history textbooks, science-fiction novels, or sacred texts, they might, with equal justice, look to some of the great texts of moral philosophy for a similar source of inspiration.

4.2 Games as Practical Theology

Games belonging to the world-builder genre can either be turn-based, real-time, or a mixture of both. Before we talk about what theological content might be implicit in these types of games, it will help to provide a brief description of the style of interface used in each.

The most popular series in the world-builder genre over the past couple of decades has unquestionably been Take-Two Interactive Software's *Civilization* games.[3] The *Civilization* series is the canonical example of purely turn-based world-builder games, meaning that all of a player's commands happen during her turn. When she clicks the red button on the map interface to finish the turn, each nonplayer character (NPC) takes a turn in a predetermined order. In order to win one of these games, the player has to bring the virtual civilization she has founded up to a certain point of development; in *Civilization II*, for example, the player wins if the society she has founded is the first to build a spaceship capable of colonizing other solar systems. The primary interface of the *Civilization* games is a map representing facets of the diegetic world such as location of cities, dominant ecology (forest, desert, mountain, sea, etc.), resources (gold, oil, iron, etc.), and improvements (farms or mines). Through manipulation of the mouse and keyboard, the player moves her units across spaces on the map and tells each one what to do, depending upon its function. Settlers found cities. Workers improve regions through construction of roads, farms, mines, railroads, etc. Military units defend and attack cities, despoil the landscape, and attack other units. Typically, the player only sees the part of the map she has explored and the landscape, the way it was, when one of her units last traversed the area in question (though this can change late in the game when the player's civilization develops satellite systems).

If the player clicks her mouse over one of her cities, a new interface is opened that allows her to direct the construction of buildings, training of units (military, workers, settlers, spies, missionaries, traders, etc.), and the percentage of working population devoted to building/training, research, or entertainment. There is also often an interface governing diplomatic interaction between the player's avatar and the avatars of rival civilizations. Through this interface, the player can manage trade of resources or technology, build alliances, bully her neighbors for resources, and declare war.

Microsoft's *Age of Empires* series is a real-time world-builder game. The interface is roughly similar to the *Civilization* interface, but instead of taking turns, all of the players perform their actions simultaneously. As soon as you direct a unit to undergo some task, such as building a monument, training soldiers, or making improvements, the game begins to do it. Since all of the other players are doing this at the same time, *Age of Empires* game-play is radically different from *Civilization* game-play. Because one can stop and think without weakening one's position in *Civilization*, the game feels a lot more cerebral and perhaps the major part of the player's joy is figuring out the algorithm and beating it. In *Age of Empires*, though, the player gets the adrenaline rush of trying to do all of the required actions quickly enough. People who compete at high levels in the *Age of Empires'* community must devise and master a huge set of keyboard macros so that they needn't take the time to point and click with the mouse. Some players find this exhilarating, but others think that it detracts from the joy of rational world building.

The Creative Assembly's *Total War*[4] games are an innovative mixture of the turn-based and real-time subgenres. Moving units and ordering citizens to build and improve cities is turn-based in exactly the same manner as in *Civilization*. However, when units are directed to engage in combat, a new interface opens and the player has the choice to direct the battle in real time. In *Shogun Total War*, this process was clunky and slow, but having the ability to issue orders in real time to one's soldiers, cavalry, archers, siege weapons, and irregular local militias in *Rome Total War* is an astounding experience. Of course, sometimes in the fog and panic of war, your orders do not get followed. The wise player takes this into account in setting up the initial disbursement of her forces.

How do all of the powers possessed by the player in world-builder games compare to the powers traditionally attributed to God in the tradition of Western monotheism? Most of the philosophers who have discussed the deity's nature and defining characteristics have regarded God as having a trio of logically distinct properties: omnipotence (all-powerfulness), omniscience (all-knowingness), and omnibenevolence (all-goodness). The major Western monotheistic religious traditions—Judaism, Christianity, and Islam —have all held that God possesses these three properties in spite of their deep disagreements about other significant theological questions (e.g., the nature of the afterlife, the reliability of certain prophets, or the sense in which God is one). Furthermore, the possession of omnipotence, omniscience, and omnibenevolence is supposed to distinguish the God of monotheistic religions (at least conceptually) from any other being in the natural or supernatural worlds.

However, coming up with a coherent and vivid conception of an omniscient, omnipotent, and omnibenevolent being is so difficult that it is not unfair to characterize it as one of the eternal tasks of the philosopher.[5] For centuries, theologians have puzzled over the apparent fact that a God who possessed one of these properties would have to be constrained in certain ways when it came to the exercise of the others. The famous "paradox of the stone," according to which an omnipotent God both *could* and *could not* create a rock that is too heavy for him to lift, shows that omnipotence is extraordinarily difficult to characterize.[6] And even if this paradox could somehow be solved, is there any sense at all to be made of the suggestion that God has the "power" (through omnipotence) to change the very laws of logic that govern the claims that we make about him? Many religious believers also think that a benevolent God would want human beings (whom he is usually, but not always taken to have created) to have as much freedom of choice as possible. But there is also a sense in which people *can't* really be free in a universe designed by a being who knows in advance how every single human decision will turn out (omniscience), right up to the end of time.[7]

Now, consider the constraints imposed upon the player of turn-based world-builder games, such as the impossibility of reacting immediately to the enemy's movements, or the constraints imposed by real-time interfaces such as the difficulty of simultaneously managing the movements of hundreds of soldiers through the game-world. Might it be possible to obtain some insight into the nature of potential conflicts among God's properties by reflecting upon how these limits on the player influence the coherence, realism, or even the entertainment value of god games? Or, conversely, might theological reflection help us to see some ways in which the games belonging to this genre could be better designed?

4.3 The Bible Tells Me So?

Left Behind Games' world-builder game *Left Behind: Eternal Forces* combines narrative material from a series of novels of the same name with some highly dubious theology. The setting is in New York City during the period that follows the "Rapture," an incident that some sects of Protestant Christianity believe to be foretold in the Bible. During the Rapture, all genuinely faithful Christians are supposedly going to be swept up instantaneously into Heaven, leaving the world in the hands of two factions that will act out the events that scripture foretells as leading up to Armageddon. In the game, these two factions are the "Tribulation Force," an association of belated converts to Christianity, and the "Global Community Peacekeepers," the army of the Antichrist. The player's goal is to build a strong, well-fed, and well-funded Tribulation Force by converting neutral

NPCs and harvesting resources from what remains of a chaotic, near-abandoned simulacrum of downtown Manhattan.

Scriptural ethics is the thesis that our moral obligations can be derived by correctly interpreting canonical scripture. This approach to morality has received enthusiastic support from many of the believers in the world's great religions. Clearly, the designers of *Left Behind* wanted the game to reflect their commitment to scriptural ethics (though they might not have used this terminology) by rewarding the player for doing what real-life believers in the game's prophetic content take to be God's will.

The game is actually a lot of fun, regardless of how seriously one takes its basic theological premise. But *Left Behind* also has some rather peculiar features that serve to undermine the designers' apparent commitment to scriptural ethics. For example, in the game's early cinematic scenes, it is explained that adherence to Christianity is strictly a matter of free, autonomous personal choice, a doctrine that has been endorsed by most of mainstream Christianity. But when the player "converts" neutral citizens into her "force" in the game, they go from acting independently of the player's will to following her every instruction without question. Furthermore, "converts," unlike neutral characters in the game, wear uniforms (a hideous purple sweater-vest) and are referred to in the game's internal tutorial as "units," rather than as "people." This is an odd way of depicting the behavior of agents who have achieved salvation through the exercise of free will.

But perhaps the strangest feature of *Left Behind*, from the point of view of scriptural ethics, is the fact that in the game's multiplayer mode, the player can actually choose to take the side of the Global Community Peacekeepers, rather than the Tribulation Force! Contemporary game designers are aware that it is difficult to sell games in the world-builder genre unless they can be played competitively online. The requirement of making a profit is surely, therefore, what dictated that online players be able to command the army of the Antichrist, and have a plausible chance at defeating the Christians. Nonetheless, allowing the player to take the side of evil completely undermines the game's whole point as an attempt to get him to act in accordance with the designers' set of ethical beliefs.

Problems with overall coherence in *Left Behind* seem to us to run deeper than just a few questionable decisions by the game's designers. It's actually rather difficult to imagine how one could possibly succeed at using the medium of video games to teach players how to act in accordance with some preordained and supposedly unambiguous set of ethical rules delivered up by an omniscient God. How could such a game be internally consistent, while still allowing for the sorts of flexible decision making that makes playing any world-builder game even minimally worthwhile?

A similar problem arises for the philosopher who tries to come up with a plausible general defense of scriptural ethics as a theory of morality. Often, God's commands are taken by religious believers to have been communicated to prophets, and the prophets' words to have been encoded in sacred texts. Thus, scriptural ethicists usually support something like the following claim:

> X is commanded by God if, and only if, X is endorsed by a prophet or X is commanded in a sacred text.

One must, of course, specify who counts as a prophet, and/or what counts as a sacred text. Moreover, the scriptural ethicist should be prepared to give a principled justification for whatever criteria she uses to separate true from false prophets and canonical from apocryphal texts, an extraordinarily difficult task. For example, one of the authors of this book once asked a priest why the Gospel of Thomas was excluded from the standard Christian Bible. The priest responded that in the Gospel of Thomas, Jesus' first miracle was recorded as turning clay statues into living pigeons, but that we know from the other Gospels that his first miracle was turning water into wine. The problem with this answer is that it simply *presupposes* that the four "canonical" Gospels are correct, when what had been asked was why the other books are taken to be correct and the Gospel of Thomas to be incorrect?[8]

Suppose that moral goodness is just whatever God commands us to do and the problem of selecting true prophets and a canon in a principled manner can somehow be solved. We still have yet another problem of *interpreting* whatever canon gets chosen. Even if a sacred text can be picked, we still must discern what God's commands are within that text. But when one studies the history of any major world religion, one finds that the sacred texts that it uses are interpreted in wildly different ways. For example, people have used the Bible both to defend and to criticize each of the following things: slavery, the emancipation of slaves, the civil rights of minorities, the persecution of Jews, the ethical superiority of white Protestant males, voting rights for women, the provision of political sanctuary for refugees, the liberation of the poor, the execution of witches, the permissibility of women priests, the permissibility of married priests, the legality of sodomy, punishment for masturbation, the legality of abortion, violence towards children, the regulation of clothing and hairstyle, the thesis that diseases are caused by sin, the inferiority of African-Americans, discrimination and violence against homosexuals, capital punishment, the persecution of Roman Catholics, prayer in schools, prohibition of work and drinking on Sundays, medical science, war, and saving the environment.[9] Over the past 2000 years, many different groups of sane and thoughtful people have strenuously disagreed about whether each of these practices is supported by the authority of scripture.

Believers' widely differing interpretations of scripture show that it is extraordinarily difficult to discern the correctness or incorrectness of moral beliefs by attending to an authoritative text. But one might also attempt to make a stronger positive argument against scriptural ethics based on different interpretations of scripture. We will call this "The Projection Argument."

The Projection Argument

1   Many of the commands that can be extracted from the Bible[10] appear to be unclear and inconsistent.

2   To read the commands of the Bible consistently, one must carefully distinguish between moral commands and nonmoral commands, holding that the moral commands are true for all time and all peoples, and the nonmoral commands were only true at a given time for a given group of people described in the Bible.

These first two premises are statements that most scriptural ethicists would agree with. In the next steps, the scriptural ethicist and her opponent part ways.[11]

3   If a person could determine what her moral duties were from the Bible, then it would be the case that conscientious readers of the Bible would not discern inconsistent moral commands in the Bible.

4   However, conscientious readers of the Bible do discern inconsistent moral commands in the Bible, typically by separating moral from nonmoral commands in different ways, and by deriving different commands from different parts of scripture.

5   Therefore, nobody can determine what her moral duty is by reading the Bible.

If this argument is plausible, a good explanation of different interpretations of the Bible is that people project their own antecedently formulated opinions concerning what their moral duties are into the Bible by citing passages that support what they already take to be morally obligatory as prophetic articulations of "moral law," and interpreting other passages differently.

For example, people enthused about denying civil rights to homosexuals in the United States almost always cite the prohibition of homosexual sex in *Leviticus* 18:22 and 20:13. But these same people almost never feel bound by the other prohibitions in *Leviticus*, such as those that forbid tattoos, earrings, wearing more than one kind of cloth at the same time, seeing a naked menstruating woman, or touching the skin of a pig, all of which are condemned in exactly the same manner as the practice of men laying with men. Furthermore, these same people almost never support the death penalty for disobedient children, prostitutes (by burning to death), blasphemers, and those who have a ghost or spirit familiar, even though these too are commanded by the author of *Leviticus*.

The Projection Argument concludes that there is no principled, consistent reading of the Bible, or (given its equal applicability to texts outside of the Judeo-Christian tradition) of any sacred text, such that we can figure out what our moral duties are by reading that text. While one may be able to *create* a consistent reading of the Bible, this is only because one already has a consistent view about ethics that is then projected into the text.

At the same time, though, it is important to realize that the scriptural ethicist cannot say that we determine what the moral law in the Bible is by using a prior notion of what the correct moral law is. If interpreting the Bible correctly requires an antecedent morality, then the Bible is no longer a place where we can *discover* all of our moral duties; we would already have to know what our moral duties are in order to read the Bible correctly.

The scriptural ethicist might argue that there is good evidence that the Bible is consistent. If so, then conscientious readers could discern the consistent correct interpretation of the Bible, and Premise Four of the Projection Argument would be false. However, such a view is enormously difficult to defend because the *prima facie* inconsistencies in the Bible extend well beyond its supposed moral commands. Examples can be drawn from, but are not limited to, the creation and flood stories, the description of the temple, and the description of events in Jesus' life. The following are a few examples of multiply told stories with clear inconsistencies:

1　The number of animals taken onto the ark.[12]
2　The events surrounding Moses' reception of the Ten Commandments.[13]
3　The events surrounding Jesus' anointment at Bethany.[14]
4　The events surrounding the resurrection.[15]

Sometimes, the appearance of contradiction in Christian scripture is merely a result of taking metaphorical language literally, and some superficial contradictions (for example, many morally relevant ones about dietary restrictions) can perhaps be resolved by appeal to humanity's evolving relationship with God. However, some are clearly contradictory, for example, *Mathew* 1 and *Luke* 3:23 list different numbers of generations relating to Jesus' genealogy. Thus, arguing that the Bible is completely internally consistent is an uphill battle, to say the least.

Most scriptural ethicists defend the claim that moral truth can be found in the Bible by asserting that it contains the infallible word of God. But the proponent of the Projection Argument is likely to conclude that the factual inconsistencies in the Bible provide evidence that there are moral inconsistencies as well. Consider the following argument to this effect.

The Argument from Fallibility

1　If the Bible contained the infallible word of God, all of its pronouncements, ethical or factual, would be true.
2　However, a contradiction concerning contingent empirical matters can never be true (e.g., it can't be true that the one and only Ark of the Covenant was solely made by Moses and solely by Belazel).

3 But the Bible contains contradictions concerning contingent empirical matters.

4 Therefore, the Bible straightforwardly entails sentences which can never be true.

5 Therefore, since the Bible is not infallible, we have no evidence that moral truth can be found in it.

The point here is that if a putative source of information contains a lot of demonstrable falsehoods (as contradictions must be), then that source of information is not reliable. Whenever we discover an empirical contradiction, we know that at least one of the contradictory claims is false. Therefore, if the nonnormative contradictions in the Bible cannot be resolved, we know that the Bible does contain falsehoods, and we have evidence against its reliability as a source of truth, whether this truth is moral or empirical.

Thus, the scriptural ethicist should either attempt to interpret the Bible in some way that plausibly eradicates the appearance of factual inconsistencies or argue that the existence of factual inconsistencies in the Bible provides no evidence for the existence of moral inconsistencies in the Bible. The apparent impossibility of the first task causes most Biblical scholars to conclude that anyone who thinks the Bible is literally true hasn't really read it.[16] The second option is at variance with the way evidence works, and as such is patently unreasonable.

In the preceding section, we noted some rather vivid inconsistencies within one of the most prominent video games thus far developed by avowed believers in scriptural ethics,[17] the world-builder game *Left Behind: Eternal Forces*. Our examination of this game revealed the existence of conflicts between the theological assumptions clearly embraced by its designers and certain elements of game-play, such as the treatment of converts to Christianity as mindless robots and the possibility of playing the game in the person of a tool of Satan's will. In this section, it has emerged that the threat of inconsistency, in fact, looms over all of scriptural ethics. We hope to have shown that, at the very least, the scriptural ethicist has to be extraordinarily careful about how she is getting her moral commands from sacred books like the Bible. This kind of care requires philosophical reflection on what makes an action moral—the same kind of reflection that someone without any significant religious commitments needs to undertake in thinking about morality.

4.4 The Power of God Compels Thee

The religious moralist could bypass any reference to sacred texts in the formulation of her ethical opinions and instead propose that things are right or wrong merely because God desires them to be so. This philosophical position is called divine command theory and requires commitment to the following idea:

An act X is morally obligatory because God (an all-powerful, all-knowing, all-good entity) commands, or would command, X.

Imagine the world from the perspective of one of the tiny settlers in *Civilization*, a member of the Brotherhood of Nod in *Command and Conquer*, or a Roman centurion in *Rome: Total War*. Each little NPC in these games justifies his existence by doing exactly what he is instructed to do via the game's interface, whether it is marching through Gaul, parachuting into enemy territory, or flying to Alpha Centauri. By so doing, he fulfills his predestined role in the grand plan of a transcendent being, that is, the player herself (and/or the player's avatar, depending upon the game). Divine command theory would, therefore, probably be the most rational approach to morality for somebody living in this rather unenviable situation.

The creation of a moral universe within world-builder games seems where the player just determines what is right by her commands seems to us to be something that the more sophisticated and imaginative game designers should be trying to rebel against. Perhaps it is no surprise, then, that most philosophers regard this form of divine command theory as having been decisively refuted over 2000 years ago, in one of the earliest dialogs of Plato.

In the *Euthyphro*, Plato represents Socrates engaged in the following exchange with a well-known religious practitioner of the day about the meaning of the Greek word for "pious:"

Socrates:	What then do we say about the pious, Euthyphro? Surely that it is loved by all the Gods, according to what you say?
Euthyphro:	Yes.
Socrates:	Is it loved because it is pious or for some other reason?
Euthyphro:	For no other reason.
Socrates:	It is loved then because it is pious, but it is not pious because it is loved?
Euthyphro:	Apparently.
Socrates:	And because it is loved by the Gods, it is being loved and is dear to the Gods?
Euthyphro:	Of course.
Socrates:	The God-beloved is then not the same as the pious, Euthyphro, nor the pious the same as the God-beloved, as you say it is, but one differs from the other.
Euthyphro:	How so, Socrates?
Socrates:	Because we agree that the pious is loved for the reason that it is pious, but it is not pious because it is loved. Is that not so?
Euthyphro:	Yes.[18]

Plato's argument may be represented as follows (substituting the term "morally obligatory" for Plato's rather anachronistic "piety"):

The Euthyphro Dilemma

1   Assume that an act X is morally obligatory because God commands or would command X.

2   Then it would be possible for God to command any act whatsoever, and that act Y would be morally obligatory because God commanded it.

3   But then our assumption in Premise One implies that an action is or would be commanded by God because he does or would command it.

4   This makes our initial assumption entirely trivial, so that it cannot be taken to rule out the possibility that just any egregiously horrifying act of cruelty Y is morally obligatory.

5   But clearly, at least some egregiously horrifying acts of cruelty cannot be morally obligatory.

6   Therefore, since Point 4 and Point 5 contradict one another, our initial supposition was false. It is not the case that an act X is morally obligatory because God commands or would command X.

The fundamental problem with divine command theory, then, is that it makes claims about God's omnibenevolence utterly *devoid of content*. Theological common sense suggests that when we say that God is morally perfect, we are saying something highly informative, since we are asserting that there are some possible actions that God either cannot or would not do. But the divine command theorist cannot consistently believe this; for a proponent of this theory, all claims of the form "God wants X because X is good" are equivalent to claims of the form "God wants X because God wants X." And this makes God sound a lot more like a willful preadolescent than the sort of being that mature adults ought to worship, love, and emulate.[19]

A world-builder game on the divine command theory model would count *any* action by the player (as "God") as good. But obviously, not all video-gamers have the best interests of the diegetic world at heart. Or even if they do, they will make mistakes by commanding things they *think* will be good for their world, but which in fact backfire for some reason. There is another solution, however. But it requires fundamentally different approaches to ethics and game design.

4.5   The Solution: Ethical Dilemmas and Game Design

In *The Brothers Karamazov*, the Russian novelist Fyodor Dostoyevsky has one of his characters make the famous proclamation that "If there's no ever-lasting God . . . everything is permitted."[20] This is a deeply strange remark; even for militant atheists, it is surely possible to recognize other thinking nondivine agents (e.g., one's mother, the police, or the leaders of one's Boy Scout troop) as having the moral authority to forbid them from performing certain sort of actions. Perhaps, though, the reason why Dostoyevsky's remark has resonated with so many people is that it reminds us how difficult and obscure the central questions of ethics can be if one starts out with the presumption that our obligations are not simply dictated to us by an all-powerful being. Anyone raised as religious, and who has come to be dissatisfied with theologically-based approaches to ethics, must surely have wondered at some point what could possibly replace the authority of such a being when it comes to deciding upon the rules for how we should all behave. It is actually surprising how *few* answers philosophers have managed to come up with to this question. But enough plausible suggestions have been made over the years to arouse the suspicion that Dostoyevsky's character might be mistaken. By examining some of these openly secular approaches to understanding the nature of morality, we'll also discover some simple but fairly revisionary ideas for the design of better world-builder games.

4.5.1 Dueling Philosophical Traditions

Many philosophers who have tried to figure out some other source of morality than the unquestionable will of God have settled upon the idea that any act is morally wrong if it *hurts* someone. For example, if a drunk driver runs into my car or a friend betrays me, I normally feel resentment because I am harmed by the relevant person's action, not just because the person has broken some rule that is written down in a religious book or accepted by everyone else in my community. And contemplation of the pain that we have caused other people also often seems to be the source of our own feelings of bad conscience.

But is the obligation not to harm others all that there is to wrongness? At least some major thinkers have argued that it is. The nineteenth-century philosophers Jeremy Bentham and John Stuart Mill claimed that the only absolutely authoritative and exceptionless moral rule that we are all obligated to follow is the "Greatest Happiness Principle" (also referred to as the "Principle of Utility," from which the ethical theory utilitarianism gets its name). The utilitarian principle is formulated by Mill in the following way:

> Actions are right in proportion as they tend to promote happiness; wrong as they tend to produce the reverse of happiness. By happiness is intended pleasure and the absence of pain; by unhappiness pain and the privation of pleasure.[21]

For everyday moral judgments, the Greatest Happiness Principle seems to provide just about the most plausible guidance imaginable. Why is it wrong to drive drunk? Because it significantly increases the likelihood of injuring someone. Why should people pay their taxes? Because the money is likely to be used to help someone more vulnerable to economic harm than the taxpayer herself.

In certain cases, however, the Greatest Happiness Principle seems to give bad moral advice. Suppose that a person could choose between buying an enormous jar of mustard that would give every member of his extended family a little extra pleasure every time one of them ate a sandwich, or paying for antibiotics that would stop just one of them from dying of an easily treatable disease. Surely the second choice is obviously the right one; the Greatest Happiness Principle, however, only dictates that buying antibiotics is better provided that nobody really, really likes mustard. Or suppose that a government imprisoned and tortured a few thousand innocent people, and this had the effect of making millions of people feel more powerful and less humiliated by daily life. Most of us (even within the United States) think that this would be a horrifically unethical thing to do, but Mill's remarks seem to imply that such an act could be morally justified—perhaps even morally obligatory—if the pleasurable sense of security, power, sexual atavism, and revenge that the torture provided to members of the general public was enough to outweigh the harm done to the prisoners.[22]

The aforementioned examples suggest that we have obligations to other human beings arising from something other than the need to aid them in the pursuit of happiness and the avoidance of harm. People seem to have rights and entitlements as well as appetites, and the fact that we have a duty to respect these things does not seem to be explicable solely in terms of anybody's ability simply to have more fun.

According to the school of thought called "deontology," our most fundamental obligations arise from the acknowledgement of these human characteristics. Immanuel Kant, the greatest and most influential deontological moral philosopher, formulates this antiutilitarian insight in terms of a principle that is meant to be as authoritative and exceptionless as the Greatest Happiness Principle, while also being immune from the objections to which Mill's principle falls prey. Kant called his principle the Categorical Imperative, which means "unconditional command." He provides several formulations of the Categorical Imperative in his book *Foundations of the Metaphysics of Morals*. The two most famous versions are as follows:

1   "Act only according to that maxim [i.e., rule] about which you can at the same time will that it should become a universal law."[23]
2   "[R]ational nature exists as an end in itself . . . Act so that you treat humanity, whether in your own person or in that of another, always as an end and never as a means only." (*Foundations*, 47)

It is hard to tell exactly why Kant thought that these two versions of the Categorical Imperative were equivalent to one another. But the core idea seems to be this: the capacity to reason is both what makes all human beings alike and what makes us different from anything else in the natural world. Because of this fundamental similarity that we bear to one another, we are required to follow a special set of rules that apply to humans and nothing else. The very fact that reason enables human beings to set our own goals entails for Kant that these goals should not be subordinated to anyone or anything else, unless they interfere with other people's abilities to pursue their own interests.

Although Kant was a firm believer in the Christian God, his views on ethics have been attractive to many people for purely secular reasons. His idea that all rules of conduct should be "universalizable," in the sense that it should be possible for them to be followed by everybody, echoes the sorts of egalitarian political sentiments that have been at least somewhat prevalent in the West since the eighteenth century. And the idea that it is simply wrong ever to use another human being for one's own ends sounds like a good general way of pointing out the need to respect certain rights such as life, liberty, and (perhaps a bit more dubiously) the pursuit of happiness.

But what about children, mentally retarded humans, higher animals such as chimps, elephants, and dolphins, and other creatures with unformed, incomplete, or impaired rationality? What sort of treatment do the rest of us owe them? This question is extraordinarily difficult for the deontologist to answer. There are also problems with some of the specific maxims that seem to pass the Kantian test. Consider the rule "Don't tell lies!" It is certainly a principle that everybody could follow, and it is also plausibly the case that all forms of deliberate deception at least partly involve using other people to further the liar's own ends. But there are also certain circumstances (e.g. when the Nazis come to your door asking for information about Jews and homosexuals in the neighborhood) where it seems like lying would clearly be the only moral thing to do.

There are other nontheological approaches to morality that have been defended in the modern philosophical tradition,[24] but none have attracted the attention of philosophers quite as much as either utilitarianism or deontology. Both of these ethical theories are highly controversial and problematic. But as the foregoing discussion shows, their problems are different than those that arise for either scriptural ethics or divine command theory. For our criticisms of these two religious approaches to ethics challenged the very *coherence* of what their proponents are trying to say. And this is something that advocates of utilitarianism and deontology don't seem to have to worry about; however plausible or implausible one might find the Greatest Happiness Principle or the Categorical Imperative, they are not self-contradictory or logically incoherent. Moreover, they give explicit voice to some of our deepest moral sentiments regarding pain, happiness, and freedom. The only problem is that advocates of both principles occasionally make highly questionable recommendations about what to do in certain specific types of situations.

4.5.2 The Playability of Ethical Dilemmas and the Quest for Greater Realism in Gaming

The player of *Civilization* wins by building an epic empire through absolutely ruthless military expansion. For one of the authors of this book, long hours of playing this game led to an obsession with leaders referred to as "the great:" Alexander, Frederick, Peter, and Catherine. All of these rulers pursued a policy of successful empire building similar to the type that is encouraged in the early *Civilization* games. They oversaw appalling losses of the lives of their own citizens and brought immense hardship to those unfortunate enough to live in the geographical areas ruled by their political enemies. Even if games like *Civilization II, Empire Earth,* or *Medieval Total War* do not provide a perfectly accurate simulation of this sort of power, they still give the player at least some idea of the oceans of blood that follow upon its exercise. Thus, anyone who has played *Civilization* deep into the night has probably experienced something like the worry that the moral hideousness of a Hitler or a Stalin will, over the centuries, shade into a respect for the power these men brandished. We have, to some extent, forgotten just how brutal the reigns of all of the so-called "Greats" mentioned earlier were, not to mention those of Philip of Macedon, Julius Caesar, or Louis the Fourteenth. And so long as the player is obsessed with diegetic empire building, the joy of winning tends to obscure one's normal human responses towards one's virtual citizens.

In *On the Social Contract*, the seventeenth-century French philosopher Jean-Jacques Rousseau remarks that

> [f]orce is a physical power; I fail to see what morality can result from its effects. . . . Let us then agree that force does not bring about right, and that one is obliged to obey only legitimate powers.[25]

The view doesn't make right sounds like plain ethical common sense to most of us most of the time, but modern life presents us with plenty of opportunities to forget it, both inside and outside of the practice of gaming. One can, after all, go onto Amazon.com and order *Leadership Secrets of Attila the Hun*,[26] a book written in the late 1980s for U.S. business executives that is not even remotely satirical![27] The dominant morality in the worlds of the majority of god games can be summed up pretty adequately by the famous line from *Conan the Barbarian*: "Crush your enemies. See them driven before you. Hear the lamentations of their women."

God games raise philosophical questions distinct from the ethical worries discussed in the previous chapter. For if the player/avatar is a God-like being in these games, then so are these games' designers, who have created the very realm within which the players' all-powerful avatars operate. The designers of these games determine how much the player gets to see of the ethical consequences of her decisions. Thus, within games that actually display simulated combat (such as *Rome Total War*), the acts of violence performed by soldiers seem eerily bland and harmless, even when compared to the very driest academic discussion of Alexander the Great's bloody conquests. After all, the player doesn't see mutilated bodies, grieving parents, starving masses, or any of the other horrible results of war.

The games' designers also determine rewards/punishments for different kinds of acts, surely a traditional "God-like" role. Some of the most innovative recent god games do manage to incorporate some ethical components into both the tasks that the player is assigned and the rules according to which the player is rewarded or penalized. In *Civilization IV*, for example, the number of map squares included in the territory ruled by the player can increase or decrease, depending upon the cultural achievements of the country. If these effects are pronounced enough, other cities will voluntarily join the player's civilization. In *Black and White* the interface changes in interesting ways depending upon whether the player chooses stereotypically good or evil actions; the ambience is more light and cheerful for the good player, and darker, sinister, and more disgusting for the evil. As these examples demonstrate, though, the approach in such games is fragmentary and *ad hoc*. There is currently no set of principles agreed upon by designers about how to incorporate such ethical concerns.

Rome Total War: Barbarian Invasion makes some attempt to be historically accurate with respect to the brutality necessary to maintain a large empire.[28] It is simply not enough in this game for the player to pour resources into an occupied city. One must also destroy civic buildings and religious structures (as actually happened during the Muslim conquest of North Africa and the reconquest of Spain) and make it in people's interest to adopt the religion of the occupier. Unfortunately though, the interface presents this merely in terms of a few clicks of the mouse to alter the building queue and then changes the ratio of happy to unhappy citizen icons.

Historically and philosophically informed games could give players the option of "winning" them *ethically*, as well as just militarily or technologically. Just as one can win *Civilization II* by being the first society to send spaceships to Alpha Centauri as well as through sheer conquest, games like the *Total War* series could be set up to reward the conquerors who do the least violence to Kantian or utilitarian moral principles, as well as being the most successful expansionists. This could easily be set up with, for example, a "utilitarian score," a "Kantian score," and an "expansion score," yielding different methods of winning.

Both utilitarianism and deontological ethics agree, though, that the moral worth of an action is in no way a function of the rewards that the action brings to those who perform it. Sometimes great unhappiness and death come because one does the right thing, and it is precisely this that confers so much nobility on the sacrifices of martyrs such as Martin Luther King Jr. and Gandhi, as well as the immense suffering endured by their followers. Moreover, great art sometimes must reflect this tragic aspect of existence. As such, video games cannot simply encourage more moral acts by granting higher scores to the players that behave the most morally (whether the morality in question is utilitarian or deontological).

In a manner analogous to many works of great literature, cutting-edge games of the future should use other mechanisms than just scoring to manipulate the human–computer interface in order to appeal to the player's moral sensitivities. The currently available game that does this most imaginatively is Lionhead Studios' *Black and White*, in which the player manages a full-scale virtual human society, but with an important twist; her influence on the population is in part exerted through an animal-like demiurge that has to be kept alive and happy, and trained to respond to simple commands. Even more interestingly, *Black and White* gives the player the opportunity to develop a curious sort of intimacy with at least this one inhabitant of the game-world, as her monkey, cow, or tiger develops from a clueless infant into a loveable magician or a vindictive monster. The player supervises the development of the creature from its birth, and has to teach it all of its basic life skills, including grooming, healthy eating, and going to the toilet via a simple system of rewards (caresses) and punishments (slaps). Eventually, the animal becomes an important intermediary between the God-like player and his worshippers in the game-world. It metes out punishment to apostates, fights off the society's military enemies, and can even comfort and aid the populace after they have been subjected to the player's divine wrath via some natural disaster or death-dealing miracle. It is difficult for any imaginative player of *Black and White* to adopt the sort of purely exploitative attitude encouraged by games like *Civilization* toward an artificially intelligent critter that she has raised from infancy as though it were a domestic pet.

This facet of *Black and White* could without too much work be incorporated into other existing games. Take *The Sims*, for example. Although the player is given no explicit goals the achievement of which would count as "winning" this game, there are a lot of strong implicit suggestions. In the first release of the game, one begins with just enough resources to build a tiny house with a few cheap appliances in a neighborhood that already contains one enormous, lavishly furnished home waiting to be occupied. A lot of players of this version of the game quickly discovered a good strategy for making their own favored Sims rich and successful as quickly as possible. The trick is to design two separate small households, each one containing a couple of freshly minted citizens of the game-world, and then to make a systematic use of the resources and personalities belonging to one household to improve the fortunes of the other. One's "favored" Sim family can call up the neighbors to banter or flirt whenever they need to keep their scores for social interaction high, or just drop over unannounced on their hapless "friends" to raid the fridge.

Once again, if the availability of this strategy is a flaw in the game, it is hardly because of any lack of realism. Exploitation between families and other social groups is a well-known part of the human experience. But it also represents a manifest violation of the second version of Kant's Categorical Imperative, since the strategy involves treating other "people" as means without taking their own (game-relative) ends into consideration. A more sophisticated and challenging future version of *The Sims* might not simply *disallow* the "squeeze your neighbors" strategy, or penalize the player for overusing it; rather, such a game could make the cost of adopting this strategy more apparent by having game-play reflect the human cost of doing so. For most of us, at least, it would be much less fun living in a giant house if the rest of the neighborhood is utterly run down and one's only friends are a tribe of characterless sycophants.

When one gets used to the idea that it is possible to believe in ethical principles that attain their authority from something other than God's will or divine revelation, a whole new vista of video game design opens up. Likewise, reflection on so-called "god games" from this perspective can at least occasionally shed some light on some of the major theological and religious traditions that have often caused philosophical puzzlement. If this last claim seems implausible or presumptuous, consider the teaching that is shared by all major theistic religions, that a God possessing some version or other of the three perfections not only exists, but engages in *particular providence*—that is, in specific, temporally discrete acts of intervention in the natural order. The incarnation of God in Jesus Christ, the parting of the Red Sea, the inspiration of Joseph Smith to translate the Book of Mormon, and the delivery unto earth of the sacred Black Stone of the Kaaba are events that have been taken by millions of religious people around the world as the results of particular providence. If there is a single major lesson about theology that can be learned from god games like the ones that we have described in this chapter, it is perhaps just this: even for a being with unimaginably vast knowledge, power, and goodness, decisions about when and how to interfere with the natural order, and how much to exert one's will upon the actions of thinking beings other than oneself, would have to be atrociously difficult and demanding.

5 The Metaphysics of Interactive Art (Puzzle and Adventure Games)

5.1 Interacting Narratives

In one famous story, the hero is locked in prison. A tiny cell encloses her in all directions. She paces back and forth, staring at the impenetrable walls, her only consolation a simple game played with a small rubber ball. Hour after hour, she throws the toy against the massive grid of stones, contemplating a life of freedom outside this bleak place of confinement. Then, one day, she notices that the very game she has been playing may be her best hope of escape—for the opposing wall has begun to crumble! With tireless energy she hurls the toy against the shattering bricks, until every last one of them has turned to dust. In its place is emptiness. She walks forward, eyes slowly adjusting to the darkness. And there, in the new space, what does she find? Nothing but another wall!

In another quite different tale, the hero is a simple man with austere appetites but an infinite fund of energy. The world that surrounds him is a puzzling, ever-evolving labyrinth. His life's vocation is to make this world a cleaner, safer place, while chasing down the rewards that are his unique birthright. Sometimes though, our hero is haunted by flickering specters that dodge around corners as he approaches, only to reemerge behind him in steady and awful chase. He restlessly pursues the woman that he loves through this strange environment—or is she pursuing him? Either way, their love is as wholehearted and inevitable as the ancient principle that like attracts like.

To anybody who didn't grow up with video games, the first of these stories might have the feel of a novel by Franz Kafka, while the second might sound like the plot of a surrealistic yet sentimental pre-World War II black and white film. But we feel pretty confident in assuming that most of our readers will already have identified them as the storylines from *Breakout!* and *Pac-Man*, respectively.

It is easy to forget that all video games tell stories because relatively few of them are remembered for their plotlines. After all, who cares how all those violent monsters got onto the moon in *Doom*? Why bother wondering how your character ended up living a life of crime in *Grand Theft Auto*? Most video games throw the player into the middle of the action so fast that there is little time to notice or reflect upon overall narrative structure.

There are two major exceptions to these generalizations. First, some very popular contemporary games have been adapted from other storytelling media, for example, the *Harry Potter* games from the bestselling books and *Knights of the Old Republic* from the *Star Wars* movies. The second exception is the once extraordinarily popular genre of Adventure Games (e.g., the *Myst* series, *Grim Fandango*, and *Broken Sword*).

Though all games in a sense *have* stories, it cannot be quite right to say that they actually *tell* stories in the way printed novels do or in the manner of your grandmother reading to you at bedtime. Rather, the player herself partially determines the story that gets told based on the decisions she makes herself, such as what sort of character to play, how to interact with the guard at the temple, or whether to risk going into the crypt without a magic lantern. Even in simple old-school games, like our two examples at the start of this chapter, players often tend to construct stories for themselves unconsciously as they make their way through levels, over power-ups, or along monster-infested corridors.

The impulse to create stories is universal, and has been around since the earliest phases of human history. No sooner had the founders of the first Mesopotamian civilization built huts to live in and invented a code of laws than they came up with the *Epic of Gilgamesh*, a heroic narrative full of gore and melodrama that would make a pretty good video game. The earliest epics, like *Gilgamesh*, the Babylonian *Enuma Eliš*, the Indian *Rāmāyana* and *Mahābhārata*, and Homer's *Iliad* and *Odyssey*, almost certainly weren't each written by a single individual. Instead, they were transmitted orally, in Greece by paid storytellers (called *rhapsodes*) who altered the tale that they were telling from place to place depending on how much they remembered and who was in their audience. If you were delivering part of the *Odyssey* to a group of merchant seamen, for example, you'd want to be sure you knew a bit of maritime lore; if your audience for the *Iliad* consisted of hard military types, you'd probably want to play up the lewdness and violence. These tales were the first examples of interactive storytelling, since what happened in the narrative depended crucially on audience feedback. It is easy to forget that this form of literary art predates the kind of stories that modern consumers find ready-made when they go to the bookstore or the movie theater.

Video games restore the art of storytelling to its radically interactive roots. Consider the games of the *Myst* series. In each installment, the player is presented with a number of different virtual "ages" that she needs to visit in order to complete the game. These are strange, geographically isolated realms full of puzzles and challenges that are made accessible via a method of magical writing practiced by the two nonplayer characters (NPCs) Atrus and Gehn. In the original *Myst*, each Age is presented as having a considerably different feel: the age of Channelwood is heavily forested and serene, the Stoneship Age is full of surreal imagery, winding paths, and secret rooms, and the Selenetic Age is barren and vaguely threatening. One of the most striking things about the *Myst* games (and the dozens of other adventure games produced in the mid-1990s that imitated their basic premise and game-play style) is how different the experience of playing them is, depending upon the order in which one gains access to each separate age. The player who arrives in the arboreal Channelwood first could easily get the impression that the art of world-constructing practiced by Gehn and Atrus was a harmless and charming pastime. But those first confronted by the tragic image of a marooned ship in the Stoneship Age could just as easily reach the conclusion that this art was nothing but a dangerous, hubristic folly.

Certainly, there is a sense in which one is playing the "same" game regardless of the order in which the various ages of *Myst* are experienced. But thinking this way makes it difficult to specify exactly what sort of aesthetic properties the game possesses. Is *Myst* a happy game or a tragedy? Is the player's own character a hero, a trickster, or a mere helper-figure to the centrally important family of Atrus?[1] Perhaps these questions are meaningless when asked about *Myst* itself; perhaps we can only answer them with respect to particular kinds of play-throughs. It is worth investigating the possibility that when the games in the *Myst* series are experienced in different ways by different players, each player is responding to an entirely different work of art, works that are in part *constituted* by the players' own creative reactions.

The idea that the player contributes to the narrative becomes all the more credible when one focuses on the fact that many video games—especially so-called "adventure" role-playing games such as *Bioshock* and *Mass Effect*—are now so enormously complicated that the designers themselves cannot possibly anticipate all of the various ways they can be played. For example, players can learn to "beat" certain games in ways that are entirely unanticipated by the designers, such as by learning the "Wall of Bones" spell in *Aidyn Chronicles: The First Mage*, or through heavy development of the "corpse explosion" spell in the nonpatched version of *Diablo II*. We will have much more to say about this point later on. First, though, we make a brief excursus into philosophical aesthetics. The idea that central aesthetic properties are creatively determined by the works' audience is far from being a new one.

5.2 Against the Audience

Here, we briefly consider two influential arguments for the conclusion that the reception of works of art is irrelevant to determining their aesthetic properties. Both speak to the intuition that there must be something besides people's personal responses, tastes, or preferences that makes Shakespeare's writings better than Tom Clancy's. Our discussion reveals that, even in spite of the need to respect this fact, the view of aesthetic properties as purely viewer-independent leaves out something important about how we go about experiencing and evaluating art.

5.2.1 The Mind-Independence Argument

G.E. Moore's *Principia Ethica*[2] contains an interesting critique of the idea that the value of a work of art could depend in any way on its audience. He asks us to reflect upon the differences that might exist between two different possible worlds, in both of which there is nobody around to respond to anything. Moore writes, "Let us imagine one world exceedingly beautiful. Imagine it as beautiful as you can; put into it whatever in this earth you most admire—mountains, rivers, the sea, trees, sunsets, stars and moon . . . then imagine the ugliest world that you can possibly conceive. Imagine it simply one heap of filth, containing everything that is most disgusting" (*Principia*, 83–4). The question that Moore wants us to consider is this: even if there is absolutely no possibility that a human being could ever live in either of them and thus experience their respective contents, "is it irrational to hold that it is better that the beautiful world should exist, than the one which is ugly" (*Principia*, 84)? If the answer to this question is "no" (as Moore thinks that it must be), the value of beautiful things must always be determined by something other than how they cause people to think or feel.

Moore's position can be summarized by means of the following two-premise argument:

The Mind-Independence Argument

1   There are some possible worlds, the contents of which it is impossible for human beings to experience or respond to.
2   These possible worlds might nonetheless contain objects that have either positive or negative aesthetic value.
3   Aesthetic value is, therefore, not determined by the experiences or responses that artworks provoke in human beings.

Since inaccessible worlds that contain works of beauty are more valuable than those that don't, aesthetic value must not be a function of an artwork's reception by its audience.

Far-fetched thought experiments like Moore's are as common in contemporary philosophy as they are dubious. They almost always raise more questions than they answer,[3] and the lack of anything approaching a consensus on them should be enough to give any opponent of audience-centered aesthetics pause about enlisting Moore's help. Is it really so obvious that we can even *conceive* of Moore's two strange, uninhabited worlds? And if we could perform such a feat of imagination, wouldn't that mean that there is a sense in which both the "trees and sunsets" of one world and the "disgusting filth" of the other were really being observed and responded to by us, even if only through the medium of speculative imagination?

This line of attack becomes clearer if we examine the first premise of The Mind-Independence Argument more carefully. The premise says that the relevant worlds are such that it is "impossible" for anyone to respond to the works. Perhaps this is because nobody lives in those worlds, or perhaps for stronger reasons such as an atmosphere inimical to conscious life. But arguably, to the extent that we ourselves are *imagining* the objects inhabiting the worlds, we are in our own universe (the "actual" world) responding to the merely possible objects within Moore's worlds. We think of them as being filled with "disgusting" things (e.g., dead fish, mildew, metastasizing tumors, and feces) or try to summon up images of their natural loveliness (e.g., rich biodiversity, the social architecture of ancient Greece and India, and Michelangelo's sculptures). But then, from the perspective of Moore's worlds, there *is* a possible world (i.e., ours) where people respond to the objects in question, so even in those worlds it is not impossible for the objects to be responded to.

Later on in the present chapter, we will examine some more substantive reasons for holding that the worlds Moore describes can't exist. First, though, we turn to another important argument against response-based aesthetics that avoids problematic thought experiments like Moore's.

5.2.2 The Objectivity Argument

Most amateur video game enthusiasts, as well as critics and journalists who write about games for a living, focus almost exclusively on audience reaction. A quick look at the user review pages on a heavily trafficked website like Gamespot.com will bring up dozens of remarks like "*System Shock 2* is a scare-fest extrordinaire, still the creepiest experience around," or "*Harry Potter and the Chamber of Secrets*: been there, done that." But one will find curiously few observations about why a particular designer might have chosen to include some effect or plot twist rather than another, and little about the other features of design beyond sentiments such as "Cool graphics!" Fans of multiplayer online gaming tend to be even more subjective, expressing most of their admiration for games like *World of Warcraft* by talking at length about how addicted they have become.

Hearing video games (or any other kind of artwork) described in these terms can become curiously unsatisfying after a while. Even if you and I have a great deal in common, how much do I really learn about what makes a particular game, song, or novel distinctive or interesting by hearing about the effect that it has had on your personal psychology? For this reason, it turns out to be deeply difficult to determine the properties of works of art solely by reference to people's reactions to them.

Common sense suggests that one can be *objective* in describing the properties that any object possesses, whether it is considered as work of art or in some other way (as a lump of metal, say, or a sequence of rhythmical noises or black squiggles on a page). But if person *A* says to person *B* "Ice cream is tasty," or "I liked *The Longest Journey* much more than *Knights of the Old Republic*," it would normally be weird for *B* to try to start an argument about the objective truth of either of these claims, since in most contexts these sorts of assertions function as little more than declarations of personal preference. Common sense just as strongly supports the famous and often-quoted Latin proverb *De gustibus non est disputandum*, which translates (roughly) as "There is no disputing taste." But what about statements like "The landscapes in *Myst* are beautiful," or "*The Longest Journey* is a better game than *Knights of the Old Republic*?" On one hand, these also sound a lot like mere declarations of personal preference. But on the other hand, they aren't supposed to be the sort of statements that simply make no sense at all to argue about. Are they?

If it is true that there is no disputing taste, then the following relatively simple argument might turn out to constitute a knockdown refutation of any response-based approach to aesthetics.

The Objectivity Argument

1   There are objective facts about what makes a work of art valuable.
2   It is always possible to engage in rational argumentation about matters of objective fact.
3   It is not possible to engage in rational argumentation about the appropriateness of a person's affective responses to a work of art.
4   Therefore, what makes a work of art valuable is not in any way a function of affective responses to it.

In "The Affective Fallacy," the literary critics W.K. Wimsatt and Monroe Beardsley suggest that trying to base philosophical aesthetics on claims about how people respond to artworks is bound to fail for just this reason.[4] For them, the style of aesthetics practiced by Internet critics is really just a symptom of epistemological skepticism (the thesis that the human mind is simply incapable of genuinely knowing anything at all).[5] They regard the truth of Premise Three of the Objectivity Argument as implying that any attempt "to derive the standard of criticism from the psychological effects of the poem"—or of any other kind of literary artwork—always "ends in impressionism and relativism" (*Verbal*, 21). It makes about as much sense, they suggest, as trying to "study the properties of wine by getting drunk" (*Verbal*, 20).

5.3 Our Humean Heritage, Part Two: A Standard of Taste

David Hume wrote a fascinating essay called *On the Standard of Taste* that addresses some of the philosophical concerns raised earlier about evaluating art. Hume was interested in discerning whether there really is an objective standard of taste in the arts. In the course of doing so, he makes some remarks that can be read as representing a response to what we have called The Objectivity Argument against "affective" approaches to philosophical aesthetics.

5.3.1 The View

According to Hume, when it comes to "judgments of taste" the most important thing for the philosopher to keep in mind is that not all such responses to works of art are created equal. Hume points out that whenever we come into contact with someone who prefers artworks that are obviously junk (e.g., games like *Extreme Paintball* or *Space Bunnies Must Die!*) or else merely second-rate works (e.g., *Hexen*, or *Baldur's Gate: Dark Alliance*) over other artworks that are acknowledged masterpieces (e.g., *Doom*, *Homeworld*, and *Grim Fandango*), "we pronounce, without scruple, the sentiment of these pretended critics to be absurd and ridiculous. The principle of the natural equality of tastes is then totally forgotten, and while we admit it on some occasions, where the objects seem near equality, it appears . . . a palpable absurdity, where objects so disproportioned are compared together."[6]

As an account of how people actually talk to one another about their tastes in the arts, this passage probably sounded more plausible to Hume's contemporaries than it does today. In a democratic culture, it is always rather risky telling people that they have crummy taste, regardless of what we might privately believe about the preferences of our fellow citizens. But Hume's observation at any rate proves nothing at all, taken by itself, since it needs to be backed up with a plausible story about why we would be justified in dismissing the responses of people who are drawn to especially rotten works of art. We ought to be able to point to some very general, relatively indisputable principles of game design in our attempts to argue that the games we prefer (and others with similar features) are better than those that we regard as inferior.

Hume proposes that such principles of creation do, in fact, exist. And he seems to be right about this. It is easy enough to think of a few general rules of composition that seem to apply to works of art in any genre, like "Avoid tiresome repetition!" or "Don't imitate other artworks to the point of outright plagiarism!" There are also much more genre-specific rules, like "Don't cut off peoples' heads!" (for photography), or "Don't switch arbitrarily from iambic to dactylic metre!" (for poetry), or "Don't kill the player's avatar too often!" (for game design).

But Hume also insists (and this is the really original, controversial feature of his aesthetics) that the truth of these kinds of principles is itself entirely dependent upon our actual practice of judging specific works of art. It is a mistake, he thinks, to suppose that a person could determine which of these rules are the most important *before* she has experienced any works of art in the relevant genre. Rather, the "general rules of beauty," as Hume puts it, are "drawn from established models, and from the observation of what pleases or displeases, when presented singly and in high degree" (*Standard*, 11).

So when a person criticizes you for napping during Beethoven's Ninth Symphony, laughing out loud during the last scene of *Hamlet*, or running away from every scary alien in *The Crystal Key*, what she is doing is perfectly rational, contrary to Premise Three of The Objectivity Argument. For although she may not be able to describe the principles that underlie her criticisms, her very ability to value these classic works of music, theatre, and game design shows that she is aware of the general characteristics to which people respond.

In fact, Hume ends up proposing that we can only ever achieve real objectivity in aesthetics by observing how the preferences of the most enlightened consumers of art tend to converge upon a small number of classic works. For Hume, it is the fact that great paintings like *La Primavera* or novels like *David Copperfield* have attracted sophisticated admirers outside of the period in which they were produced that lets us know that they have genuine aesthetic value.[7]

Even in a relatively novel medium like video games, we see this sort of phenomenon beginning to take place with older classics like *Joust*, *Pitfall!*, *Zork*, and *King's Quest*. It is precisely because they have been replayed so many times, and because they have inspired such a host of clever imitators who follow the "rules of beauty" first brought to light by the designers of these early games, that we regard them as classics in the first place. Of course, this process is fallible, and sometimes great works get neglected while mediocre stuff gets overpraised. But Hume remarks that even the most objective knowledge that we get from the hard sciences is fallible in the same way. In addition, Hume's treatment of these issues suggest that one's ability to pass double blind tests for the nonnormative properties of a work of art is a good guide to one's expertise with the normative properties. For example, someone who can reliably discern from taste alone the kinds of grape that make up wine (or in Hume's example, one who can tell that a wine tastes like metal) will tend to have much better opinions about wine quality (metallic wine is not good) than one who cannot do this. In virtue of all of this, Hume is able to plausibly suggest that even though normative aesthetic properties are a function of our considered responses, nonetheless the achievements of the greatest artists can "maintain an universal, undisputed empire over the minds of men" in a way that "theories of abstract philosophy" and "systems of profound theology" can simply never aspire to (*Standard*, 18).

5.3.2 A Problem for Neo-Humeanism

Hume's proposals are closely echoed by some controversial claims that have been made by recent literary critics about the nature of literary art. Moreover, contemporary neo-Humeans extend Hume's audience centered perspective far beyond mere normative aesthetic properties such as the work's overall beauty. According to Stanley Fish, an influential member of the "reader response" school of criticism, the very *meanings* of literary texts themselves (as opposed to just their goodness and badness), "are not extracted but *made* and made not by encoded forms but by *interpretive strategies* that call them into being. It follows that what utterers do is give hearers and readers the opportunity to make meanings (and texts)."[8]

Fish is suggesting here that written texts and acts of speech do not count as being *meaningful at all* until they have been responded to.[9] Before that, they are only meaningful *in potentia* (as Aristotle might have put it). And one and the same text might potentially bear *contradictory* aesthetic properties, because for Fish the artwork is not complete until a creative viewer interprets it.[10] On this view, Moore's unwitnessed "beautiful" and "ugly" worlds would, in fact, be neither beautiful nor ugly at all, since no one has actually experienced the contents of either world.

Perhaps the most difficult issue raised by Fish's remarks is the question of what counts as a legitimate response to a literary text. Can a reader really "make meanings" in Fish's sense while reading *A Tale of Two Cities* if she has never even seen London or Paris on a map? How about if she just reads every second page? Some critics from the reader-response school have tried to distinguish between readers who have "literary competence"—by which they presumably mean the possession of an adult vocabulary, a basic understanding of the relevant literary genres and minimal rationality—and readers who do not. But, (as we have argued in our paper, "Computability Theory and Aesthetic Competence") such proposals turn out to be maddeningly provisional, vague, and unworkable when subjected to close scrutiny.[11]

5.3.3 Artist-Centric vs. Audience-Centric Aesthetic Properties

In the *Broken Sword* series of adventure games, the player's character George Stobbart travels around carrying a large collection of improbable stuff, from poisoned darts and sewer keys to a bag of dog biscuits and a plastic clown's nose. To make progress through the game, the player has to figure out which inventory item George needs to use in which situation. Some of the solutions to these puzzles are more or less self-evident: when the player needs to make a quick escape down a manhole into the Paris sewers, selecting the sewer key from George's inventory will clearly be the most natural choice. At other places in the game, though, things can get quite unintuitive. At one point in *Broken Sword II*, George has to put out a dangerous fire by fitting an overheated CO_2 cylinder into a spritzer bottle using a pair of his girlfriend's underwear as a protective glove.

It is not impossible (for a talented player, after hundreds of hours of game-play, at any rate) to write out a complete strategy for beating one of these games, or for any traditional adventure game designed upon similar lines. One could simply match each item from George's inventory with the task it performs. There are dozens of these guides (or "walkthroughs," as they're usually called) to playing commercial video games available free on the Internet. Overuse of them is not much fun, though, partly because it is "cheating" in a sense, but mostly because much of the enjoyment of these kinds of games is completely lost if the player's avatar never goofs up. The *Broken Sword* games are full of clever jokes and character development, most of which takes place when George tries to use the wrong object for any given job (e.g., the clown nose to pick a lock, or the underwear to bribe a potential informant). He gradually emerges as a humorously likeable, albeit incurably pompous and self-satisfied character in the broadly Dickensian tradition. To a player who experienced the game via the rigorous use of a walkthrough, however, George would just come across as another efficient, but more or less faceless action hero.

Nonetheless, such walkthroughs for adventure games are used reservedly by all but the most patient and rigorous gamers. It is no small thing to come up with this sort of a strategy for beating a game like *Myst, Broken Sword*, or any of the other large-scale commercial adventure games, and (as noted earlier) many such strategies involve sequences of actions never conceived of by the designers of the games.

But, this raises an important question. In what sense is playing a video game really an artistically creative act? If we can answer this, it would help us to get a clearer sense of whether the player's actions and decisions might be described as coconstituting the work of art in something like the way that Fish claims a reader's acts of interpretation help to constitute the very meaning of a work of literature.

5.3.4 *Turing Machines and the Halting Problem*

We may begin by taking for granted the fact that the artists, programmers, and designers who produce a piece of game software play a highly significant role in determining the constitution of particular computer games. As mentioned earlier, though, certain aesthetic properties that these games have arise as the result of events in gameplay that the game's authors might very well not have anticipated taking place. Before we consider the role that the player has in all of this, we will need to undertake a fairly significant digression in order to consider what part the computing machine itself—home PC, multiuser network or gaming console—plays in generation of aesthetic properties.

Today there is an enormous amount of variety in the way that contemporary personal computers and gaming consoles are designed, the types of components they are made out of, and the sorts of programs that they are built to run. But all of them can be understood as being to some extent based upon the abstract idea of a Turing machine (free simulations of which can now be manipulated online).[12] A standard Turing machine consists of a piece of tape infinitely long in both directions which is divided into an infinite number of cells, each with either a 0 or a 1 written on it, and a counter which follows a given set of instructions to either write a 0 or a 1 on the tape or to move left or right.[13] For example, if we denote the location of the counter by boldfacing the number in a tape's cell, the following illustrates the execution of a Turing machine program, where each row represents the tape. For the second to tenth row, the machine has just been changed either by the counter moving to a new place, or by the counter writing on the tape.

```
......0 0 0 0 0 0......
......0 1 0 0 0 0......
......0 1 0 0 0 0......
......0 1 1 0 0 0......
......0 1 1 0 0 0......
......0 1 1 1 0 0......
......0 1 1 1 0 0......
......0 1 1 1 0 0......
......0 1 1 1 0 0......
......0 1 1 1 0 0......
```

We will define a standard Turing machine program to consist of a series of commands, all having the following form.

> If the machine is in state m and the counter reads n, then write/move o and then go to state p.

Here the variables m and p range over the natural numbers, and n can be equal to either 1 or 0, and o can be equal to either 1, 0, L (for left), or R (for right). The only restriction we impose is that each line be well defined; we prohibit multiple lines that give contradictory instructions. Thus, the following is *not* a Turing machine program.

> If in state 1 and the counter reads 1, then write 0 and go to state 1.
> If in state 1 and the counter reads 1, then move L and go to state 2.

The machine can receive at most one instruction for where to move or what to write, given whatever the counter is reading in a given state. Likewise, the machine can receive at most one instruction for what state to move into given the state it is in, what the counter has read, and what it has written or moved. So the following is also *not* a Turing machine program.

> If in state 1 and the counter reads 1, then write 0 and go to state 1.
> If in state 1 and the counter reads 1, then write 0 and go to state 2.

To illustrate some of the points we want to make about Turing machines in what follows, we'll describe the coding and behavior of some very simple Turing machine programs. Working through these sorts of examples is a skill that is usually taught to beginning computer scientists, and is also a rather fun variety of puzzle solving in its own right; the reader is, therefore, invited to follow along with our descriptions of how such a hypothetical machine might behave when "told" to calculate a variety of basic arithmetic functions.

Here is an acceptable Turing machine program, a program that makes the machine do what is executed by the aforementioned portrayal of a series of tapes (see Program 1).

If in state	and the counter reads	then write/move	and then go to state
1	0	1	1
1	1	R	2
2	0	1	2
2	1	R	3
3	0	1	3
3	1	L	4
4	0	R	
4	1	L	4

Program 1: standard Turing machine that prints three ones to the left of the initial counter place.

We can show how this program executes *via* the following.

(0 0 0 0 0 0 0 0) Go to state 1.
1- Since the counter reads 0, write 1
(0 0 1 0 0 0 0 0), and go to state 1.
1- Since the counter reads 1, move R
(0 0 0 0 0 0 0 0), and go to state 2.
2- Since the counter reads 0, write 1
(0 0 0 1 0 0 0 0), and go to state 2.
2- Since the counter reads 1, move R
(0 0 1 1 0 0 0 0), and go to state 3.
3- Since the counter reads 0, write 1
(0 0 1 1 1 0 0 0), and go to state 3.
4- Since the counter reads 1, move L
(0 0 1 1 1 0 0 0), and go to state 4.
4- Since the counter reads 1, move L
(0 0 1 1 1 0 0 0), and go to state 4.

4- Since the counter reads 1, move L
(0 0 1 1 1 0 0 0 0), and go to state 4.
4- Since the counter reads 0, move R
(0 0 **1 1** 1 0 0 0 0).

With the example of these machines in mind, we can define a *Turing-computable function* as all those functions that can be computed by a Turing machine. A function can be computed by a Turing machine if there exists a Turing machine program such that any tape starting in canonical starting position (with the function's inputs separated by one space and the counter on the beginning of the leftmost input) will, after running the program, halt with that function's output on the tape and with the counter at the leftmost edge of that output. Program 1 computes the zero place function "is equal to three."

To better see how this works, consider the simple Turing machine for the two-placed addition function. Just to make this as simple as possible, we will only consider adding positive natural numbers (and so not have to worry about adding zero) (see Program 2).

If in state	and the counter reads	then write/move	and then go to state
1	0	1	2
1	1	R	1
2	0	L	3
2	1	R	2
3	0	L	4
3	1	0	3
4	0	R	
4	1	L	4

Program 2: standard Turing machine that adds two positive natural numbers.

To see this in action, consider the tape in the canonical starting position with the inputs being the numerals two and three, and then run the program.

(0 0 **1 1** 0 1 1 1 0) Go to state 1.
1- Since the counter reads 1, move R
(0 0 1 **1** 0 1 1 1 0), and go to state 1.
1- Since the counter reads 1, move R
(0 0 1 1 **0** 1 1 1 0), and go to state 1.
2- Since the counter reads 0, write 1
(0 0 1 1 **1** 1 1 1 0), and go to state 2.
2- Since the counter reads 1, move R
(0 0 1 1 1 **1** 1 1 0), and go to state 2.

2- Since the counter reads 1, move R
(0 0 1 1 1 1 1 1 0), and go to state 2.
2- Since the counter reads 1, move R
(0 0 1 1 1 1 1 1 0), and go to state 2.
2- Since the counter reads 1, move R
(0 0 1 1 1 1 1 1 0), and go to state 2.
2- Since the counter reads 0, move L
(0 0 1 1 1 1 1 1 0), and go to state 3.
3- Since the counter reads 1, write 0
(0 0 1 1 1 1 1 0 0), and go to state 3.
3- Since the counter reads 0, move L
(0 0 1 1 1 1 1 0 0), and go to state 4.
3- Since the counter reads 1, move L
(0 0 1 1 1 1 1 0 0), and go to state 4.
3- Since the counter reads 1, move L
(0 0 1 1 1 1 1 0 0), and go to state 4.
3- Since the counter reads 1, move L
(0 0 1 1 1 1 1 0 0), and go to state 4.
3- Since the counter reads 1, move L
(0 0 1 1 1 1 1 0 0), and go to state 4.
3- Since the counter reads 1, move L
(0 0 1 1 1 1 1 0 0), and go to state 4.
3- Since the counter reads 0, move R
(0 0 1 1 1 1 1 0 0).
Execution of Program 2 when beginning with blank tape

Given our conventions, the initial state,

(0 0 1 1 0 1 1 1 0) Go to state 1,

is equivalent to feeding the numbers two and three into the program, and the output,

(0 0 1 1 1 1 1 0 0),

is equivalent to the number five. Given that this holds for any two inputs, it is in this sense that the machine computes the addition function for positive natural numbers.

Here are a couple more definitions that will turn out to be important to our later discussion. First, we can define the Turing-computable sets of natural numbers as those for which there exists a Turing machine program that computes the characteristic function (the function that halts on "1" for members of the set, and halts on a blank tape, and hence "0," otherwise). We also define Turing enumerability, which occurs whenever there exists a function that halts on "1" for members of the set, but may halt on anything else or not halt at all for nonmembers of the set. A set of natural numbers will be Turing-computable whenever that set and its complement (the set of natural numbers not in the initial set) are both Turing-enumerable.

These hypothetical machines are not merely interesting because they were precursors to the modern digital computer. They are also provably *equivalent* to modern digital computers, in the sense that any numerical function computed by a modern digital computer is also Turing-computable (and vice versa). Given enough time, memory, and energy, a Turing machine can do whatever a modern digital computer can. One immediate entailment of this is that if one can prove that there is something that Turing machines cannot in principle accomplish, then one has proven that modern digital computers cannot do that thing either.

In 1936, Alan Turing proved an even more surprising result about what computers cannot do. Turing showed that, strictly as a matter of logic, there can be no solution to what computer scientists refers to as the "halting problem." It is, in other words, simply impossible to write a computer program that will output a "1" whenever it is fed another program and input that causes that other program to "halt" (i.e., it doesn't just keep running forever) and a "0" when the other program would not halt on that input. The unsolvability of the halting problem is one of the most important limitation theorems in the history of mathematical logic, and it played a crucial role in the events that led up to the development of the first modern digital computers. We think it also has some important implications for the questions about artworks and aesthetic properties that have been the focus of the present chapter.

The details of Turing's proof of this result need not detain us,[14] though a few points are in order such that the reader understands its full import. Consider the following Turing machine program (see Program 3).

If in state	and the counter reads	then write/move	and then go to state
1	0	1	1
1	1	R	1

Program 3: standard Turing machine that prints 1s forever.

Whatever this Turing machine is fed, the end result is that it never halts. If it reads a 1, it moves to the right. If it reads a 0, it prints a 1 and moves to the right. So if you had an infinite amount of time and resources, this Turing machine would go on forever.

Program 3 does not halt for any inputs, but some programs halt for some inputs and not others. Program 4 is an example.

Program 4 halts if it is fed any positive number (since positive numbers are represented by strings of ones) but just keeps moving to the right if it is fed zero (since zero is represented by nothing on the tape).

If in state	and the counter reads	then write/move	and then go to state
1	0	R	1
1	1	R	

Program 4: standard Turing machine that moves to the right forever if fed a blank tape, and moves to the right once if fed with a non-blank tape.

Turing showed that one could effectively enumerate all of the Turing machine programs so that each program corresponded to a unique natural number. He was also able to show that there exists a program for a "Universal Turing Machine" such that if it is fed the number of an arbitrary Turing machine followed by a zero, and then some input, it would return the correct output for that machine. For example, if the given four programs corresponded to the first four numbers in the enumeration, and we fed the Universal Turing Machine a two (that is, two ones in a row, standing for Program 2), followed by a zero, followed by a natural number (string of ones equal to that number), a zero, and another natural number, then the Universal Turing Machine would output the sum of the two numbers, just like Program 2 does.

What turns out not to be possible is the implementation of a Turing machine that when fed two numerals, the first being the number m of a Turing machine, the second being any other number n,[15] halts on one if program number m halts on number n, and halts on zero (a blank tape) if program number m does not halt on number n. By using an ingenious method of proof called diagonalization,[16] Turing was able to show this problem (now called "the halting problem") to be insolvable.

To see the significance of Turing's result in the present context, imagine the following rather weird type of computer game. Suppose that instead of a maze to run around in, or a series of worlds to visit, the player is presented with a completely explicit description of some randomly chosen computer program and input and asked to determine whether on not the program is ever going to halt on that input. The player's job is to figure out which program will halt in less time than the computer itself does.[17]

Here is a simple illustration from the BASIC programming language of the difference between a halting program and one that never halts: 10 PRINT "HELLO WORLD"/20 END is a program that would halt in less than a second, whereas 10 PRINT "HELLO WORLD"/20 GOTO 10 would never halt at all. Even for somebody with no programming experience at all, it is pretty easy to figure out why the second of these two programs will never halt, while the first will quite quickly. For more complicated examples, of course, the player would have to have a fairly sophisticated understanding of the code in order to have any chance of making an accurate guess.

Turing's theorem about the halting problem shows that (given the provable equivalence of Turing machines and modern digital computers) it is logically impossible to come up with an algorithm that the computer can always use to beat all possible players of this imaginary game. Turing's result entails that *no computer*, no matter how large or powerful, could ever be explicitly programmed with a perfectly general process for making up these sorts of game-winning strategies.

Since the game we just described is included in the set of all computer games, it follows that there is *no general strategy for beating all computer games*! So to the extent that it makes sense to talk about a perfectly general strategy being instantiated when we get through the worlds of *Myst*, the Old Republic, or the continent of Norrath, our play-through of the game instantiates a property that could not be instantiated in a computer program, and hence that is not "already there" in the lines of code that make up a finished game from the point of view of its designers.[18] It is no surprise then that programmers are so often taken aback when players craft novel strategies for beating their games.

These observations suggest an argumentative strategy for the neo-Humean to defend his position about the nature of art and aesthetic properties. Since no computer program could embody a perfect general strategy to win computer games, the property "being a winning strategy" is brought into existence by an act of creativity on the part of the player. But this observation gives us a precise manner for distinguishing audience-centric from work-centric aesthetic properties. In our view, computationally tractable properties are objective features of the work that exist independently of any act of gameplay. But noncomputationally tractable properties such as being a winning strategy (considered in full generality) are a product of the player's interaction with the game.

5.4 Conclusions

The main philosophical idea that we have discussed here is the thesis that aesthetic properties of artworks are a function of the particular types of responses that they provoke from human beings who experience them in the proper way. From our argument, it follows that the claim is true for at least an important class of artworks: those that require the person experiencing them to adopt a general strategy of interaction before any focused emotional response to the content of the work is even a possibility. Video games represent a paradigmatic example of this kind of work, since the very structure of the narratives that they are designed to deliver depends crucially upon the player's input.

Of course our argument here raises as many questions as it answers. Within the broader context of debate in philosophical aesthetics, the most pressing question is this: even if we are right about the demarcation between objective and audience-dependent properties with regard to computer games, why think that this has anything to do with controversial aesthetic properties of other kinds of artworks?

This question is motivated by a concern that the procedures we have described for coming up with game-winning strategies seem to be distinct from the types of affective responses that one might take to be the distinctive product of great artworks. Perhaps when it comes to the appreciation of beautiful paintings or symphonies,[19] sometimes all that is involved is a sudden powerful feeling, the experiencing of which doesn't require any sort of prior decisions or strategies of interpretation. In our essay "Computability Theory and Literary Competence," we have argued at length that this two-stage analysis of aesthetic experience clearly does apply to works of literary art. One can't even begin to have the sort of emotional experiences that fans of T.S. Eliot get from reading *The Waste Land* until one has parsed the sentences, decoded the vocabulary and understood at least some of the allusions that the poem makes to other works of literature. The strategies that the reader undertakes for accomplishing these things are bound to be so widely varied and diverse that by the time she gets to the end of the poem, there is an important sense in which it truly is a different work of art for her than it was for someone who developed different strategies of interpretation. To the extent that such general interpretive strategies are involved in the appreciation of just any artwork, we can always ask whether these strategies can be explicitly programmed in full generality into a digital computer. If they can't, then by our theory, the relevant properties are audience-centric. If, in full generality, the relevant strategies can be translated into programming code, they are an objective part of the artwork itself.

The issue of what is meant by a "general strategy" is not optimally clear, nor is it clear what is meant by explicitly programming such a thing into a computer. Does the unsolvability of the halting problem mean that humans will always be able to outthink machines? Or might it make sense to say that a digital computer itself may (if not now, then perhaps someday) instance nontrivial and noncomputable properties such as that of coming up with a perfectly general game-winning strategy? These are difficult and important questions to which we will now turn, as part of our broader discussion about the nature and limitations of artificial intelligence.

6 Artificial and Human Intelligence (Single-Player RPGs)

6.1 The Problem

People are justifiably amazed when they are exposed to contemporary RPGs such as *Elder Scrolls IV: Oblivion*.[1] The diegetic realms of these games are astoundingly realized; one's avatar can wander around for days having surprising interactions with random inhabitants of cities, towns, and wild places. Older computer RPGs such as *Baldur's Gate* and *Neverwinter Nights* were vastly more linear, meaning that the progression of game-play was tightly circumscribed according to a narrative. First, the player had to help defend the town. Next, she killed all the orcs in the swamp. Then, she was sent to retrieve the amulet out of the spider-infested caves. Then, she had to bring the amulet to the wise man in the next town. Etc. Etc.

In addition to having an astonishingly well-rendered visual interface, a gargantuan number of discrete quests, and towns and cities full of buildings that the player can enter and explore, *Oblivion* is overwhelmingly non-linear. As the player's avatar meets new people, she will be exposed to numerous sets of connected quests from different agencies, including various guilds (thieves, assassins, fighters, wizards, imperial guards), quasi-political trade organizations, religious groups and their deities, as well as hundreds of individual people with their own agendas. The player of *Oblivion* also has complete freedom to send her avatar wherever she wants. Individual side-missions and sets of quests can be embarked upon in almost any order the player desires. The avatar can have dozens of active quests going on at any given time (and part of the game's genius is an interface that makes this tractable). Equally important, the avatar can have *no* active quests going on, choosing instead to wander the earth as a mere observer.

All of these having been said, no computer RPG has come close to realizing the radical open-endedness of tabletop games such as *Dungeons and Dragons*. Great tabletop game-masters achieve non-linearity by crafting detailed maps of the diegetic world, with regions left indeterminate so that they can later devise maps of smaller areas on the fly, changing the quests assigned to players as a game develops, and acting out the personalities of non-player characters. Some of these features of game-play will be devised ahead of time, by the GM herself or by the authors of commercially available "modules" such as those of the *Forgotten Realms* series. But many will be created in real time as game-play proceeds. During an average campaign, tabletop game-masters must routinely be responsible for dozens of NPCs, all of whom must be imbued with enough character and intelligence for players to feel that their avatars inhabit a fully articulated universe.[2]

Strangely, the closer the computer RPGs get to achieving this standard of realization, the further away they can sometimes feel. In the *Elder Scrolls* series of games, the player actually sees the faces of the NPCs with whom her avatar interacts. The interface is so good that no two of the thousands of NPCs have the same face. With *Oblivion*, the NPCs' facial expressions, demeanor, and level of helpfulness actually change based on the player character's charisma and actions. The NPCs also converse openly with one another, and the avatar can sometimes learn important information by listening in on conversations. They even sleep in beds in their own houses, a fact especially crucial if one's avatar is infected with vampirism. It is uncanny.

But often it is too uncanny, and there is something distinctively creepy about it. The more realistic the NPCs look, and the more varied the possible interactions one's avatar can have with them, the more the player becomes aware of how the NPCs still have a tiny range of possible behaviors compared to those available either to actual people or to the diegetic people conjured up by the *D & D* game-master's human intelligence. After enough *Oblivion* game-play, the player tires of hearing the same snippets of conversation between the NPCs over and over again. And when the player is not interacting with them, the NPCs tend to stand still or walk in circumscribed paths.

The life of an NPC professor at *Oblivion*'s Arcane University is a paltry thing when compared with that of a real life professor of philosophy. The wizard professor spends all of her time staring into space, sleeping, repeating the same contribution to a conversation with her colleagues, and giving identical pat speeches concerning quests on each play-through of the game. The boring diegetic professor actually works as perhaps unintentionally effective parody; both authors know several academics who daily approximate this level of incessant somnambulating. But in fact even the dullest and most routine-bound real-life professor does vastly more things in the course of a day than even the most carefully imagined NPC.

Real-life professors' activities illustrate the overwhelmingly flexible adaptive richness characteristic of humans and other biological animals. Human beings (and animals) quickly and rationally change their behavior in response to incoming stimuli. When the biological human's office door is blocked by a chair left by the evening cleaning crew, he knows to move the chair. When students ask questions during seminars, he is (at least sometimes) able to respond in a way that addresses their concerns and encourages more student input. And as RPGs get better and better in every way, the lack of this richness in the NPCs becomes more and more noticeable.

Psychologists call the visual version of this paradox of more detail leading to less convincing game-play the "uncanny valley effect." Increasing realism in the portrayal of everyday objects causes them at the same time to seem more disturbingly unreal. When graphical capacities were bad enough to force designers to resort to obviously cartoony depictions of the diegetic realm, players could easily identify with their avatars by thinking of themselves as inhabitants of a cartoony realm. But as advances in graphics allow greater approximation to photography or movies, players cannot help but attend to the differences between the game depictions and actual photographs or film.[3]

One of the clearest examples of the uncanny valley effect is the indescribably creepy digitally CGI animated film *The Polar Express*. The film's animated simulacrum of Tom Hanks (in his role as "the conductor") has inspired Cthulu-like terrors in many viewers, including one of the authors of this book, who suffered serial nightmares after viewing half of the movie. The Tom Hanks creature is sinister and unsettling precisely because it looks so very much like a filmed human, yet at the same time clearly is not.

With *Oblivion*, the use of artificial intelligence in game design has (just barely) progressed to the point at which something similar to the uncanny valley effect crops up. But in this case, the problem arises with respect to what we will call the "cognitive interface"—i.e., all of the facets of the computing machine that users mentally categorize in order to accomplish their tasks. To differentiate cognitive from sensory interface, consider again *Oblivion*'s professors at the Arcane University. The graphical resolution and speed of change on the monitor are facets of the sensory interface. On the other hand, the fact that some part of the monitor is a *representation* of an NPC professor is part of the game's cognitive interface. The sensory interface consists of the raw materials such as the colors on the screen perceived by the player. A game's cognitive interface is what those raw materials represent and how they function in the relevant program. Clearly, these two facets of any game are inseparable. Without a sensory interface there would be no cognitive interface. Without a cognitive interface the sensory interface would be (to borrow the words of William James) "a blooming, buzzing confusion."[4] The type of uncanny valley effect we are presently concerned with is not the sensory one (where good graphical capacities lead us to notice how the characters look creepily like, yet unlike, photographic and film depictions of real people), but rather a cognitive analog (where characters behave intelligently enough to cast in bold relief the ways in which they are not).

The only conceivable solution to the cognitive uncanny valley problem would be the development by computer scientists, game designers, psychologists, and roboticists of a genuine artificial intelligence. Given all of the other advances in computer engineering over the past half century, one is entitled to be surprised that this task has not been accomplished yet. So what, exactly, is the problem?

In order to answer this question, we will need to take a close, extensive, and carefully critical look at a radically new[5] theory of human and machine cognition that philosophy, psychology, linguistics, and computer science researchers developed in the previous century. This theory, which is sometimes referred to as the "Computational-Representational Understanding of Mind" (CRUM), is the view that cognitive processes are computations upon language-like (or "linguaform") representations.[6] Explaining exactly what this amounts to and exploring the main video game relevant problems with it are the main tasks of this chapter.

The term "artificial intelligence" (AI) is used slightly differently by gamers than it is in the academic community.[7] In academia, AI research usually focuses on trying to get computers to engage in plausibly human-like linguistic and inferential behavior. While the restrictive manner in which NPCs verbally communicate in games such as *Elder Scrolls* is a significant part of the cognitive uncanny valley problem, it is only one instance of the NPCs' failure to exhibit flexible adaptive richness. Among gamers, "AI" most often refers to the skill with which a computer opponent can tailor its strategic and tactical behavior to defeat the player. Such tailoring is often lacking in ways that surprise even the programmers. For example, in *Oblivion* a character who can jump high enough and fire a bow can win all of the gladiatorial combats, because all she needs to do is leap up on a parapet and shoot arrows at her opponents. The opponents fail to adapt in the ways that human gladiatorial opponents no doubt would (hiding from the arrows, throwing things up onto the parapet, jumping up and grabbing the character's foot, etc.). Instead they just keep hitting their weapons against the stone columns below the player's avatar. Game reviewers commonly refer to this sort of problem as an instance of "bad AI."

On the linguaform CRUM model of artificial intelligence, a biological human's decision to jump up on a parapet is no different in principle from how a computer might be explicitly programmed to make an NPC jump up on a virtual parapet. In the language of the computer's program there are linguistic expressions, symbols, or lines of code standing for the NPC and parapet, which the program utilizes under appropriate circumstances to make logical inferences that deliver the judgment that the NPC in fact should leap upon the parapet.

For CRUM to succeed, computing machines must be programmable to model the flexible adaptive behavior characteristic of human intelligence in a compelling way. Otherwise, CRUM looks at best like a description of how some machines accomplish tasks related to human intelligence, rather than as a plausible theory of human intelligence itself. Unfortunately though, attempts to vindicate CRUM have almost always faced what is often called the Computational Paradox. This is just the fact that while digital computers can do with panache many things that are extremely difficult for humans (e.g., adding humungous sums), many tasks that are extraordinarily easy for humans (e.g., running away when someone has jumped up on a parapet and begun to shoot arrows) have been nearly impossible to get machines to do.

6.2 How We Got to CRUM, Part One: Philosophical Background

The idea that intelligence involves the computational processing of linguistic information has been widely held since the first half of the twentieth century. It originated in an influential essay by the visionary mathematical logician Alan Turing (whom we already know from the previous chapter's Turing machines). Turing was the first contemporary thinker to propose a decisive behavioral test to determine whether or not any computing machine was a genuine embodiment of human-like intelligence. In order to pass the famous "Turing Test,"[8] a machine has to trick a real human being through conversation alone into thinking that she is really interacting with another person. According to Turing, this "imitation game" is a suitable criterion for AI because "[t]he question and answer method seems to be suitable for introducing almost any one of the fields of human endeavor that we wish to include. We do not wish to penalize the machine for its inability to shine in beauty competitions, nor to penalize a man for losing in a race against an airplane. The conditions of our game make these disabilities irrelevant."[9]

Turing's assumption that all forms of human endeavor involving the use of intelligence can be tested for via *conversation* should be highly controversial. To get a sense of why this idea has nonetheless seemed so natural to many researchers in AI, we will have to look at a number of different philosophical theses that came to seem commonsensical in the previous century.

Once again, Bertrand Russell's ideas provide a helpful fulcrum for our task. In Chapter One, we explicated Russell's *Problems of Philosophy* era theory of perception. Here we examine his linguaform theory of cognition from the same period. The two are intimately related. As we will show, Russell's conceptions of the nature of meaning and belief arise from his explanation of how we could have beliefs about the external world in spite of the fact that we only ever directly perceive the data provided by our senses.

6.2.1 Our Russellian Heritage, Part Three: A Linguaform Account of Belief and Meaning

For a system of mental phenomena to be linguaform, it must be at least in principle translatable into a natural language such as English, and also have a combinatorial syntax and a compositional, representational semantics. A "representational semantics" is a system in which certain expressions stand for other objects, in the sense that "The White House" and "The current U.S. President's home" stand for the same object. Combinatorial syntax determines the manner in which such entities can be combined into grammatical units. For example, "George W. Bush is a mammal," is a grammatical string of words in English, while "is mammal George W. Bush a" is not. "Compositional semantics" refers to the manner in which stringing together (and for example in the case of pluralization, changing) such units creates new meanings from previous ones. With "George W. Bush is a mammal," the meanings of the two representational units "George W. Bush" and "mammal" are connected with the non-representational (or "syncategorematic") units "is" and "a" to express a complex thought.

It should not be controversial to claim that natural languages such as English and artificial languages such as first-order symbolic logic are lingua-form in this sense. But it should be controversial to claim that the human mind's paradigmatic tasks (perception, belief, reason, and action) can be explained in terms of computational operations performed upon entities that are linguaform in this sense. Russell's early philosophical account of our knowledge of the external world made such an explanation much more plausible with regard to perception and belief. Understanding Russell's conception is a matter of fully grasping the implications of one curious claim: "Every proposition which we can understand must be composed wholly of constituents with which we are acquainted" (*Problems* 32).

For Russell, "knowledge by acquaintance" is a certain kind of relation "with anything of which we are directly aware, without the intermediary of any process of inference or any knowledge of truths" (*Problems* 25). Knowledge by acquaintance is first-hand experience of something. Being a phenomenalist (see Chapter One), Russell ultimately concludes that we don't really know Bill by acquaintance, even if we have met him personally; rather, we know by acquaintance *the sense data caused by Bill* (e.g., the brownness of his hair, the tone of his voice, the suffocating stench of his cologne).

By way of contrast, we have "knowledge by description" of an object when we know that certain sentences, those that serve to distinguish that object from other objects, are true. For Russell, physical objects (as opposed to the sense data they cause) and other people's minds are not known by acquaintance, but rather by description. "We shall say that an object is 'known by description' when we know that it is 'the so-and-so', i.e., when we know that there is one object, and no more, having a certain property; and ... we do not have knowledge of the same object by acquaintance" (*Problems* 29). For example, I know Mary by description if I know that she is the best *Guitar Hero* player on the block. I can know this without having met her, or in other words, without being acquainted with the relevant sense data caused by her.

All of this so far is pretty unproblematic. But then Russell makes the surprising suggestion that names like "Moses" are really disguised descriptions, so that my thought that "Moses existed," is really a thought of the form "The so-and-so existed." Perhaps it is something like, "The person who received the Ten Commandments, led his people out of bondage, and parted the Red Sea existed."[10] For Russell, the English word "Moses" is translated into a much longer phrase in the language of *propositions*.

Russell provides a complex and rather arcane description (and one that he modified at various points throughout his long career) of what sorts of entities propositions are supposed to be.[11] In order to show how CRUM is neo-Russellian, we will simply assume that a proposition is a sentence in the "language of thought."[12] Such sentences are supposed to exist (in some sense) in our brains. According to this view, when we speak or think, we subconsciously translate a sentence from the language of thought into a natural language (such as English).

If this *language of thought* is the same for all people, no matter what language they speak, then sentences of different languages that have the same meaning (such as "Snow is white" in English and "Schnee ist weiss" in German) both correspond to the same sentence in the language of thought. The hypothesis that there is a language of thought is supposed to explain such data as: (a) how children are able to learn to speak and understand natural languages so quickly with (supposedly) so little help or teaching, (b) how deaf people who learn a first language such as American Sign Language late in life were able to get about in the world before having a natural language, and (c) why the world's languages are (again, supposedly) so similar to one another.[13]

If we read him in the way just described, then Russell's statement that "Every proposition which we can understand must be composed wholly of constituents with which we are acquainted" might be understood as, "Every sentence in the language of thought must be such that the referring words in that sentence refer only to things with which we are acquainted." Since our ability to understand a language is supposed to require translating natural language sentences into sentences of the language of thought (and since Russell's views committed him to a parallel position concerning natural language and a language of propositions), Russell's claim implies what we will call the Translation Thesis: every sentence is translatable into a sentence whose referring words denote only things with which we are acquainted.

On Russell's view, some words name objects and properties with which we are acquainted and some do not. For example, words that name color sensations are words that name things with which we are acquainted. Words that name physical objects such as "table" name things with which we are not acquainted. Russell then asks how we can have knowledge that sentences involving the word "table" are true, when we do not have any non-inferential, direct knowledge of (physical) tables. Remember (from Chapter One) that Russell believed we infer the presence of the table from our sensations of sense data. So the words that name the sense data that allow us to infer that a given table exists can themselves be used to replace the word "table" in our sentences.

At this point, it starts to become a little clearer how the Russellian view of language suggests a model for AI and robotics. A sense data language must at the very least have ways to refer to every place in our visual field, the different colors we can see at those places, and the different sensations of taste, touch, hearing, and smell as well as relations between those sensations (i.e., "this tastes sweeter than that"). The phrase that translates the word "table" would have to be quite complicated to be at all plausible. Now imagine that you are trying to devise a machine that can recognize tables as tables. Suppose you had two detector grids that were functionally analogous to human eyes. At each grid location is a set of input devices measuring properties of light hitting that location. These measurements would be translated into numbers, so that for each location on the grid there would be an ordered set of numbers feeding into the central processor. Then, just as the Russellian mind must compare its sense data with an extraordinarily long sense data language translation of "There's a table," our robot could compare its input numbers with a sentence of code that allows it to respond "yes" when queried if it is seeing a table, when there is a table in normal lighting conditions in front of its detection grids. In this sense it is clear that Bertrand Russell (who was one of the inventors of modern formal logic, and hence ultimately the digital computer) did articulate a program for artificial intelligence.

6.2.2 The Language of Thought and Benign Homuncularism

The initiation of bodily action is one of the mind's paradigmatic tasks. In fact, perception and action are intimately related. For example, when you manipulate your fingers to tie your shoes you constantly perceive where your fingers are and how the laces feel, and this perception must be utilized in completing the task. But once this perception is explained in terms of sentences in a language of thought, it is hard to see how the mind could command the body to action without doing something like issuing inner verbal commands. Every command the mind makes to the body would have to use sentences describing the body's perceptual states (e.g., what it feels like to hold the shoelace between thumb and forefinger).

Jerry Fodor is the cognitive scientist who has most explicitly thematized such a neo-Russellian account of human action. In the following illustrative passage, Fodor describes how he thinks an individual mind accomplishes the prosaic task of tying its body's shoes.

> This is the way we tie our shoes. There is a little man who lives in one's head. The little man keeps a library. When one acts upon the intention to tie one's shoes, the little man fetches down a volume entitled *Tying One's Shoes*. The volume says such things as: "Take the left free end of the shoelace in the left hand. Cross the left end of the shoelace over the right free end of the shoelace ..." etc.... When the little man reads "Take the left free end of the shoelace in the left hand," we imagine him ringing up the shop foreman in charge of grasping shoelaces. The shop

foreman goes about supervising that activity in a way that is, in essence, a microcosm of tying one's shoe. Indeed, the shop foreman might be imagined to superintend a detail of wage slaves, whose functions include: searching representations of visual inputs for traces of shoelace, dispatching orders to flex and contract fingers on the left hand, etc.[14]

This explanation of shoe-tying perfectly captures two of the main features of Fodor's influential philosophy of mind: (1) his belief that all mental tasks are carried out in a linguaform manner, and (2) his hope that homuncularism can be benign if each set of homunculi is progressively dumber, bottoming out in those that perform tasks that even the simplest machine could handle.

Fodor's brand of "benign homuncularism" can best be understood by comparing his model of action with the homunculus fallacy discussed in Section 2.2.2.2. The homunculus fallacy occurs when a mental task is explained by positing in effect the existence of another "miniature person" inside the agent performing yet another mental task in need of the same explanation. The paradigm case of such pseudo-explanation is explaining vision by appeal to an "eye of the mind" that somehow views sense data inside of us. To the extent that the actual sensing of external objects is in need of explanation, the eye of the mind's supposed internal scrutiny of sense data requires even more.

Of course, the eye of the mind idea would not be a fallacy if there were an independent explanation of what the eye of the mind actually is that did not itself involve an appeal to the phenomenon of vision. Fodorean homuncularism is benign because the chain of explanation is supposed to be finite, and the final homunculi—the "wage slaves" of his shoe-tying example—are doing something purely mechanical.

An extended analogy with the way that video games are designed will prove helpful here. For the methods that contemporary game designers use to develop the extraordinarily complicated behaviors of game programs turn out to bear a strong structural similarity to the workings of the human mind as Fodor describes it.

6.2.3 The Fodorean Mind Considered as a Design Team

At the lowest level, a personal computer or a gaming console such as the Xbox is purely mechanical, and just consists in registers having certain numerical values in them (i.e., electrical charges in places in the central processing unit). Programs that work at this level (written in machine language or machine code) simply tell the machine whether to add or remove numerical values in a given register.[15] It would be impossible to program very much in such a code, though, so often there is an intervening layer of assembly language. Most current assembly languages express machine code sentences in an easier-to-grasp way,[16] and (more importantly) they also allow macros, which express complicated machine language procedures in terms of very simple commands. Higher level programming languages such as C++ and Visual Basic are machine-independent, i.e., so abstracted from machine code that the same programs work on different types of computers. Just as the assembler translates all of the macros down to a language of dumb machine level commands concerning numbers in registers, higher level programs and applications have compilers, which translate these languages into an assembly language or the machine codes of specific machines.

Applications such as the 3D modeling tool *Maya*,[17] used by game designers and digital animators, are even one more level removed. People can be trained to use these programs via graphical interfaces without being proficient in programming languages. And at the very highest level, one finds design tools like the "level editors" that are packaged with some modern games (e.g., *The Elder Scrolls Construction Set* for the *Elder Scrolls* games, or the *Siege Editor* for *Dungeon Siege*), which allow players to design their own maps and levels for commercially produced RPGs.

The artistic success of latter-day computer RPGs, with their enormously rich and detailed worlds and highly non-linear gameplay, is largely attributable to this diversity of functions in the design process. On most design teams for complex, commercial games there will be programmers, writers, and conceptual artists who specialize in working at different levels in this hierarchy, from line-by-line coders all the way up to 3D illustrators and animators. A person who is great at the kind of creative statistical tinkering at which paper RPG-ers often excel can design a game's combat system line by line in C++, while a writer who is relatively new at coding can put together long passages of interactive dialogue through the use of a small set of macros or a flowcharting interface like the one provided by the programming tool *AllClear*.[18] And a studio art or graphic design major who has never written a line of code in his life can design the shrubbery and the monsters that populate the gameworld in a program like *Maya* almost as easily as he could with a set of pastels or a paintbrush.

Fodor's insight with respect to benign homuncularism is that the language of thought could work just like a hierarchically organized game design team. At a very high level, the mind commands the body to do various things, such as tying one's shoes. At a slightly lower level this compiles into commands to bring into being certain organizations of bodily parts that correspond to certain perceptual states. At the lowest level it assembles down into just telling certain neurons to fire in certain ways. The top level corresponds to a high level programming language while the bottom level corresponds to the machine code for our body. The homuncular fallacy is avoided, because at bottom, our bodies' actions are controlled by a thoroughly unintelligent nervous system. If this all works, then CRUM accounts not just for perception and belief, but also for action, and (assuming there exists a computationally tractable model of inference to tie it all together) we begin to see how CRUM might give us a plausible model of real-world intelligence.

6.3 Our Chomskyan Heritage: The CRUM Synthesis

At this point, a brief digression becomes necessary. Before we spend any more time exploring the particular constellation of ideas about perception, belief, desire, and action known as CRUM, it is worth examining in a little more detail a problem associated with what we referred to earlier as the Computational Paradox. Given that computers are so much better than humans at certain tasks, why should we think that human thought is computational?

An interesting answer to this question—one that is highly suggestive within the context of thinking about the possibility of AI—is provided in the writings of the enormously influential American linguist Noam Chomsky.

6.3.1 *Generativity*

Here's a strange fact: a significant percentage of sentences you hear in your lifetime have never been uttered before and will never be uttered ever again.[19] So how do you understand them? It can't be the case that we associate some primitive fund of personal experiences with each individual sentence in a correlation that somehow gives the meanings of those sentences. If this were the case, you wouldn't be able to understand a new sentence that you've never heard before out of the blue. But this is something that even very primitive speakers of human languages clearly can do.

The solution to this puzzle involves noting that, while there is a potential infinity of sentences, there are only finitely many words. However, the meaning of a sentence is not just a function of the words in the sentence. Among other things, the order of those words matters. "I killed the Troll with my compound bow," means something, while "bow Troll I with the compound killed my" does not.

In his early writings, Chomsky suggested that the only reason people can recognize the first sentence above as grammatical and the second string of words as ungrammatical is because they have tacit, in-born knowledge[20] of a finite set of rules concerning the proper way words and phrases are put together. According to Chomsky, it is the job of the linguist to explicitly state these rules.

Chomsky argued that linguistic theory must be generative, meaning that it should show how a lexicon and finitely stateable set of rules can generate all of the sentences of a language. In his early work, Chomsky used the term "generative" in a manner that entailed that all generative processes could be modeled by a digital computer.[21]

6.3.2 Competence

Here is where the Computational Paradox raises its ugly head. If Chomsky is correct that all language users have tacit knowledge of a computationally tractable linguistic theory, then the parts of our brain governing syntax are computational. But as a matter of fact we are all much worse than digital computers in doing precisely the kind of thing that Chomsky says we all do as a matter of course. We speak and write ungrammatically all the time, and regularly mischaracterize the grammatical properties of other people's speech and writing.

Our tendency to make various errors using language is especially striking when one compares adults' linguistic behavior to that of the natural-language "parsers" that were built into some of the classic text adventure games of the mid-1980s, such as *Zork*, *A Hitchhiker's Guide to the Galaxy*, and *A Mind Forever Voyaging*. Instead of clicking a mouse or mashing buttons on a controller, the player of these games had to type instructions out in full sentences on a computer keyboard (e.g., "Kill the troll," "Throw the amulet into the well," "Flee from the Eldrich Horror!") to move his avatar from room to room, solve puzzles, and escape from enemies. The programmers who designed these wonderfully literary and imaginative games tried to make their programs as receptive as possible to player inputs, but the limitations of natural language programming at the time were such that even the most experienced text-adventure gamer was bound to be told at least a fair amount of the time "Your input does not make sense," or "Try to put it in a different way" when the game could not make sense of his (often perfectly grammatical) sentences. Modern descendants of these rudimentary natural language parsers[22] suffer from similar problems (not to slight the mammoth intellectual achievement represented by *Microsoft Word*'s recent grammar checkers). Yet there is a certain sense in which they are also much better at "understanding" human languages than we are ourselves, for they can decipher much longer sentences than any biological humans can. And when the player does make a grammatical mistake while inputting commands, these game programs catch it every single time. So if we humans really do have a complete understanding of the possible rules of grammar for any natural language built into us from birth, how did these games ever get so much smarter than us?

Chomsky tries to dodge this embarrassing question by invoking what he calls the performance/competence distinction. As we noted above, according to Chomsky, a speaker's tacit, subconscious knowledge of grammar facilitates her use of language. It is a basic methodological principle of this approach to hold that the grammar tacitly known does not in any straightforward way *determine* the language that is spoken and understood by speakers of the language. Rather, the grammar can at best be understood to describe the verbal behavior of an *ideally competent* speaker, someone with no cognitive shortcomings whatsoever. For example, the ideally competent speaker is understood as being able distinguish between strings of words of arbitrary length that are grammatical sentences and those that are mere nonsense. The ideally competent speaker was also represented by Chomsky as being immune to mistakes due to "noise" such as low blood sugar, inattentiveness, or a faulty primary education. Of course no actual human speaker is ideally competent in this way. However, the behavior of the ideally competent speaker is supposed to be perfectly described by the competence theory that is (supposedly) known by all existing speakers of the language.

If this makes sense, then Chomsky has a well-motivated response to the first part of the Computational Paradox. The reason why even a very crude digital grammar parser can recognize the grammaticality of extra-ordinary long sentences and human beings cannot is merely due to "performance limitations" forced upon human beings by the smallness and slowness of our all-too-human brains.

6.4 Against CRUM

Chomsky's performance/competence distinction goes a long way toward protecting CRUM from the objection that computers do lots of things much better than human brains. But it doesn't affect the other part of the Computational Paradox. The kind of flexible adaptive behavior character-istic of human cognition has not been replicated by computers with very much success. Remember that, according to CRUM, any instance of flexible adaptive behavior is really an instance of (mostly) subconscious linguaform reasoning. So CRUM stands or falls with the success or failure of using linguaform academic AIs to perform the sorts of tasks that video gamers look for in game AIs, like creating worthy NPC adversaries. In Chapter One we spent some time presenting an alternative view to Russell's theory of perception. Here we will focus on canonical problems for the other three *explananda* of CRUM: belief, action, and inference.

6.4.1 *The Underdetermination of Content*

Michael Wheeler raises an interesting point in his discussion of the way in which CRUM treats our thoughts as "representations" of the outside world. "One core philosophical question that accompanies any form of represen-tationalism is this: how does one decide that a particular representational state bears one content rather than another" (*Reconstructing* 59)?

The problem exists in two stages. The first concerns attributing specific beliefs with determinate content to people when there may not be enough evidence to tell conclusively what that person really believes. But when one thinks carefully about some of the everyday difficulties associated with this task, a deeper philosophical problem arises. Perhaps there is often simply *no fact of the matter* about which determinate beliefs people have. That is, at the deepest level, human beliefs might just not have the kind of determinate content that would always guarantee attribution. But (as we will argue) if they do not, then the hope of getting a character in a video game to carry out a convincing conversation with us by devising a method of explicitly translating natural language sentences into a computer analog of the language of thought is hopelessly naïve.

6.4.1.1 *Fixing Content: The Psychological Problem*

The psychological states that we classify as beliefs paradigmatically accomplish two things. First, they help us to build up a personal representation of the way the world is. And second, they determine (along with desires) the actions that we take. In trying to determine what people believe, we listen to what they assert and watch what they do. If they are being sincere, what they assert is a good guide to how they perceive the world. And (if we understand their desires), so is how they behave.

Unfortunately, it is often the case that what people assert and what they do come disastrously apart in quite radical ways. We all know people who claim that one of the most important facets of having a good life is understanding the Bible, but who have nonetheless never read it, even in a translated language, not to mention never having undertaken the rational course of learning the original languages and embarking on a historical study of the Bible's composition. It is tempting to say about such people that even though they really do think that they believe that understanding the Bible is the most important of life's goods, in fact they don't believe any such thing.

Often the case is not so clear. In the course of our evolving relationships with people, our actions and self-professed beliefs are sometimes slightly at odds. Anyone who has been blessed with the opportunity to make a transition from great friendship to deep and lasting love realizes that there is a penumbral area in between where it is just not clear whether the lovers believe they are "just friends" or something else. Darker examples involving the family are the stock in trade of Freudian psychoanalysts. The child claims to love his father, but while individuating himself as an adolescent he finds himself angry, resentful, and behaving in a non-loving manner. The Freudian response to these phenomena is to posit determinate subconscious beliefs to explain the child's behavior. For the Freudian, no matter how much you protest, in some sense you really believe that your father wants to castrate you, and you experience deep fear as a result.

Such attributions rest on the fallacious view that the facts about what a human being believes must always be determinate. To the Freudian who obnoxiously insists that the woman in your dream must represent your mother, you should always reply that there is no reason to think that she represents anyone in particular. Likewise, the behavior of an adolescent may simply be a function of the general irritation that accompanies hormonal shifts and the physical discomfort caused by a rapidly changing body. There is no reason whatsoever to think that a malicious, mother-obsessed miniature agent buried in the subconscious directs all of a person's actions from its determinate fund of beliefs and desires.[23]

The fact that what we believe is often radically indeterminate is a serious problem for CRUM. If perception, belief, and action are all explainable in terms of inferential processes on linguaform entities residing in the brain, there will be a strong temptation to think (as some latter-day Freudians have)[24] that the linguaform entities responsible for action and belief can be identified with a determinate set of beliefs as expressed in natural language. Given the manifest implausibility of this hypothesis, the defender of CRUM must tell a different story about how a determinate set of sentences in the language of thought could give rise to such broad diversity and unpredictability in the personal behavior (both verbal and otherwise) of competent language users.

Or perhaps, *pace* CRUM, the internal states that cause our sincere assertions and actions are radically non-linguaform. That is, perhaps it is false to explain human beliefs in terms of a set of sentences somehow encoded in people's brains. More radically, perhaps the category of "belief" is analogous to concepts from folk-physics such as the kind of "impetus" that Aristotle explained. The vast majority of people polled, including undergraduate physics majors, falsely predict that objects move according to Aristotelian principles. For example, if an object is tied to a string and spun around, and the string is cut, the object will travel a straight line along the tangent of where it was on the circle of spinning. Nearly everyone wrongly predicts that the object will instead spin around in widening circles because of the "impetus" granted to it by the spinning.[25] Given the way our minds work and our place in the ecosystem, it is perhaps inevitable that we predict and explain the world in terms of such categories, but that does not mean they reflect the true nature of the universe. Likewise, the fact that it is very natural for us to understand people as acting out of a determinate fund of linguaform beliefs does not mean that they actually do.

From an evolutionary perspective, this makes sense. Darwinian natural selection presumably selects for people who assert things that help them survive in their ecological niche, not for people who assert the whole truth and nothing but the truth. If the very notion of determinate belief were like "impetus" in this regard, then one would expect to see plenty of the sorts of psychological ambiguities and indeterminacies that we have described in this section.

In what follows, we will not argue that people simply do not have beliefs, or that we should stop attributing beliefs to people. Rather, we will argue that determinate human beliefs do not play quite the broad explanatory role that it is very natural for us to think they do. If this is the case, then the CRUM hope of understanding action as a result of a subconsciously presupposed determinate set of sentences in the language of thought is absolutely chimerical.

6.4.1.2 *Fixing Content: The Semantic Problem*

In a classic paper from 1982,[26] the contemporary American philosopher Mark Wilson discusses a scenario that would not be too out of place in some time-travel based RPG such as *Chrono Trigger* or *Dragon Warrior*. He describes the inhabitants of an obscure island, who happen to be the descendents of shipwrecked Druids. These isolated, latter-day Druids (having never beheld anything like an airplane before) are surprised when a crew of American flyboys crash land onto the island. Wilson notes that in such a circumstance, nothing in the Druids' earlier usage of the words "house" or "bird" prohibits them from calling the plane either "metal bird" or "flying house," while at the same time maintaining that birds and houses are incompatible categories of things. In the future, airplanes might come to be viewed as paradigm instances of either houses or birds for the Druids' descendents.

In a case such as this the linguist's task of discerning a complete, determinate set of truths about the meanings of "house" and "bird" in the Druidese language starts to look hopeless. Years later, the flying-house dialect Druid descendents might claim that a central component of the meaning of "bird" is that birds are not made of metal. The metal-bird dialect descendents would disagree with this. Yet both might also (quite reasonably) claim that the meaning of "bird" did not change in their respective dialects.

The strangeness of Wilson's example is no guide to the ubiquity of the phenomena he discusses. The study of lexical semantics[27] by linguists has amply verified Wilson's contentions. The semantics of even very common, widely-used referring expressions such as "man" and "walks" has proven to be more complex than anybody would have predicted.[28] Perhaps the main problem is that while speakers of the same language agree on the inferential roles of the *compositional* expressions in a language (e.g., the quantifiers "every," "some," "more than," "six," or "the," modals such as "can" and "must," productive morphological changes such as pluralization, and cross-dependent phenomena such as conditionals and anaphora) they often have vastly different conceptions of the meanings of *referential* parts of speech— i.e., the parts of speech (in English most nouns, adjectives, verbs, and adverbs) that in some sense refer directly to different aspects of the world.

Such implicit disagreements are rarely an impediment to communication. Consider the authors of this book. We find it both enjoyable and productive to argue with one another about our favorite games; one of us is a devoted RPGer while the other is addicted to the old adventure games of the mid 1990s. The RPGer is always talking about strategies for "leveling up" and finding "Easter eggs." The adventure gamer has only the very haziest idea of what these terms mean, but can discourse at great length about the relative merits of "Myst-clones" and the horrors of "pixel-hunting." The RPGer has next to no idea what those terms mean. So there is a sense in which each of us means something different by the very word "gaming," yet we continue to discuss and argue about our favorite hobby. But if this word meant utterly different things when each of us used it, then such conversations would not be possible, because we would not understand each other at all.

One wants to respond that communication works only because there is enough overlap of meaning, when meaning itself is still to be construed in linguaform terms. Perhaps the word "gaming" has a core or "focal" meaning (expressible in something like a dictionary definition), and people with different areas of expertise can communicate successfully in virtue of understanding this core concept. If this were at all plausible for words in general, then there would be no deep problem of underdetermination facing CRUM. A set of sentences about the focal meanings of each word would be encoded in the language of thought within the mind of anyone competent at using the language.

But from Wilson's discussion (and, as we will show, from reflection on contemporary lexicography) it follows that almost all words that represent facets of our shared world are like those used by the Druid descendents. There are objects that are capable of being considered *either* as paradigm instances of that to which the word applies or as paradigm instances of that to which the word does *not* apply. Prior to their interaction with the flyboys, the airplane could have become either a paradigm instance of a bird, or a paradigm instance of a non-bird for the Druids.

It is not too difficult to find further real-life examples that support Wilson's hypothesis. Consider online RPGs like *World of Warcraft*. Most of us are quite comfortable thinking of these applications as "games." But when their historical predecessors, text-based "Multi-User Dungeons" first came online, people were unsure how to classify them. At the time, it seemed rather odd to think of mere online chat and exploration as a form of gaming, even if a person was doing it through the persona of a dwarf or a wizard. The writings of the early twentieth-century philosopher Ludwig Wittgenstein contain a fascinating, lengthy discussion of why these sorts of innovations make it impossible to come up with a durable definition of the word "game" itself.[29]

Or, to take an even more philosophically puzzling example, consider what one might take to be a paradigm example of a term that can be clearly defined: "number." From the time that the ancient Pythagoreans allegedly drowned the person who discovered that the square root of two is not expressible as a fraction, people who have tried to introduce new kinds of numbers have had a hard time of it. The names of proposed new classes of numbers are themselves very telling: "negative," "irrational," "imaginary," "non-standard," and "surreal." Today "imaginary" numbers like the square root of negative one are considered genuine instances of different kinds of "number," but this has only quite recently been the case. Students of the history of "number" realize that nothing in the meaning of the word uniquely determines whether or not the elements of new kinds of abstract mathematical structures get counted as numbers. No such appeal will explain why (to his evident and justifiable dismay) Hamilton's quaternions[30] never received their own epithet as a kind of weird number, while complex numbers did.

Wilson's point has a fascinating consequence. If word meaning is under-determined, then it has the property of being inextricable from broader theory. That is, if either of an inconsistent pair of properties can without error come to be seen as central to a predicate's meaning, then one cannot at a given time fully specify the meaning of that predicate in terms of definitions.

These observations about the nature of word meaning are not new. Over 200 years ago Samuel Johnson recorded them eloquently in the *Preface* to his dictionary:

> Kindred senses may be so interwoven that the perplexity cannot be disentangled, nor any reason be assigned why one should be ranged before the other. . . . The shades of meaning sometimes pass impercept-ibly into each other, so that though on one side they apparently differ, yet it is impossible to mark the point of contact. Ideas of the same race, though not exactly alike, are sometimes so little different, that no words can express the dissimilitude, though the mind easily perceives it, when they are exhibited together; and sometimes there is such a confusion of acceptations, that discernment is wearied, and distinction puzzled, and perseverance herself hurries to an end, by crowding together what she cannot separate.[31]

Attempts by contemporary lexicographers to build knowledge bases from machine readable dictionaries have led to a robust verification of Johnson and Wilson's claims.[32]

If all of this is correct, then the neo-Russellian Translation Thesis that we described near the beginning of this chapter is hopeless. According to this thesis, every sentence of a human language is translatable into a sentence whose words refer only to things with which we are acquainted. If referring words do not have a determinate set of analytically true sentences individu-ating their meanings, then the beliefs we attribute to one another in natural language simply cannot be translated into sentences in a CRUM-style language of thought.

The Russellian picture is profoundly misleading. When two people talk about something, they do not agree about meanings because they share the same meaning-giving sentences in the language of thought. Rather, their agreement is based on two things: (1) identical grasp of the compositional aspects of meaning and the inferential role of non-referring expressions (aspects revealed by compositional semantics done in the tradition of

Richard Montague), and (2) agreement "not to disagree" about the meanings of referring expressions. Because of the normative constraint articulated in (2), people may without error take themselves to be talking about the same kind of thing when they talk about (e.g.) games, even though nothing in their heads or in the heads of expert game designers or in the outer world uniquely fixes "the meanings" of the relevant terms.[33] As long as people find disagreements that are actually worth arguing about, they take themselves to agree on the meanings of the terms in which the argument is carried out, while disagreeing about some aspect of the way the world is. It is only when they decide that no discovery (through empirical means or reasoned argumentation) could even be relevant to the disagreement that their disputes become "merely semantic."

So how might AI researchers ever get machines to communicate through language in such a way that it would be rational to attribute the kinds of beliefs characteristic of biological humans to those devices themselves? It should by now be clear that, in order to do so, they must model the pragmatic aspects of conversation that allow biological humans to converse and argue coherently given the underdetermination of meaning, and then build machines that can be subject to such a normative pragmatics of language use. Unfortunately, it is much easier to take the Russellian approach, modeling conversational ability in terms of an internalized set of sentences and associated inferences. The reason for this is simply that most of the art of computer programming itself concerns linguistically representing explicit inferences and orders in a formal programming language.

This having been said, some very high level design work, such as creating a forest or a system of caves in the graphic design application *Maya*, involves manipulating a graphical user interface rather than coding linguistic commands. While people don't usually refer to using such a graphical interface as "programming," there is a sense in which it is, since the results (when compiled down to machine code) are an integral part of the resulting game program. Perhaps the pragmatics of conversation can be captured in some way analogous to the non-linguistic "programming" carried out by the artists on a video game's design team. At present it is not at all clear how this could be done.[34] But, at any rate, what should be clear is that the beliefs we express in natural language do *not* hold as a function of a corresponding language of thought sentences in our brains.[35]

6.4.2 The Framelessness of Action

We biological humans have yet to recover from the blow to our collective vanity engendered on May 11, 1996, when the computer program Deeper Blue defeated world chess champion Gary Kasparov in a six-game tournament. Our champion was defeated by the machine at a game taken by its players to require precisely the combination of creativity and analytical skill that is constitutive of human intelligence at its best.

But things were really not that simple. The tournament rules allowed Deeper Blue to be reprogrammed every night by a team of its human helpers, a team that included chess experts analyzing Kasparov's play from the previous day. On its own, Deeper Blue did not possess enough flexible adaptive richness to defeat the human champion.[36]

Hubert Dreyfus was the first major philosopher to call attention to the overwhelming difficulty of getting computers to mimic the human ability to assess a situation quickly and determine the relevant course of action out of large sets of alternatives.[37] This difficulty in AI research is now known as the Frame Problem, and it is generally conceded to be the biggest obstacle confronting real world artificial intelligence.

In his classic paper on the Frame Problem[38] Daniel Dennett asks his reader to imagine a robot placed in a room and programmed with the following information: his power source is on a nearby cart, and there is a ticking time bomb somewhere in the room. Suppose that the robot is also equipped with some programming analog to the human desire for self-preservation. What will the robot do? Almost certainly try to wheel the cart out of the room before the bomb goes off. Could the robot be expected to succeed at preserving itself in this sort of scenario? Quite possibly it could, Dennett points out, barring mechanical failure, and supposing that the bomb *is not located inside the cart*!

Now consider what would happen if a human being were to be placed in the same scenario (with the power source replaced by something similar— some food or medicine, say) and provided with the same information as the robot. Any sensible person who did not want to get blown up would of course check to make sure that the bomb was not in the cart before she fled the room with it. This example does not of course show that all human beings are better problem-solvers than all robots. One could, after all, program the robot to go through the extra step of looking on the cart for the bomb, and checking for other contingencies also (e.g., the presence of a trip-wire in the room's doorway, the presence of dangerous puddles between itself and the outer hall). Perhaps it is possible to provide the robot with a large enough "expert system" to determine what to do in such situations. The robot would then need to search through *all* of its internal representations of possible situations and plans of action. But the search space would be so outrageously large that it would become likely that the robot would still be running through its options when the bomb exploded!

Dennett's thought experiment is supposed to draw one's attention to the wonderful capacity that human beings have of ignoring irrelevant possibilities (e.g., "Perhaps there's an evil, invisible goblin in this room who'll throw the bomb after me as I leave") and attending to the features of our environments that are most salient to the actions we wish to perform (e.g., "The bomb is on the cart!"). Perhaps one could program the robot with heuristics such that only relevant parts of the search space are ever exploited, and for many involved in classical AI research, the term "the

Frame Problem" refers to such heuristics programming. Unfortunately, nobody is even close to the kind of success that would allow an artificial intelligence to survive even in simple real world situations like those of Dennett's thought experiment. Savvy players of games that rely heavily upon NPCs learn to put these virtual characters in situations analogous to that of Dennett's poor, doomed robot. This is exactly what is going on in *Oblivion* when the player maneuvers her avatar up onto the parapet to kill the gladiators, who then keep on mindlessly attacking the stones beneath her.

The ability of humans to use language effectively in spite of the sorts of semantic indeterminacies described in the previous section is itself a paradigm instance of our flexible adaptive richness. We constantly learn new things that shake up our previous conceptions of the world. Just as we can tell effortlessly which objects and actions in a given context are relevant, we are usually able to discern which facets of word meaning are relevant in discerning how to go on when faced with new information. We are usually able to learn to communicate with one another even when we have quite different conceptions of the world, and when we express these conceptions in radically different ways. Computers are very bad at this.[39]

We ourselves are not absolutely reliable at this. For example, the belief that somebody is abusive and loving at the same time is inconsistent with most people's core beliefs about love. If one merely wanted consistency one could continue to believe that an abusive person is loving by changing one's ancillary beliefs about the nature of love.[40] The resulting set of beliefs would still be consistent, albeit harmful. In some respects, then, biological humans do share more in common with Dennett's robot than we would like to think.[41] Nonetheless, humans are often very skilled at maintaining relevant consistency in a way that helps us further our goals. And until this ability is better captured by computers, game-based artificial intelligence will always suffer from the cognitive uncanny valley effect. Reflection on the Frame Problem should therefore increase one's suspicion that the basis for many of our most distinctive abilities may not be inferential/linguaform in the manner posted by CRUM.

According to CRUM, my ability to use a hammer is based on the ability of a series of homunculi to make inferences about the hammer's physical properties and environmental surroundings, and deliver linguaform commands. So human action is grounded in inferences involving linguaform concepts expressible in the language of thought. But common sense says that the reverse is true. My grasp of the concept of "hammer" is partly constituted by the *ability* to hammer. If I can describe everything that can be described about the physical construction of a hammer, and can also describe with complete perspicuity how somebody else might use it to knock nails into a piece of wood, there is nonetheless something absolutely crucial missing from my understanding of the type of object it is if I'm simply unable to get it to work.

We have already discussed (in Chapter Two) the radical Heideggerian conclusion that the reason we can directly perceive the world is because objects in the world exist "for" us as things that can be manipulated with a specific purpose. If this Heideggerian inversion is correct, then purposive action must be understood prior to understanding linguaform belief, because the contents of linguaform beliefs are in large part a function of such purposive actions (and at a basic level not vice versa).

Moreover, if I lacked practical abilities with all of the key terms in my description of the hammer, I couldn't be said to understand the word "hammer" at all. Say I had never held an object in my hand, and had never done anything analogous to putting nails into wood, had never handled wood or metal, etc. In this case, the descriptions would be empty. If the neo-Russellian Translation Thesis says that every sentence is translatable into a sentence whose referring words denote only things with which we are acquainted, these reflections suggest a more holistic version of Russell's thesis, formulated in terms of practical abilities. That is, every sentence we understand must be such that the referring words can at least be described in terms of practical skills we actually possess. Of course the sort of "understanding" at issue here comes in degrees, but nonetheless at root it is based on interaction with the world.

These conclusions are discussed at far greater length, and applied to recent research in so-called "real-world robotics," in Michael Wheeler's excellent book *Reconstructing the Cognitive World*. Doing justice to the rich and provocative work of Wheeler and others in this tradition would take us too far afield here.[42] Note, however, that if they are right, then it might be the case that developing convincing artificial intelligence for video games will require computers that can move themselves and accomplish tasks in the real world. If human conceptual mastery (characterized by flexible adaptive richness at both the cognitive and behavioral levels) is in part a function of Heideggerian real-world problem solving, then perhaps the same will be true of future robots. Unfortunately, such a machine would probably have better things to do than play *Oblivion* with us, but we can always dream.

6.4.3 Our Turingian Heritage, Part Two: The Limits of Mechanized Inference and Chomsky Halted

Part of what makes CRUM unique is the central role that it affords to the making of linguaform inferences. Since perception, belief, decision, and action are all accounted for in terms of operations on sentence-like entities within the mind, there is a sense in which (according to CRUM) all mental processes are explained in terms of the phenomenon of inference. But the very invention of digital computers was *itself* the result of attempts to make inference processes entirely mechanical! The success of digital computers at performing this task has both motivated and made more plausible the

Russell/Fodor accounts of perception, belief, and action. Unfortunately, even here there lurks a fundamental problem.

6.4.3.1 A Brief Note on Mechanizing Inference

The invention of the modern digital computer was the result of an accumulation of discoveries over the first two-thirds of the twentieth century. First, the philosophers Gottlob Frege, Bertrand Russell, and Alfred North Whitehead developed formal languages to express mathematical proofs more rigorously.[43] Second, Alonzo Church, Kurt Gödel, and Alan Turing developed methods to mechanically specify sets of numbers. Turing's method was discussed in the previous chapter. Gödel's method led to the ability to assign unique numbers to fragments of formal languages, which in turn led to a method for mechanically specifying sets of sentences.[44] Turing's method involved the description of abstract "universal" machines that could achieve such specification. But then at this point, the main logical machinery was in place to actually build machines to check the validity of inferences that could be stated in a formal logic. Finally, Richard Montague described a method for mechanically translating between natural language sentences and sentences of a formal language.[45]

The combination of these innovations led to an explosion of computational linguistics and added to the intuitive plausibility of something like Fodor's view. It seems natural enough, after all, to imagine a computer programming language playing the role of Fodor's language of thought and Montagovian computational linguistics handling the transitions between natural, spoken language and Fodor's "inner" language of the mind.

In 1944, the mathematician John Von Neumann led the team that built the first computing machine along the lines of Turing's universal computer, i.e., it had an architecture that mapped program memory and inputs into the same address space, treating programs themselves as inputs.[46] From a computer science standpoint, the most important facet of both Von Neumann and Turing's machines is that they are *universal* in the sense that there is a clear separation between the hardware that performs very simple tasks, and different programs that utilize the equivalent of GOTO loops to call on different parts of the program stored in the machine. Despite the differences (not only are Von Neumann computers actual, they also have named registers and the ability to put any numeral in a register), the two kinds of computers can in principle compute the same set of functions, and indeed the same set of functions computed in-principle by every existing modern computer.

The fact that Turing machines can compute everything that Von Neumann machines can raises the question of whether Turing machines might be universal in another, somewhat stronger sense. Perhaps the set of sets of numbers checkable by *just any* machine is equivalent to the set of

Turing-computable sets of numbers. This view is called Turing's Thesis (and given the possibility of Gödel numbering, an analogous claim can be made about the set of sets of machine checkable inferences).

J.B. Rosser was the first to explicitly propose that the very fact that one can prove that Turing, Gödel, and Church's accounts of computable sets of numbers are identical[47] supports the idea that Church, Gödel, and Turing must have correctly analyzed the informal, everyday notion of computability that all of us have when we try to think in the abstract about what numerical tasks might be possible for just any machine to perform.[48] This claim is now known by logicians and computer scientists as the Church-Turing Thesis. If (in such different ways) all of these thinkers ended up surprisingly characterizing the same sets of numbers, then it is plausible to think that each was correct. Given that Turing machine computability is equivalent to the Von Neumann computability of contemporary computers, the Church-Turing Thesis entails that if a function is intuitively *computable at all*, then it can be computed by a modern digital computer (given enough space, time, and energy resources).

In the context of CRUM, the importance of the Church-Turing Thesis cannot be understated. Since CRUM is a characterization of perception, belief, action, and inference in terms of computation, and the Church-Turing Thesis entails that computation is to be identified with what contemporary digital computers in principle can do, it follows that digital computers can in principle perceive, believe, act, and infer.

6.4.3.2 Chomsky Halted

The Church-Turing Thesis gives some of the most interesting logical results of the previous century a great deal of further philosophical interest. If the thesis is true, then mathematical results about the *limitations* of what digital computers can in principle accomplish are also results about what is simply *not computable at all*. Turing, Church, and Gödel proved the three most important such formal limitation results. Where "Von Neumann Computable" is identified with what a modern digital computer can in principle do, the three logicians' results are equivalent to the following.

1   *The Unsolvability of the Halting Problem* (Turing)
     There is no Von Neumann computable procedure to determine of any arbitrary computer program m and input n whether m stops for n or runs indefinitely.
2   *The Non-Decidability of First-Order Logic* (Church)
     There is no Von Neumann computable procedure to determine of an arbitrary sentence of first-order logic whether it is logically true, rather than being either contingent (true only in some logically possible worlds, but not others) or logically false.

3 *The Non-Enumerability of Arithmetic* (Gödel)
    There is no Von Neumann computable procedure for enumerating all of
    the truths of arithmetic.

For our own argumentative purposes, it is essential to note that all of these
theorems describe cognitive skills that *people* clearly do have. Just as
people have the cognitive ability to differentiate grammatical from non-
grammatical sentences, they have the ability to: (1) parse programming
code and predict input–output relations, (2) imagine logically possible
worlds that make sentences written in a formal, logical language true or
false, and (3) prove the truths of arithmetic.[49]

The Chomskyan program for cognitive science commits one to a ready
explanation for the existence of these skills in biological human beings.
From the performance/competence distinction, it follows that successfully
accomplishing each of the above tasks requires only following a specifi-
able procedure. Given performance limitations, human beings can only
follow these procedures for so long, but the cognitive scientist's job is
to spell out how this is done in full generality. Given the requirement of
generativity, we know that cognitive scientists can do so, as the full procedure
will be such that it can be stated finitely. And given the Church-Turing
Thesis, we know that such an effective procedure will be Von Neumann
computable.

But wait! Turing, Church, and Gödel proved that there is *no* Von Neumann
computable procedure available to someone (or some machine) for the
accomplishment of these tasks. Something has got to give, then: either some
aspect of the Chomskyan program or the Church-Turing Thesis itself.[50]

The existence of the digital computer was supposed to show that CRUM
applies to language as it is used by at least *something* in the natural world.
It was supposed to sanction confidence about the prospects for artificial
intelligence along the lines originally suggested by Turing and taken up
by advocates of the neo-Russellian and Fodorean views of the mind. But
the limitation results listed above should give us pause. One can either argue
that the kinds of inferences discussed in CRUM (such as those by which
the Russellian forms the belief that she sees a table, or those by which
the Fodorean ties her shoe) are not inferences that a computer can do, or one
can give up on generativity. But if one gives up on generativity then one
has to admit that human thought itself may not consist of effective procedures that can be finitely stated by the cognitive scientist and AI programmer. This is a fundamental dilemma at the heart of all research and
philosophical thinking about AI.

6.5 Conclusions

We hope to have left the reader with something of an appreciation for how
difficult it would be to develop truly convincing AI. It is also extraordinarily

hard to develop a decent theory of human intelligence that has the kind of technology-creating explanatory ability that is possessed by fundamental sciences like physics. CRUM is the most articulated theory in this regard, but as we have shown, it is beset by fundamental problems.[51]

If our culture manages to avoid entering another dark age, we predict that CRUM will play a role analogous to classical physics. The problems that it faces do seem insurmountable to us, just as insurmountable as Newton's failure to plot Mercury's orbit. To get this right, physics had to move beyond classical physics. But the new theories had to also explain why classical physics got so much right, and justify the continued use of classical physics in contexts where it is inevitable to do so.[52] As long as humanity desires to manipulate and understand nature, classical physics will of necessity be with us. If CRUM is analogous, then it would be the height of folly to conclude from our critique that academic and commercial research into CRUM should be abandoned.[53]

Finally, nothing we have said above entails that computers cannot in principle do what humans can do. In the case of the limitation results, we do know that a computer cannot follow an explicitly programmed effective procedure to enumerate all of the truths of arithmetic, but it is not by any means clear that humans can do anything analogous. Given the under-determination of linguistic meaning, it is clear that paradigm CRUM approaches to programming will not yield anything approaching human conversational abilities. But non-CRUM approaches to artificial intelligence may do better.

The linguaform understanding of human thought and action that is implied by CRUM seems to us to arise in part from a natural, but outdated conception of how computers should be programmed to accomplish specific goals. As noted above, modern video games are so complicated that there is a sense in which they are not really "programmed" at all. First, they are almost always designed by a large, non-hierarchical team. Second, the design work is so complicated, and employs so many macros above the machine code, that the eventual behavior of games often surprises the very designers.

We propose the following solution. Say that both CRUM and Heideggerian robotics receive the research support they deserve, and that this research forms part of a feedback loop with related commercial applications of artificial intelligence, including (perhaps especially) video games. If, in a slow, piecemeal fashion the AI in future games is improved to the point at which the uncanny valley effect disappears, it is likely that the computer agent will be so enormously complicated that the computational basis for its intelligent behavior will remain a mystery.[54] Nonetheless, this does not rule out the creation of new kinds of intelligent beings by biological humans. And if your metaphysical beliefs incline you to the view that the universe needs as much intelligence as it can get, this should be a cheering prospect.

7 Epilogue: Video Games and the Meaning of Life

7.1 Philosophy: Puzzle or Quest?

Over the preceding six chapters we have moved rather abruptly from talking about the nature of the human mind to a discussion of the ethics of violence, then from a skeptical analysis of religious ethics to constructive arguments about the aesthetics of gaming. Taking this patchwork approach has been something of a necessity for us, given the extraordinarily diverse and multi-faceted nature of the young art form of video game design. But it also represents an approach to philosophy that is distinctive of the twentieth-century, Anglo-American tradition within which both of this book's authors were schooled—the tradition of so-called "analytic" philosophy.

It is worth considering the possibility that an alternative approach should be taken toward the philosophical issues raised by video games. Many philosophers, both inside and outside of the academy, have nursed the suspicion that perhaps there is really only *one* big philosophical question, and that discussions of ethics or aesthetics or the nature of the mind or the philosophy of religion are only valuable insofar as they help to answer it. This question, of course, is "What is the meaning of life?" Philosophically inclined people who regard this question as coherent and worthy of rigorous reflection usually imagine that a satisfactory answer to it would provide information about all kinds of things at once: how we should live, what caused us to exist in the first place, what makes us different from the rest of nature's works, and how to conceive of the relationship between God and humankind.

So which games have the most to tell us about philosophy's biggest question? We start with the most obvious candidates, games with characters the meanings of whose lives are transparently and dramatically clear: traditional high fantasy Role Playing Games (RPGs).

7.2 Heroes of Our Own Journeys

Imagine what your life would be like if you were the hero of one of these games—*Baldur's Gate*, say, or *Aidyn Chronicles*, or *Jade Empire*, or *Elder*

Scrolls. From the moment you were born, you would have been marked out by destiny to fight some monumental battle or go on some elaborate quest with the fate of your people (or perhaps your fellow elves, sprites, or goblins) resting in your hands. Before you picked up your first broadsword or magical scepter, you would have acquired legions of determined enemies, many of them equipped with fearsome weapons or skills of their own, not to mention faces that looked like something out of a butcher's worst nightmare. Especially galling might be the thought that, no matter how clever or brave or independent you felt in the midst of your adventures, there would always be some invisible stranger peering over your shoulder, computer keyboard or gamepad in hand, controlling your every move. Who needs this kind of stress?

Then again, life would at least in some respects be much simpler. People around you would for the most part know (or be able to guess) how enormously special you were. After all, not everyone is fated from the dawn of the universe to find the lost magical orb and rescue civilization from a fate worse than death. Furthermore, even though the world you inhabited might be a savage, dangerous place, it would at least come with helpful instructions and simple choices:

> "Fight the ogre!"
> "Be careful of trap doors!"
> "Would you like to drink the green potion?"
> "Do you want to go into the Cave of Doom?"

The everyday world would be a lot less confusing for everyone if we all received large, glowing messages like these from out of the ether at crucial turning points in our lives.

It is easy to chuckle at the idiosyncrasies of the genre when one is away from one's console or personal computer. Even diehard fans of the fantasy RPG genre have been known to crack up in mid-Boss Battle at the sheer goofiness of some of these games. But one of the reasons why they are such fun is that the heroes and heroines live out their lives in such structured, predetermined ways. So why do all of us (but especially gamers) get such a kick out of pretending to be these sorts of people, if only for a short while? Is it just escapism, pure and simple? Or is there something we think we can learn about our place in the cosmos from slaying dragons, hunting treasure, and carrying around the One Ring to Rule Them All on a two-dimensional, backlit screen?

Trying to answer such questions about one's preferences in gaming (or anywhere else in the arts) is always a useful thing to do. But when one begins to look for ideas in the writings of major Western philosophers about what might explain the deep and perennial attraction of role-playing, one comes up against a startlingly uniform pattern of skepticism, pessimism, and outright hostility.

7.3 The Philosophical Critique of Role-Playing

A lot of famous philosophers have really hated actors. Plato was the first. In the *Republic*, he manifests a deep distrust of all forms of art that rely upon imitation. A painter's attempt to imitate reality by drawing a lifelike picture of a bed was a bad enough form of trickery and deception. But the imitation of other humans (real or imaginary) was far, far worse. He has the character of Socrates make the following remarks:

> [D]oes this also follow from our earlier statement, that each individual would do a fine job of one occupation, not of many, and that if he . . . dabbled in many things, he'd surely fail to achieve distinction in any of them?. . . . As for someone who is not of this sort, the more inferior he is, the more willing he'll be to narrate anything and consider nothing unworthy of himself. As a result, he'll undertake to imitate seriously and before a large audience all the things we just mentioned—thunder, the sounds of winds, hail, axles, pulleys, trumpets . . . even the cries of dogs, sheep, and birds.[1]

The professional player of roles, Plato assumes, is someone who tries to be good at everything, and as a result becomes no good at anything—not even imitation, apparently, since there is no sign of willingness on Plato's part to treat acting as a worthy skill in and of itself.

The great nineteenth-century philosopher Friedrich Nietzsche was less concerned to specify what was undignified or contemptible about the practice of acting itself, and much more interested in characterizing the evil influence that he thought acting had on both the character of the performer and the morals of the audience. In his logically obscure, but highly suggestive *Thus Spake Zarathustra*,[2] he makes the following melodramatic pronouncements:

> Spirit, hath the actor, but little conscience of the spirit. . . .
>
> Tomorrow he has a new belief, and the day after tomorrow a newer one. Quick senses he has, like the people, and fickle moods.
>
> To overthrow—to him that means: to prove. To drive crazy—that means to him: to convince. And blood strikes him as the best of all arguments.
>
> A truth which slips only into fine ears, he calls a lie and nothing. Verily, he only believes in Gods that make a great noise in the world! (*Zarathustra* 36)

Nietzsche's view seems to be that the most successful actors are those who are best able to influence the thoughts and opinions of other people through noise, rhetoric, and spectacle rather than rational argumentation. And a side effect of constant imitation is that the performers end up having no firm beliefs or commitments themselves.

We have never really understood this prejudice against actors and play-acting. In fact, most of the actors that we have met have been generous and amiable people. But a deeper and more pertinent objection to the opinions expressed here by Plato and Nietzsche is that there is obviously a sense in which *all* human beings are actors. Everyone who has ever spent time at an American high school, or worked in an organization with a fairly rigid hierarchy, knows that a large percentage of every civilized person's life is spent playing artificial roles, whether that of the smiley cheerleader, the pensive geek, the perpetual comedian, the dutiful employee, or the stern boss.[3] Some of these roles come naturally to us, of course, but whether they do or not usually has remarkably little to do with how well we are expected to perform them.

7.3.1 Archetypes

The Swiss psychologist and cultural theorist C.J. Jung wrote eloquently about the unavoidable element of role-playing in civilized life. Jung is best known among philosophers for his belief in what he called the "collective unconscious." He thought that the memory of every human individual functions as a storehouse of the most important, recurrent, and affecting experiences that have been shared by all or most of the other members of our species. There is an important sense, he thought, in which we all share exactly the same notions of fatherhood, motherhood, the afterlife, and (most controversially) the gods.[4] Jung's views aren't taken seriously by contemporary psychologists as a predictive model of human thought and behavior, but they have had an enormous effect on modern thinking about literature and mythology. Because of this, they have also had a significant impact upon the ideas of the people who design traditional RPGs.[5]

Another closely related feature of human psychology that Jung thought was universal was the tendency that each of us has to identify very strongly with some "arbitrary segment of the collective psyche."[6] People are prone to fall into the habit of thinking of themselves in everyday life as playing the character of the epic hero (for example), or the loving mother figure, or the devious trickster. Jung refers to each of these roles that a person willingly tries to play as that individual's "persona."

Jung's description of the tendency that every human being has to take on one or more of these roles represents an interesting explanation of the popularity of Massively Multiplayer Online Role Playing Games (MMORPGs). If Jung was right, then it is far from accidental that the most successful such games tend to be based loosely upon ancient myth. The popularity of *Everquest* in the late 1990s and *Worlds of Warcraft* about ten years later have never been equaled by games set in sci-fi universes (*Eve Online, Earth and Beyond*), simulations of everyday life (*The Sims Online, Second Life*), or even popular scenarios from contemporary culture (*Harry Potter*).

But Jung also regarded the adoption of a persona as psychologically unhealthy. He points out that the word "originally meant the mask worn by an actor signifying the role he played" (*Relations* 137). This phase of psychological development should be regarded (he claimed) as a transitional stage on the way to a preferable state that he called "individuation." He described this latter phase of a person's psychological development as the process of "becoming a single, homogenous being" (*Relations* 147). Jung's opinions thus represent a continuation of the old philosophical tradition of distrusting actors; the only real difference between his brand of disapproval and Nietzsche's is that Jung counts as acting *every* form of role-playing that human beings engage in, rather than just the type that is done by professionals in front of a paying audience.

Most fans of role-playing games would probably object to Jung's attitude. What he says about the psychological need to abandon one's persona sounds depressingly similar to the remarks of non-gamers who insist that those of us who take pleasure in role-playing do so because we are unwilling to take part in the so-called "real world." There is, of course, a crucial difference between the adoption of a Jungian persona and the participation in RPGs; the latter sort of activity is a form of *play*. This means at least two things. First, the participants in tabletop and online RPGs engage in these pastimes voluntarily. Second, they normally derive pleasure and amusement, rather than any sort of stress or psychic disequilibrium, from their absorption in these games. But the Jungian has an obvious response here. People often do voluntarily enter into unhealthy psychic states, whether it is something as simple as self-delusion about an otherwise obvious but uncomfortable truth (e.g., truths such as "My spouse is cheating," or "My boss is a jerk") or something as complex as a full-scale neurosis. And even individuals who have been subjected to intensive therapy often strongly resist getting out of these states, which shows that there must be something like pleasure associated with them.

Still, there is obviously a difference between the momentary thrill that one gets from a vivid fantasy or delusion and the sort of thing that happened between Chris and Alayne, the couple whose online wedding in *Second Life* was described in Chapter One. And for serious online role-players, the personalities that their virtual characters develop can often be much more stable and long-lived than the quasi-mythic Jungian roles that we play in other areas of daily life. If we are really going to take seriously the question of whether it is "healthy" to engage in serious play-acting, then we should examine philosophical debates concerning potentially more permanent roles. In this context, the fascinating recent philosophical discussion of the phenomenon of multiple personality disorder (MPD) is highly salient. The comparison of MMORPG players to people with a medically diagnosable psychological condition might seem rather far-fetched, and more than a bit insulting. But there are some provocative similarities.

7.3.2 *Multiple Personality Disorder and the Autonomy Argument*

Diagnoses of MPD began in the United States in the early 1970s, and grew exponentially throughout the mid-1980s, around the same time the popularity of tabletop RPGs first started to take off. Even more interestingly from our point of view, observers of this diagnostic trend in clinical psychology have noticed that, while multiples often have traumatic experiences in their early childhood and exhibit symptoms of various other types of neurosis throughout their early lives, the actual emergence of "alters" (the discrete personalities) is rarely observed by anyone outside of the medical profession before treatment begins. In fact, the tendency that victims of MPD have of referring to themselves with two or more different proper names, and of associating different memories from the past with each of the personalities attached to these names, is very often *triggered* by specific sorts of interactions between doctors and patients—when the patient is under hypnosis, for example, or has been asked to discuss troubling memories of her past. These facts suggest that the extra personalities of multiples emerge in something like the same sorts of collaborative, interactive contexts as do the characters of committed tabletop and online role-playing gamers.

Philosophers who have written about MPD have been interested in both the question of whether it deserves to be classified as a "real" disease and the question of how it might best be treated. In his recent book on the subject, *Rewriting the Soul*,[7] the philosopher Ian Hacking argues that these two questions are much more closely related than one might think. A clinician who is convinced that a patient already has a set of discrete personalities buried somewhere in her psyche will often make a proactive attempt to get patients to "fragment," and begin speaking in these other voices. Doctors who are more skeptical of the idea that MPD represents a genuine ailment might be more hesitant about trying to induce this behavior for fear that they end up making things worse.[8]

Hacking's own conclusions on this topic are startling. He abstains from trying to answer the "reality" question about MPD with a simple "yes" or "no." But he is aggressively critical of therapists who are strong believers in the "reality" of alternate personalities in patients who have not yet exhibited them. Just about the worst thing that the clinical psychologist can do, he thinks, is to encourage patients to speak in the different "voices" of hidden personalities that have not already become manifest. For if a psychologist makes it her principal goal to bring these personalities out into the open, "the end product is a thoroughly crafted person, but not a person who serves the ends for which we are persons. Not a person with self-knowledge, but a person who is the worse for having a glib patter that simulates an understanding of herself" (*Rewriting* 266). A person who is forever play-acting cannot, Hacking thinks, be truly "autonomous." He proposes that "in the modern image, it is we ourselves who must choose the ends" that we pursue and that "we can be fully moral beings only when we understand why we choose these ends" (*Rewriting* 264). He identifies this way of thinking about the human good with the opinions of a broad and diverse group of modern philosophers, including Jean-Jacques Rousseau, Immanuel Kant, and Michel Foucault.

Hacking's view that self-knowledge is incompatible with role-playing can be taken as representing a further continuation of the old philosophical tradition that distrusts the whole practice of pretending to be a different person than one "really" is. Philosophers have tended to suppose that the practice of role-playing, whether it takes a form as innocuous as performing in a stage play or a movie or as drastic as developing an "alter" in a therapeutic environment, cannot but represent an evasion of the serious, adult responsibilities that require one to be consistent in one's demeanor, public manners, and one's first-person avowals of the form "I am . . . ."

If there is a general argument against role-playing that can be extracted from the claims of the philosophers we have examined here, then it is the following:

7.3.2.1 Autonomy Argument

1 In order to be psychologically and morally sound human beings, we must choose the ends that we pursue freely and autonomously.
2 Autonomy in the choosing of one's own ends is not possible without self-knowledge.
3 The practice of role-playing (i.e., thinking or speaking of oneself as a character in a fictional narrative) reliably impedes one's access to self-knowledge.
4 Therefore, one should not engage in the act of role-playing.

Somebody who accepts the autonomy argument against role-playing need not believe that all the first-person utterances of the role-player are simply *false* (the position that we referred to as "naïve fictionalism" in Chapter One). It is perfectly consistent with all four of the statements listed above to say that such utterances might be completely true. What is not consistent with the Autonomy Argument, however, is the possibility that the first-person avowals of the role-player contain the type of information about the person uttering them that provides for psychologically valuable self-knowledge.

The Autonomy Argument should provoke at least some immediate suspicion in light of what we concluded in Chapter One about the vagueness of the self. As we'll see in the next section, though, the argument also has more serious problems.

7.3.3 Role-Playing by the Rules

When the designers of computer RPGs actually sit down and try to figure out how their stories are supposed to go, they spend a lot of time worrying about whether or not they are getting it right. Even with action-based RPGs like *Diablo* or *Dungeon Siege*, where the point isn't storytelling so much as hacking one's way through piles of animated monsters, people in the game industry recognize that there are certain narrative elements that players expect. And they know that, if they do not deliver, then however pretty a game's graphics look and however many cool magic spells or explosions it contains, the player will sense that something is out of whack.

There are even books about storytelling that have been written deliberately as "how-to" manuals for avoiding this problem. One of the most famous and widely used is Christopher Vogler's *The Writer's Journey*. With patient and elaborate detail, Vogler lays out what he thinks are the essential elements of a well-constructed "hero's journey" narrative. Such a story must include elements like the "Meeting with The Mentor," the "Supreme Ordeal," the "Return with the Elixir," and so on.[9] The differences that seem to exist between stories like Homer's *Odyssey*, J.R.R. Tolkien's *Lord of the Rings*, the *Star Wars* movies, and *Final Fantasy VII* are superficial variations on an entirely predictable pattern, according to Vogler. Furthermore, the "pattern of the Hero's journey is universal, occurring in every culture, in every time. It is as infinitely varied as the human race is and yet its basic form remains constant. . . . The repeating characters of world myth such as the young hero, the wise old man or woman, the shapeshifter, and the shadowy antagonist are the same as the figures who appear in our dreams and fantasies" (*Writer's* 14).

Anyone who reads fantasy novels by authors such as Steven Erikson, Neil Gaiman, George R.R. Martin, Terry Pratchett, or J.R.R. Tolkien, or who regularly plays fantasy RPGs, will be bound to find many of the story elements Vogler describes very familiar indeed. But the existence of the patterns in storytelling that he describes is itself rather mysterious. Why the need for all this repetition? Don't we in fact value *novelty* above all else in the games we play and the stories we tell? If one were anxious to try *Ogre Smasher II*, but a trustworthy fellow gamer pointed out that it was really just the same as the first game, one probably wouldn't shell out fifty bucks for the sequel. Surely, what we want is *better* graphics, *new* styles of combat, and *surprising* twists and turns of plot in the games to which we devote our hard-won leisure time.

Or do we? Vogler isn't by any means the first thinker to suggest that the idea that people want novelty in storytelling is something of an illusion. He is, in fact, directly paraphrasing Jung when he proposes that the characters within every version of the hero's journey narrative, "reflect different aspects of the human mind . . . our personalities divide themselves into these characters to play out the drama of our lives" (*Writer's* 14).

A curious philosophical thesis is implicit in these remarks. Our preferences in stories (and therefore, one supposes, also in games) are irrevocably founded upon our sense that what happens in them mirrors the narrative structures of our own lives. If every story with a hero has the same fundamental structure, then it must be because at some level of abstraction we all share the same fundamental set of concerns as the heroes of our own life stories.

The idea that hero stories mirror how we see our own lives, if it's at all plausible, puts us in a good position to respond to the Autonomy Argument. If the practice of role-playing illuminates crucial aspects of our lives that would otherwise be hidden from us—specifically, the structural features of an individual's life that make her a hero, an antagonist, a shapeshifter, or a prophet—then Premise Three of the Autonomy Argument is clearly false. It is simply not the case that the practice of role-playing impedes one's access to the knowledge necessary for personal sovereignty, freedom, and independence. The fantasies that we indulge in about ourselves when we pretend to be characters in a fictional world teach us about our place within the "real" world, and this is precisely the sort of self-knowledge (one must surely assume) that will aid in the pursuit of true autonomy within our lives.

So *does* every human life really embody the sort of "drama" that Vogler describes as lying beneath the mundane surface events of daily life? It certainly does not feel that way while we are waiting in line at the drugstore, riding the bus, or brushing our teeth before work on a Thursday morning. Then again, all of us sense at times that we are engaged in personal struggles that have some of the same nobility and significance as Ulysses', Hamlet's, or Anakin Skywalker's. Even if we don't have bloodthirsty Orcs eternally spawning in our backyards, challenges like getting decent grades in school, pacifying some of our crazier relatives, or keeping our spouses and lovers happy can often have the same general feel to them as the monumental tasks undertaken by the fantasy hero. Maybe it all comes down to how we choose to look at our lives—which details we choose to recognize and reflect upon and which we choose to ignore or treat as meaningless—when it comes to deciding whether each of us is the hero of her own journey.

For the philosopher, however, the way people choose to see the world is never the most important issue. Philosophy is always concerned with how things *really are*. The question of whether a human being's life really does share a common structure with the hero's journeys that we see in RPGs and adventure games might seem like an odd one to expect a fully objective answer to. But in fact, that is exactly what Aristotle tries to provide in some profoundly surprising and unusual passages from Book One of the *Nicomachean Ethics*.

7.4 The Human Function

Aristotle's *Ethics* is one of the earliest books to go beyond merely giving its readers advice about how to be happy (like the books one might find in the "self-help" or "spirituality" sections of a modern bookstore) and get down to the issue of what the word "happiness" means.[10]

Aristotle thought that the young men who were his students in fourth-century BCE Athens had been getting mostly bad advice about happiness from their peers and elders. He warns his students right from the outset of the *Ethics* (which was originally written as a set of lecture notes) not to think of happiness as deriving solely from "pleasure, honor," or "wealth." Aristotle realized the importance of these things; however, he thought that none of them were "self-sufficient," by which he means "that which when isolated makes life desirable and lacking in nothing" (*Ethics* 12). Money and honor are no good taken by themselves, unless one deserves the honor and one knows what to spend one's money on. And even someone who is experiencing a lot of pleasure can surely imagine her situation being improved by having even more, which provokes a state of mind that Aristotle plausibly describes as "slavish" (*Ethics* 6).

Aristotle's view about the true nature of human happiness seems strange by modern standards. He thought that the only way we could reach a satisfactory conclusion on this subject was by first figuring out "the function of man." Just as the function of a can opener is to open cans, and the function of an Axe of Troll-Slaying is to slay trolls, so (he thought) human beings are *for* something. But why think this about ourselves? And assuming that this peculiar claim is actually true, what on earth could each of us be "for?"

If there's such a thing as a single "function" that we all share, then our lives are more like those of the heroes of fantasy RPGs than any of us would normally think. Each and every one of us is here on the planet because she has a real, meaningful job to do, even if it is not something quite as dramatic as tracking down Sephiroth or paying a visit to the Cracks of Doom. Many people would probably be greatly comforted by this piece of news. And even for those of us who don't feel the need to turn to philosophy for the reassurance that there is some overall point to our lives, knowledge about something as crucial as "the human function" could hardly be received with indifference.

Perhaps the oddest thing about Aristotle's discussion is the fact that it seems so *obvious* to him that human life serves some definite purpose or other. He does not feel the need to talk about God's plan for us, or to use any of the rather opaque language about "self-actualization" that one often hears from motivational speakers or the authors of self-help books. Instead, he merely observes that it would be very surprising if we did not have a function, given that all the significant parts out of which we are made clearly do: "as eye, hand, foot, and in general each of the parts has a function," he proposes, "may we not lay it down that man similarly has a function apart from all these?" He also makes the point that the jobs we take on in order to make a living clearly have a function. "Have the carpenter, then, and the tanner certain functions or activities, and man has none?" (*Ethics* 13).

Aristotle is surely right that it would be weird if a person who was employed in some field that does have a function (e.g., garbage collecting for sanitation engineers, estimating risk for actuaries, and so on) didn't have any clear function at all when simply considered as a human being. And given that our eyes are for seeing, our ears for hearing and our hearts for circulating blood, nature would have arranged things very oddly if the functions that each organ served didn't aid in the performance of some overall function carried out by the whole person. On the other hand, the analogies that Aristotle based his argument on are far from perfect. The whole point of the argument is to equate human happiness with the performance of our characteristic function. But many people hate their jobs, and seeing things certainly doesn't make our *eyes* happy in any coherent sense.

Perhaps more significantly, there is an important dissimilarity between ourselves taken as individuals and all of the components that make up our bodies taken one at a time. Individual human beings have free will—we can choose which tasks to perform over the course of our lives. Our freedom is of course constrained by our physical and intellectual limitations—nobody can simply choose to be turned into gamma rays and bounced off the moon, nor to come up with the solution to some intractable problem in higher mathematics. But the very fact that how we are built doesn't take away our ability to *reject* certain tasks that our lives seem to present us with has led many thinkers writing subsequent to Aristotle to regard his "function argument" as a huge philosophical red herring.

Curiously enough, Aristotle himself clearly did believe in the causal significance of free will.[11] He tried, in fact, to build the possibility of free will into his own carefully worded characterization of the human function. The task that nature equips every human being to perform, he thought, is to live out "an active life of the element that has a rational principle" (*Ethics* 13). According to Aristotle, the capacity to freely use our reason is the one and only thing that separates human beings from the rest of nature. By using reason to govern our actions, we therefore must be performing the sole function for which we are better suited than anything in the universe.

What is the relationship between this mysterious "rational element" in human nature and everything else that makes us who we are? Here our RPG analogy can help us out. The rational element of a player character in a traditional, third-person style role-playing game is *you*, the player. Everything about the character's heritage and environment, and many of her skills and deficits, strengths and weaknesses, are pre-determined by the game's designers. But what she actually does with these abilities is up to the person with the controller, at least within a significant range of possibilities. Perhaps a human being's ability to reason allows her to exert something like the same sort of control over her own physical behavior in the "real" world that a player of RPGs can over the behavior of her avatar.

This particular analogy with games is rather a tricky and ambiguous one, though. For it can also be used in a slightly different way to illuminate the discomfort that many modern philosophers have had with the whole idea that human beings have a pre-established function. Consider the behavior of certain anti-heroic characters in some of the more sophisticated RPGs and adventure games. In *Final Fantasy VII*, Cloud spends much of the story resisting the call to complete the dangerous tasks that the game sets out for him. In *Grim Fandango*, Manny only becomes interesting enough to be worth playing once he has utterly rejected the function assigned to him as a minor bureaucrat in the Land of the Dead. And in some classic comedy games the whole idea that the hero has one unmistakable function to perform is aggressively spoofed. Poor Leisure Suit Larry makes his way through innumerable tests and trials as the result of nothing more than an overactive sex drive. And Guybrush Threepwood, the hero of the classic series of *Monkey Island* games, has most of his adventures through pure bad luck and misplaced curiosity.

Perhaps the authors of these games thought in some implicit way that not only a philosophically adequate understanding of human freedom, but also a proper appreciation of the role of chance and serendipity in our lives, are impossible to reconcile with the belief that we have any specific "function" whatsoever. Perhaps instead, we must each seek out meaning in our own lives without the sort of help that Aristotle thought he could provide for his students.

Taken to its logical conclusion, this strongly *voluntarist* attitude presents a stark and unconsoling picture of the human condition. A voluntarist is anyone who believes that human beings can make a real, substantial difference to what happens in our world—or at least within ourselves—through the exercise of free will. To get a firmer sense of precisely what this position entails when it comes to trying to figure out the meaning of life, we need to turn to the work of a very different sort of philosopher from Aristotle, and also to reflect upon some of the features of a very different sort of game.

7.5 "Thrown" into the Void

One of the most startling beginnings to any video game (and at least part of the reason for its phenomenal popularity) is the first few seconds of *Myst*. The player is presented with the image of a closed, ancient-looking book hovering against a black, star-filled void. The image of a hand hovers over the book; this tiny icon is the only direct point of contact that the player ever has with the diegetic world of the game. A single click on the surface of the book, and the pages flutter open to reveal a picture of the game-world, to which the player is instantly transported.

The world of *Myst* is filled with puzzles, and one occasionally comes across friendly or malevolent non-player characters (NPCs) who ask the player's rather mysterious avatar for help. But unlike the traditional RPGs, one is never presented with instructions about how to proceed. There are no obvious villains to fight, magic spells to learn, or elixirs to retrieve. The player can choose to become embroiled in an interesting, highly dramatic story upon which the fate of worlds depends, or she can merely explore the fascinating universe of the game without any greater goal.

In the mid-1990s, the early games in the *Myst* series enjoyed huge popularity and inspired dozens of imitators.[12] Many experienced gamers hated the slow pace and the ambiguity of these "point and click" adventure games. But the *Myst* series also attracted a whole new audience of computer users to video gaming, many of whom (especially women) had never been thought of as part of the traditional market. Is there a philosophical view about the meaning of life that can explain the appeal of the *Myst* games and their many clones?

We think that such an approach can be found by returning to the writings of one of the twentieth century's most influential philosophers, Martin Heidegger. Heidegger characterizes the situation of human beings in the universe in unmistakably anti-Aristotelian terms in his 1927 work *Being and Time*. According to Heidegger, every single human being is in a condition of "thrownness" into "the there" (*Being* 33).[13] From the time that a person first becomes capable of thought, she is irreversibly and thoroughly implicated in the habits and routines of "the world." This state of affairs, according to Heidegger, makes it impossible for us to attain the kind of detachment and objectivity that would be required to come to a true understanding of our Aristotelian function.

Heidegger gives an ambiguous, albeit highly suggestive description of how we acquire the sense that there is some ultimate purpose each of our lives is meant to serve. The human being, he claims

> . . . always has understood itself and will understand itself in terms of *possibilities*. Furthermore, the project character of understanding means that understanding does not thematically grasp that upon which it projects, the possibilities themselves. Such a grasp precisely takes its character of possibility *away* from what is projected, it degrades it to the level of a given. (*Being* 136)

What Heidegger seems to mean here is that, when each of us tries to think about the various available projects that we could choose to undertake over the course of our lives, we do not (and cannot) think of them as being in any way settled in advance. A human being's future is not a long series of inevitabilities, responses to some inexorable vocation, or courses of action that we are somehow built in order to act out. Only a being that lacked freedom could ever regard its own future as a "given." Heidegger's philosophy of human nature is therefore quite starkly incompatible with Aristotle's, since the Aristotelian worldview represents us humans as being able to understand our own singular "function," and so as being able to achieve precisely the kind of foresight that Heidegger thought was impossible.

Heidegger's emphasis on the radical nature of human freedom was taken up by other philosophers from the existentialist school of thought. Jean-Paul Sartre, who was perhaps the most famous existentialist, expressed this commitment by saying, "man is a being whose existence precedes his essence."[14] For human beings, according to Sartre, it is useless, deceptive, and philosophically unsound to try to explain or justify what we *do* by appeal to what we essentially *are*. Sometimes, of course, this is obviously true: if you steal other people's underwear, nobody will be impressed if you try to account for your actions by saying "I'm just an underwear-stealing kind of guy." But for Sartre, it is just as nonsensical to say in any context whatsoever that you either did or must do some action X because "I'm a Christian," "I'm an alcoholic," "I'm just excitable that way," or even "I'm only human."

Many of the existentialist philosophers were deeply pessimistic about the human condition, to the extent that they were sometimes willing to describe our lives as being devoid of meaning. Heidegger thought that a full and authentic understanding of our place in the world inevitably produces *angst* (a German word meaning something like "deep distress") (*Being* 174). For Sartre, the thought that one's life has *any* meaning and purpose, the pursuit of which can transform one into what one was not before, is an act of fundamental "bad faith."[15] This is rather a strange view. Isn't freedom supposed to be a valuable thing to human beings? Granted, the sort of freedom that Heidegger and his followers were talking about was something more basic, and undeniably scarier, than the relatively mundane (albeit no less important) types of freedoms exalted in documents such as the *Declaration of Independence*. The existentialists seem to think that an authentic human existence should be lived free not only from governmental coercion and religious repression, but also from the "thematic" restrictions on behavior imposed by a sense of duty, the obligations of public service, or personal fidelity to any species of higher power, divine or otherwise.[16]

In the last scene of *Riven*, the game that was released as a sequel to *Myst*, the player's character has rescued the other characters in the game-world from a horrible fate, and has received their gratitude and faithful friendship in return. But then the earth opens up, the images on the screen tremble, and the perspective suddenly shifts dramatically. Now the player is looking at the game-world from out of the same "starry expanse" that she began from at the start of *Myst*. All the puzzles and adventures that she has become intimately concerned with for the previous thirty or so hours of playing time suddenly seem distant and inconsequential. But just at this moment, a voice-over informs the player that the void from which she came now seems more welcoming, and less lonely than one would think from its mere appearance. The stars and the blackness fill up more and more of the screen, and the game's credits begin to roll.

Writing the ending of the game in this way was an artistic risk by its designers; there is no RPG-style reward of experience points, treasure, or world-domination given to the player, and some gamers probably found the story's conclusion rather strange and alienating.[17] But perhaps the existentialists would have approved. They did not, after all, have anything against the formation of long-term projects or deep friendships and allegiances over the course of a human life. They merely thought that there was something dishonest about a person's *identifying* with these projects in such a way as to make crucial practical decisions seem easier and more automatic. Heidegger thought that life was lived most authentically when a human being learns to exhibit a kind of "resoluteness" in the face of the angst that inevitably haunts each of us when we look forward into our own personal futures (*Being* 273). The mere possibility of cultivating this mental attitude is perhaps not enough to provide human life with the robust meaningfulness in which Aristotle and traditional religions ask us to believe. But it might at least be enough to endow the relationships we form and the tasks that we choose to undertake—not only in game worlds like those of *Myst* and *Riven*, but in the "real" world that we all share—with a temporary, ephemeral meaningfulness that can cure us of the bleakest forms of pessimism.

7.6 The Game of Life

We have now looked at two starkly incompatible philosophical views about the meaning of life. Would it make any sense to regard one or the other of them—the Aristotelian's or the existentialist's—as clearly *right*? How could one possibly even begin to adjudicate between them?

On our way toward an answer to these questions, let us take a look at a radically different type of computer game from any of those that we have discussed in the book so far. In 1970, the British mathematician John Horton Conway came up with a set of rules for a zero-player game (i.e., a type of game that plays itself). The action of Conway's game takes place on a two-dimensional grid of squares, just like the Cartesian planes with X- and Y-axes in geometry textbooks. Every single move in the game is determined in advance by what the rules say, together with an initial distribution of filled-in squares somewhere on the grid.[18] Conway nicknamed his invention the *Game of Life*, because he thought that it could serve as a representation of how animal populations thrived or diminished over a given expanse of space and period of time.

Each initially filled-in square on the grid is supposed to represent a single "live" individual, or (even better) a minimal unit of some population group like a family or a tribe. The fundamental idea is that any organism or group of similar creatures will be unlikely to survive and prosper if there are either too many or not enough of their own kind in close proximity. One's chances of survival increase up to a certain point when one belongs to a community, but start to go down again once that community becomes overcrowded. Anyone familiar with the gameplay of commercial games like *Civilization*, *The Settlers*, and *Empire Earth* will at some point have had to come to grips with this state of affairs. The following three relatively simple "rules" of Conway's game are designed to reflect the basic structure of the phenomenon.

- Fill in any empty square on the grid that has exactly three "neighbors" (i.e., adjacent squares) already filled in. That square is now "live."

- Erase any block on the grid that has fewer than two or more than three "neighbors" already filled in. That square is now "dead."
- Any live cell with two or three live neighbors should be left alone, to "survive" into the next "generation" (i.e., subsequent applications of all three rules to the new pattern).

Repeated applications of these rules to an initial pattern of filled-in blocks on the grid will often result in a stable pattern of "live" squares that will resist any further change in later "generations." For example, a "game" that begins with the distribution of filled-in squares shown in Figure 7.1 will stabilize after four "generations."

The reader is invited to figure this out using some graph paper and pencil with a good eraser—be warned that it's tricky, though, since the rules are understood as applying to the grid *simultaneously*, rather than in any particular sequence. At the end of four applications of the rules given above, one's grid should have reached the state depicted in Figure 7.2.

Conway's game has some fascinating properties.[19] But what interests us in the present context is the sense in which it can be understood as a representation of how living creatures like ourselves actually behave.

Of course, there is no general agreement among biologists or social scientists about what conditions are needed for human and other animal communities to flourish. But it is easy to imagine simple changes to Conway's rules to accommodate such diverse opinions. An optimist about the ability of densely clustered populations to provide for themselves could, for example, change the third rule so that only a square with more than *five* neighbors will "die" off in each generation. From the initial distribution shown in Figure 7.3, an application of this new set of rules would, after six "generations," give the result shown in Figure 7.4—the seed of a pattern that would eventually spread outward to infinity!

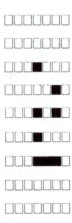

Figure 7.1

Figure 7.2

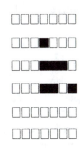

Figure 7.3

Figure 7.4

As one can see from these examples, the smallest change in initial conditions and rules of development may produce a startling change in the circumstances of life. But that doesn't mean that our attempt to forge lasting social bonds with one another is an utterly chaotic and unpredictable process. In fact, the *Game of Life* appears to show just the opposite. The most elaborate and intricate patterns can be generated in a quite spontaneous and unplanned way from a relatively simple set of rigid, underlying principles.

The idea that human life follows such patterns is strongly echoed within the following passage from Charles Darwin's *The Origin of Species*:

> . . . considering the infinite complexity of the relations of all organic beings to each other and to their conditions of existence, causing an infinite diversity in structure, constitution, and habits, to be advantageous to them, I think it would be a most extraordinary fact if no variation ever had occurred useful to each being's own welfare, in the same way as so many variations have occurred useful to man. . . . This principle of preservation, I have called, for the sake of brevity, Natural Selection.[20]

It is not at all crazy to think of the Theory of Evolution as an attempt to describe the processes of adaptation, reproduction, and migration that are modeled by the *Game of Life*. The only real difference lies in the levels of specificity at which each tries to provide a model of the organic world.

It might be helpful then to consider how questions about the "meaning of life" would be answered by someone who observed *us*—we complicated human inhabitants of the modern world—in the same way that we observe the virtual creatures (i.e., the dark spaces in the grid) in Conway's *Game of Life*. From such an utterly detached point of view, would we all appear to share a "function" that made us unique within the natural world? Or would we seem to be radically free in our actions in the way that the existentialists thought that we must be?

Perhaps the picture that we get from Conway's quasi-Darwinian representation of how populations disperse is simply too austere to help us answer the deepest philosophical questions about whether or not the lives of human beings have some overarching meaning or purpose. But Daniel Dennett disagrees. In *Darwin's Dangerous Idea*, Dennett argues that all philosophical discussions of the meaning of life must begin with an acknowledgement of how the forces of nature first identified by Darwin influence our everyday dreams and desires, and our sense of what is truly valuable in the world. "Whenever Darwinism is the topic," he observes, "[o]ne of the precious things that is at stake is a vision of what it means to ask, and answer, the question 'Why?' Darwin's new perspective turns several traditional assumptions upside down, undermining our standard ideas about what ought to count as satisfying answers to this ancient and inescapable question."[21] It is difficult to disagree with the claim that, whatever high-flown ideas we might have about a human being's ultimate purpose or highest obligations, what we say should at least be consistent with the well-supported theories about human nature that the science of biology can provide us with. Rethinking the central question of the present chapter in these terms will also help us to reconcile the Aristotelian and Heideggerian intuitions mentioned earlier on.

7.7 Conclusion: The Games We Choose

Let us revisit Aristotle's idea that all human beings share a common "function." Aristotle certainly didn't have our survival instinct or the capacity to reproduce in mind when he made this claim. But the biological perspective upon human life that we have been investigating shares at least this much in common with Aristotle's approach: both see human freedom as operating within the scope of rigid and unalterable constraints. A human individual, according to Aristotle, cannot choose whether or not to be a rational being; one can only choose whether or not to act according to the guidance provided by one's inborn rational faculty. Similarly, since humans are, after all, animals to which the generalizations of biology clearly do apply, our deepest motivations will normally have at least some of their roots planted firmly in the impulses to survive, to provide protection for our kin, and to reproduce.

At the same time, Dennett urges us to resist the temptation to suppose that there is simply no point at all to what we do with most of our time unless it furthers these basic goals.[22] He uses a provocative example to show how hard it is to take biological determinism seriously. Consider the phenomenon of sleep. People rarely if ever think that their need for regular sleep adds any meaning or value to their lives. Whatever other differences might exist among people's widely varying conceptions of the meaning of life, pretty much everyone—even the existentialists—seems to agree that a well-lived life must be an *active* one, to at least some minimal extent. Our preference for doing things is also made evident by the kinds of video games that we choose to play; one can imagine the kind of reception that a video game called *Naptime*! would be likely to get from fans of RPGs, war games, first-person shooters, or even relatively sedentary adventure games like *Myst*. But as Dennett points out, "Mother Nature doesn't see it that way at all. A life of sleep is as good a life as any, and in many regards better—certainly cheaper—than most" (*Darwin's* 340). After all, sleep does two important things for us. It renews our metabolic functions, which makes us much more energy efficient for performing all the fun, but relatively short-term tasks associated with reproduction. And it keeps us out of harm's way, provided we have managed to find a reasonably safe little cave or apartment where we can lay down our heads. Here is at least one place where knowing the basic biological facts does nothing whatsoever to change our opinions about what is important in human life.

Accounts of the meaning of life that aim for consistency with the basic facts about human biology need not be wholly incompatible with what existentialists have to say about the human predicament. To see why this is, it is worth reflecting upon one crucial feature of human life that is entirely left out by John Conway's game-like simulation, i.e., the element of time. All the little cells on Conway's grid ever get around to doing is being born, dying, or waiting passively for the next "generation" to go by. There might be some creatures on the planet (sea sponges, fungi, tree sloths, one of the authors' cats, and perhaps even a few people) whose histories can be summed up in this way without much of note being left out. But it is impossible to say this about all of us. For whatever other features philosophers have traditionally thought make us unique (e.g., our capacity to reason, the fact that we are made "in the image of God," or our curious habit of dropping bombs on one another) there is certainly one thing that we have more of than any of our fellow Earthly organisms: *leisure*. Many human beings (including the vast majority of those who are ever likely to read this book) are left with a significant amount of free time after they have succeeded in stockpiling some food, finding a sexual partner, and protecting their kids from the world's more predictable dangers. Perhaps the philosophical quandaries that the existentialists raised about human life as a whole have almost as much force when asked about just the leisure portion of a healthy, provided-for adult human's life. And perhaps, therefore, philosophical questions about the meaning of life are better re-phrased as questions about what we are to do with ourselves *after* we have finished fulfilling all of our basic, unalterable biological "functions."

Of course, it is often far from easy to tell which of the things we spend our time on are genuine leisure activities and which are really just sophisticated attempts to further our goals as animals. Take recreational hunting for example; on the one hand, it looks a lot like what our evolutionary ancestors did to provide basic nourishment for themselves and their families. But in the modern United States, shooting a small bird out of the air with an expensive shotgun is hardly the most efficient way of fending off malnutrition. Or take *haute couture*; surely there is no more certain sign that people have spare time on their hands than seeing them dress in outlandish clothes from fashion magazines. Then again, many of the apparent excesses of the garment industry probably arise in some Darwinian manner from the urge to attract extra notice from desirable sexual partners.[23]

The idea that our lives acquire their meaningfulness from our leisure-time activities[24] should have a special attraction to anyone who has managed to get this far in the present book. After all, consider what this suggestion implies for the activity of video game playing! Far from being a frivolous pastime, gaming might turn out to be one of the most important things that we human beings do. As we mentioned in the Preface, it is unlikely to be a complete coincidence that the ancient Greeks invented philosophy around the same time that they first began to indulge in ritualized game playing.[25]

Likewise, existentialism only attained broad cultural cachet during the early 1960s, the point at which New Deal economic policies and the industrial revolution had spread material affluence and leisure to all social classes in the West for the first time in human history.

Perhaps it is possible to spend too much of one's time, energy, and intelligence killing onscreen aliens, searching for elixirs in dungeons, perfecting kung-fu moves on an Xbox controller, and plotting world domination. But any philosopher who thinks carefully and objectively about the human condition should also realize that video games enrich our lives, and provide us with the sense that it is worth spending more time on the planet. This is something that is hard to attain, difficult to keep, and worth holding on to.

Notes

Preface

1 Huizinga, Johan. *Homo Ludens: A Study of the Play Element in Culture*. Boston: The Beacon Press, 1955; hereafter cited in text as *Ludens*.
2 The answer to the first riddle is supposed to be "time." The difficulty of coming up with an answer to the second question has earned it the name of "The Liar Paradox," a problem that is debated extensively by contemporary philosophers.
3 The first example of a text in which this understanding of the business of philosophy is defended seems to have been the satirical work *On What Is Not*, by the ancient sophist Gorgias. Other influential characterizations of philosophy as a fundamentally frivolous enterprise can be found in Muhammed al-Ghazali, Abu Hamid. *The Incoherence of the Philosophers*. Trans. Michael E. Marmura. Provo: Brigham Young, 2002; Marx, Karl, and Engels, Friedrich. *The German Ideology, Including Theses on Feuerbach*. Amherst: Prometheus Books, 1998.
4 See Hobbes, Thomas. *Leviathan*. ed. Richard E. Flathman and David Johnston. New York: WW. Norton, 1997; Wittgenstein, Ludwig. *Philosophical Investigations*. New York: Prentice Hall, 1999.
5 Push-pin was an inane gambling game invented in the sixteenth century. One played it by putting pins on the brim of a hat and then tapping the hat to make them jump over each other.
6 See Mill, John Stuart. *Utilitarianism*. ed. George Sher. Indianapolis: Hackett Publishing Co., 1981, 8–11.
7 Falzon, Christopher. *Philosophy Goes to the Movies*. London: Routledge, 2007; Alhoff, Fritz, ed. *The Philosophy of Wine: A Symposium on Thinking and Drinking*. London: Wiley–Blackwell, 2007; Solomon, Robert, and Higgins, Kathleen, eds. *The Philosophy of (Erotic) Love*. Kansas City: University of Kansas, 1991; Carroll, Noel. *The Philosophy of Horror: Or, Paradoxes of the Heart*. London: Routledge, 1990.

1 I, Player: The Puzzle of Personal Identity (MMORPGs and Virtual Communities)

1 For a more detailed account of Chris and Alayne's courtship, see C-Net News. "It's a Nice Day for an 'Everquest' Wedding." 1 Dec 2007 <http://news.com.com/Its+a+nice+day+for+an+EverQuest+wedding/2100-1043_3-6038936.html.>
2 Stetson Kveum pointed out to us that one can distinguish on this basis between two classes of video RPGs. For example, while the *Elder Scrolls* games and *Baldur's Gate* use recognizable variants of the *D & D* character system, action RPGs like *Paper Mario* or *Legend of Zelda* do not. As a result the distance between the

player's and avatar's abilities is narrower in the latter kind of game. If your dexterity is too bad to work the controllers, you won't get far in *Zelda*. Interestingly, most adult players tend to feel much *less* inclination to identify with their avatars when playing *Zelda* type games.

3 Neal Hebert has made this point in a number of helpful conversations with the authors.

4 Less naïve forms of fictionalism need not entail that the relevant class of sentences are false or that the relevant objects don't exist. This depends upon one's philosophy of fiction. For a good typology of different types of fictionalism, see Stanford Encyclopedia of Philosophy. "Fictionalism." 25 Jan 2008 <http://plato.stanford.edu/entries/fictionalism/>. Fictionalism has been defended by philosophers as a viable attitude toward many types of discourse, for example, statements about God (by Nietzsche), claims about the external world (by Berkeley) and even claims about *everything whatsoever* (by the Greek skeptic, *Sextus Empiricus*). The best modern book on the subject is Kalderon, M., ed. *Fictionalism in Metaphysics*. Oxford: Clarendon Press, 2005. Sadly, even contemporary Western varieties of fictionalism are fairly crude compared to debates that Indian metaphysicians have been having for the last few thousand years. For an introduction to the classical Indian debates about the reality of the external world, the self, and persistence through change, see Dasgupta, Surendranath. *A History of Indian Philosophy: Volumes 1–5*. Delhi: Motilal Banarsidass, 2004. Our own substantive conclusions in this chapter have certainly been shaped by a beginning study of Dasgupta's classic. We hope at some point to explicitly explore analytic debates about the self in light of classic and contemporary Indian philosophy.

5 Do not try this! Given the mass of these gentle creatures, it is an astonishingly cruel thing to attempt.

6 There is quite a bit more to say about the issue of getting truths out of fiction. See Sirridge, Mary. "J.R. Tolkien and Fairy Tale Truth." *British Journal of Aesthetics* 15.1 (1975): 81–92.

7 Parmenides, "The Way of Truth." *Early Greek Philosophy*. Ed. Jonathan Barnes. London: Penguin Books, Inc., 1987. 135; hereafter cited in text as "Way".

8 Descartes, René. *Meditations on First Philosophy*. Trans. John Cottingham. Cambridge: Cambridge University Press, 1986. 20; hereafter cited in text as *Meditations*.

9 Hume, David. "Of Personal Identity." *Personal Identity*. Ed. John Perry. Los Angeles: University of California Press, 1975. 161; hereafter cited in text as "Personal".

10 Parfit, Derek. "Personal Identity." *Personal Identity*. Ed. John Perry. Los Angeles: University of California Press, 1975. 218–219.

11 See the essays in *Personal*.

12 See Keefe, Rosanna. *Theories of Vagueness*. Cambridge: Cambridge University Press, 2000.

13 Clark, Andy, and David Chalmers. "The Extended Mind." *Analysis* 58 (1998): 10–23.

14 This, some other odd scientific possibilities, and their implications for conventional views of personal identity are discussed colorfully in Daniel Dennett, "Where Am I?" 15 Jan 2008 http://www.newbanner.com/SecHumSCM/WhereAmI.html.

15 Hofstadter, Douglas. *Gödel, Escher, Bach: An Eternal Golden Braid*. New York: Basic Books, 1979 contains a discussion of the possibility that ant farms possess a group mentality over and above what the individual ants possess. In Hofstadter's most recent book (Hofstadter, Douglas. *I Am A Strange Loop*. New York: Basic Books, 2007) he describes how the vagueness of the self allows

people's identities to overlap so strongly that a dead loved one literally continues to exist in the survivor. For another more wide-ranging discussion of collective intensionality, see Tollefsen, Deborah. "Collective Intensionality." *Internet Encyclopedia of Philosophy*. 15 Jan 2008 <http://www.iep.utm.edu/c/coll-int.htm>. For an excellent fictional depiction of how a collective "pack" mind might operate in an alien species, see Vinge, Vernor. *A Fire Upon The Deep*. New York: Tom Doherty Associates, 1992. As individual members of Vinge's fictional "packs" die off and are replaced, the pack mind must confront issues of personal identity. In the orderly progression of things, these groups/persons end up choosing new members of the pack that constitutes them in terms of how those members' skills and attributes will help the group/person in her plans and projects. At least in the novel, this seems to contribute to the continuity of the pack's "self" over time, and suggests the philosophical view that one's plans and projects are fundamental to one's selfhood.

16　See Scott Berg, A. *Max Perkins: Editor of Genius*. New York: Penguin, 1997.

2　The Game Inside the Mind, the Mind Inside the Game (The Nintendo Wii Gaming Console)

1　Video Game Chartz. "Video Game Chartz—Nintendo—Sony—Microsoft." 1 Aug. 2007 <http://www.vgchartz.com>.

2　Merrill Lynch analyst Yoshiyuki Kinoshita has estimated that by 2011 over 30% of the US households will own a Wii. Game Daily. "Merrill Lynch: 30% of U.S. Households to Own Wii by 2011." 1 Aug. 2007 <http://biz.gamedaily.com/industry/feature/?id=15309>.

3　Mascaró, Juan., trans. *The Bhagavad Gita*. London: Penguin Books, 1962. Plato, *Republic*. Trans. G.M.A. Grube. Indianapolis: Hackett, 1983; hereafter cited in text as *Republic*.

4　Descartes, René. *The Philosophical Writings of Descartes, Volume I*. Trans. John Cottingham, Robert Stoothoff, and Dugald Murdoch. Cambridge: Cambridge University Press, 1985; hereafter cited in text as *Writings*.

5　Russell, Bertrand. *The Problems of Philosophy*. Oxford: Oxford University Press, 1983. 2; hereafter cited in text as *Problems*.

6　Descartes was the first philosopher to defend this premise from the perspective of a recognizably modern scientific worldview. Descartes argued that properties like color and hardness are not features of things in themselves, but rather depend for their existence upon the mind of the perceiver. Interestingly, he must have entertained something like Russell's actual argument, as the very reason Descartes gives for hardness being a mental property is that perceptions of hardness differ in a way that depends upon conditions of observation. See *Principles of Philosophy*, Part II, 4 (*Writings* 177–292).

7　Perception is actually pretty bizarre both in people and in animals. See Wolfe, Jeremy, et al. *Sensation and Perception*. Sunderland: Sinauer Associates, 2005, for some fascinating case studies that demonstrate this.

8　For some interesting and detailed philosophical reflections on this sense of strangeness, see Nagel, Thomas. "What Is It Like To Be A Bat?" *Philosophical Review* 83 (1974): 435–51.

9　There are many other arguments that philosophers have offered for phenomenalism. Russell himself was also moved by the inability of natural science to account for perception in certain ways, and thought that this failure should motivate a belief in sense data. See Russell, Bertrand. *An Inquiry into Meaning and Truth*. London: George Allen and Unwin Limited, 1940. A.J. Ayer thought that dreams and other illusions were indiscernible from veridical perceptions, and used this to argue that in non-illusive sensory settings we are also perceiving sense data. See Ayer, A.J. *The Foundations of Empirical Knowledge*. London: Macmillan, 1958. Ayer's view and Russell's natural science argument both represent interesting and controversial strategies for defending the claim that we have only indirect access to the external world. Russell's argument should more properly be thought of as an example of what the great American philosopher Wilfrid Sellars described as a tension between the "manifest" and "scientific" images. See Sellars, Wilfrid. "Philosophy and the Scientific Image of Man." *Frontiers of Science and Philosophy*. Ed. Robert Colodny. Pittsburgh: University of Pittsburgh Press, 1962. 35–78. Resolving or dissolving this tension is a task that motivates a great deal of work in contemporary philosophy. Ayer's dream argument (fascinating though it is) is effectively demolished in Austin, J.L. *Sense and Sensibility*. Ed. G.J. Warnock. Oxford: Oxford University Press, 1962; hereafter cited in text as *Sense*. Since neither of the two other arguments contrasts in an especially interesting way with enactivist accounts of perception, we concentrate here on the two arguments that are presented in detail in the main body of the chapter.

10 Note that these considerations do not show all forms of relativism to be false. One might bite the bullet and accept the problematic contradiction as true. Perhaps less toxically one might also just accept the unappetizing conclusion (for strong enough forms of relativism) that error itself is simply impossible. This being said, carefully articulated forms of relativism do admit the possibility of people being mistaken. And a carefully articulated phenomenalism might be able to succeed here as well. The classic modern discussion of these issues is in Wright, Crispin. *Truth and Objectivity*. Cambridge, MA: Harvard University Press, 1992.

11 For a further discussion of this proposal, see (*Sense* 81).

12 Noë, Alva. *Action in Perception*. Cambridge, MA: MIT Press, 2004. 168; hereafter cited in text as *Action*.

13 See Seager, William. *Theories of Consciousness*. London: Routledge, 1999. 114.

14 The phenomenalist can avoid this problem by assuming that the sense data presented to the eye of the mind does have a focal point. But then we must ask whether the eye of the mind (here viewing the focused sense data) itself selects focal points. If it does, then we have the erroneous snapshot conception of vision: looking at objects in the world would really be like the eye of the mind focusing on pictures that are already focused.

15 See Heidegger, Martin. *Being and Time: A Translation of* Sein Und Zeit. Trans. Joan Stambaugh. New York: SUNY University Press, 1996; hereafter cited in text as *Being*.

16 Berkeley, George. *Principles of Human Knowledge and Three Dialogues Between Hylas and Philonous*. London: Penguin Classics, 2004.

17 See Wikipedia. "Metamerism." 25 Mar. 2008 <http://en.wikipedia.org/wiki/Metamerism_%28color%29>.

18 See Stone, M. David. *P.C. Magazine*, "Color Matching—Metamerism and Metameric Pairs." 25 Mar. 2008 <http://www.pcmag.com/article2/0,1895,1807992,00.asp>.

19 Metamerism is much easier to come by when the objects are darker colors or greyish/whitish in color. For any two objects with these kinds of colors, it is much more likely that they will exhibit metamerism in a wider variety of lighting situations. According to Noë, metamerism is in fact so ubiquitous that if one picks an arbitrary object with a given surface spectral reflectance (SSR) there will be an indefinite number of distinct objects that are of the same color but which have different SSRs. In part, the disconnection between SSR and the colors we perceive results from the fact that humans have three different types of cones in their eyes. Short, medium, and long wavelength cones are differentiated

by their propensity to activate when impinged upon by different wavelengths of light at the same intensity. But the long wavelength cone will fire at the same frequency if impinged upon by a long wavelength or medium wavelength of a higher intensity. This is the main reason that objects with such different SSRs can produce the same inputs to the nervous system. See *Action* (151–52).

20 See especially, Color Cube. "Chromatic Adaption." 15 Mar. 2008 <http://www.colorcube.com/illusions/chrmadptb.htm>.

21 These technical problems in the visual arts were first clearly discussed in 1856 in Ruskin, John. *The Elements of Drawing*. New York: Dover, 1971.

22 For a definition, see Factmonster. "Angry Fruit Salad." 16 Jan. 2008 <http://www.factmonster.com/computers/jargon/A/angry-fruit-salad.html>.

23 The famous and hugely influential psychologist James Gibson first introduced the helpful notion of *affordances*, which are facets of a creature's real-world environment that provide the relevant opportunities for action (Gibson, James. *The Ecological Approach to Visual Perception*. Hillsdale; Lawrence Erlbaum, 1979). According to Gibson, the members of each species develop within their evolutionary niches to perceive facets of the environment that they need to use. Given the differences in their evolutionary histories, it is hardly surprising, then, that these perceptions turn out to be different for dogs, pigeons, and people. Gibson wanted to suggest that we can explain why so many incommensurable properties can be correctly perceived by members of different species without supposing that they might not inhabit a single, shared reality. They are simply focusing on different aspects of reality.

Gibson's insight, as we have described it so far, is perfectly consistent with phenomenalism. The idea of affordances becomes anti-phenomenalist only when you add his view that animals *directly perceive* the affordances. But this looks like little more than a cheat. Doesn't talk of "directly perceiving" signals about the usefulness of objects in one's environment really just represent a failure to address what we described as the empirical problem of the external world? The mere claim that we have evolved to survive in a hostile environment should surely not make redundant any attempt by psychologists, physiologists, or neuroscientists to explain how perceptual contact with that environment is achieved. But this is just what Gibson (and perhaps also Heidegger) seems to be doing. A version of this anti-Gibsonian argument is presented in Fodor, Jerry, and Z. Pylyshyn, "How Direct is Visual Perception? Some Reflections on Gibson's 'Ecological Approach'." *Cognition* 9 (1981): 139–96.

24 For this kind of account to work, it needs to be extended beyond mere visual properties to include all of the other sensory modalities. This does not seem that problematic, though. There are aural analogs to everything we've said above (including strong analogs to the visual push–pull effect and metameric pairs), and our ability to detect the location of something due to the properties of sounds we hear is not radically different from the way that we view relational and non-relational spatial properties with our eyes.

We have not discussed one problem that Noë does not face to our satisfaction. On his account factual color properties (F-properties) are also relationally determined. What makes all red things the same color is a function of our shared evolutionary heritage. But then the perspectival P-properties (e.g., the ways red looks different from different perspectives) are doubly relational. In the case of shape, Noë was able to explain how perspectival properties are external and objective by reducing the relational properties to non-relational properties of the whole system of the observer plus the non-relational factual properties in the environment. It's not clear how this can work with colors, since the factual properties are already relational.

25 See Canfield, Jack, and Mark Victor Hansen. *A 2nd Helping of Chicken*

Soup for the Soul. Deerfield Beach: Health Communications Inc., 1995. 235–36.

26 Snopes.com. "Legend in His Own Mind." 1 Aug. 2007 <http://www.snopes.com/sports/golf/innergolf.asp>. The mystery golfer's first appearance in print can be traced to Zigler, Zig. *See You at the Top*. Gretna: Pelican, 1975, where the service member is unnamed. In some motivational speaking seminars the officer was referred to as "Major James Nesmeth," but military records reveal that no one of that name served in the US military during the Vietnam War.

27 Real meditation stemming from Indian religions and philosophies is vastly harder work than Western consumers of the New Age tend to realize. In fact, on most Indian accounts, the primary purpose of the physically demanding part of yoga (the asanas) is part of and prior to the inner battle of attaining true meditation.

28 Rushall, B.S., and L.G. Lippman, "The Role of Imagery in Physical Performance." *International Journal for Sport Psychology* 29 (1997): 57–72.

29 Urban Dictionary. "Truthiness." 21 Nov. 2007 <http://www.urbandictionary.com/define.php?term=truthiness>.

30 One of the authors of this book used to show *The Matrix* to his large introductory philosophy classes and have them write papers using examples from the film to either defend or criticize phenomenalism. Of the approximately 1000 students subjected to this, well over two-thirds of them chose to defend Russellian, Kantian, or Berkeleyan phenomenalism over Austin's non-phenomoenalist position.

31 In some cases this is nearly unbearably depressing. Positive thinking has been shown to have absolutely no effect on cancer survival rates. See Harrington, Anne. *The Cure Within: A History of Mind-Body Medicine*. New York: W.W. Norton, 2008. This being said, even though the mortality outcomes are the same, those who were given intensive group therapy describe the cancer as causing less suffering. So though mind-over-matter therapy does not seem to change the relevant matter, to the extent that medicine is aimed at pain remediation for the sake of pain remediation, rather than just survival, some such therapies certainly *should* be encouraged and covered by insurance companies.

32 Simlog. "Muscle Memory." 20 Nov. 2007 <http://www.simlog.com/muscle-memory.html>.

33 Andersen, J.L., and P. Aagaard. "Myosin Heavy Chain IIX Overshoot in Human Skeletal Muscle." *Muscle Nerve* 23.7 (2000): 1095–1104. The bodybuilding community became aware of this data by reading Bryan Haycock's "Muscle Memory, Scientists May Have Unwittingly Discovered Its Mystery." 20 Nov. 2007 <http://www.thinkmuscle.com/articles/haycock/muscle-memory.htm>.

34 This is a major theme in Dennett's fascinating *Consciousness Explained*. New York: Back Bay Books, 1991.

35 See Clark, Andy. *Being There: Putting Brain, Body, World Together Again*. Boston: MIT Press, 1997, and Clark, Andy, and David Chalmers. "The Extended Mind." *Analysis* 58 (1998): 10–23.

36 Kohler, I. "The Formation and Transformation of the Perceptual World." *Psychological Issues* 3.4 (1964): 1–173.

37 An anonymous referee notes that Insomniac Games' *Resistance: Fall of Man* contains a neat unlockable mini-game in which the previous level is presented with the screen reversed. But since the controller still works the same way in this part of the game, the entire visual interface has not been truly reversed, so the player doesn't even get to what we have described as the "hilarity" stage.

38 Suzuki, D.Z. *Mysticism: Christian and Buddhist*. London: The Buddhist Society, 2002; Hanh, Thich Nhat. *Living Buddha, Living Christ*. New York: Riverhead Books, 1995.

3 "Realistic Blood and Gore": Do Violent Games Make Violent Gamers? (First-Person Shooters)

1   See Barton, Carlin. *The Sorrows of the Ancient Romans*. Princeton: Princeton University Press, 1993.

2   See the information made available at US Bureau of Justice Statistics. "Criminal Offender Statistics." 11 Dec. 2007 http://www.ojp.usdoj.gov/bjs/crimoff.htm.

3   While some might argue that this is merely "prior restraint," and not censorship, it is essential to note that the code was generated under threat of having one (with criminal penalties attached) externally imposed upon the industry by the United States government. "Prior restraint" that is caused by justifiable fear of being fined and imprisoned is a form of censorship. As a result of the ESRB ratings system, many games that would have been made have not been.
    Depressingly, in this context, even the threat of clearly unconstitutional legislation is enough to change behavior. When laws censoring games pass, the game industry must spend obscene amounts of money getting them overturned in courts (see Ars Technica. "Judge Rules Against Video Gaming Law." 2 Apr. 2008 http://arstechnica.com/news.ars/post/20060825-7597.html). If it is cheaper for the industry to bow to the would-be censors than to fight unconstitutional legislation in court, then the attempt to censor has been successful.

4   There have been other moral panics about video games. Exidy's *Death Race* and Mystique's *Custer's Revenge* led to organized protests in the late 1970s and early 1980s. However, there was nothing on the order of congressional hearings, threats of legislation, and a film-style ratings system.

5   From the following discussion, it should be clear that the concern with violence is separable from Plato's broader metaphysics and his epistemological critique of all representational art in Book IX of the *Republic*.

6   On the other hand, one of Plato's most distinctive and famous philosophical opinions was that moral virtue is really just a species of *knowledge*. See Plato. "Meno." in *Five Dialogues*. ed. G.M.A. Grube. Indianapolis: Hackett, 2002. 78. Given that depictions of violence in art do, after all, show us features of reality that we seldom otherwise get to see, it is perhaps just barely conceivable that Plato might have had a more permissive view of FPS games than the ESRB appears to. The closest that Plato ever comes to addressing this issue directly is in Book Four of the *Republic*, when he has Socrates tell the story of a character named Leontias who, having glimpsed the corpses of some executed enemies of his city, could not stop himself from going over to look at them from close up, addressing his own eyes as he did so with the words "Look for yourselves, you evil wretches, take your fill of this beautiful sight" (*Republic* 115). It is hard to tell from the context whether Plato intends to be offering a criticism of Leontias' voyeurism or a qualified endorsement of his intellectual curiosity.

7   Aristotle. *Poetics*. Trans. Kenneth A. Telford. South Bend: Gateway Editions, Ltd. 11; hereafter cited in text as *Poetics*.

8   A useful survey of various attempts that have been made by Aristotle's interpreters to explain the phrase in terms of modern psychology is provided in Sparshott, Francis. "The Riddle of *Katharsis*," in *Centre and Labyrinth: Essays in Honour of Northrop Frye*. Ed. Eleanor Cook. Toronto: University of Toronto Press, 1993. 14–37. Sparshott himself is refreshingly skeptical about the whole endeavor.

9   The *locus classicus* of this view in aesthetics is Immanuel Kant's *Critique of Judgement*. Trans. J.H. Bernard. New York: Hafner Press, 1951.

10   In conversation, Emily Beck Cogburn stressed this analogy as well as the interesting manner in which it ties to Kant's views about the importance of detach-

ment in aesthetics. The fact that novel readers need to render the landscape in their own minds implies that there is a sense in which readers of novels are stereotypically less passively enthralled (and hence more "disinterested" in the aesthetically relevant sense) than watchers of films.

11   A fascinating recent study that seems highly relevant in the present context has shown that both levels of testosterone and aggressive behavior spike upward in adult males when they are given the opportunity to handle a gun. See Klinesmith, Jennifer, Tim Kasser, and Francis T. McAndrew. "Guns, Testosterone and Aggression: An Experimental Test of a Mediational Hypothesis." *Psychological Science* 17 (2006): 568–71.

12   Anderson, Craig A. "Violent Video Games: Myths, Facts, and Unanswered Questions." *Psychological Science Agenda* 16 (2003) (also available at: http://www.apa.org/science/psa/sb-anderson.html).

13   See the data reported in Gentile, Douglas. *Media Violence and Children.* Westport: Praeger, 2003.

14   See Mathiak, Klaus, and René Weber. "Toward Brain Correlates of Natural Behavior: fMRI during Violent Video Games." *Human Brain Mapping* 26 (2006): 948–56. This provocative data was brought to the attention of the wider gaming community in Baily, Ronald. "Video Violence = Real Violence? Bomb, blast, and strafe in peace." http://www.reason.com/news/show/34982.html (accessed 21 Jan. 2008).

15   Raine, Adriane, Todd Lencz, Susan Bihrle, Lori LaCasse, and Patrick Colletti. "Reduced Prefrontal Gray Matter Volume and Reduced Autonomic Activity in Antisocial Personality Disorder." 25 Jan. 2008 http://archpsyc.ama-assn.org/cgi/reprint/57/2/119.

16   See U.S. Department of Justice, Bureau of Justice Statistics. "Since 1994, violent crime rates have declined, reaching the lowest level ever in 2005." 2 Apr. 2008 http://www.ojp.usdoj.gov/bjs/glance/viort.htm.

17   For example, in an otherwise excellent article, video game historian and theorist Mark J.P. Wolf writes, "A major study conducted by Craig A. Anderson and Karen E. Dill and featured in the *Journal of Personality and Social Psychology* found that 'violent video game play was positively related to aggressive behavior and delinquency,' and that 'exposure to a graphically violent video game increased aggressive thoughts and behavior.' " Mark J.P. Wolf. "Morals, Ethics, and Video Games." in *The Video Game Explosion: A History from PONG to Playstation and Beyond.* ed. Mark J.P. Wolf. Westport: Greenwood, 2008. 283–91.

18   Anderson, Craig A., and Karen E. Dill. "Video Games and Aggressive Thoughts, Feelings and Behavior in the Laboratory and in Life." *Journal of Personality and Social Psychology* 78 (2000): 777. Hereafter cited in text as *Aggressive.* The only evidence Anderson and Dill present that concerns long-term behavioral dispositions of this group is the students' grade point averages, and their research shows that playing of violent video games by college students makes no statistical difference to grade point average. Given the plausible supposition that delinquent behavior is inversely correlated with grade point average, this should give anyone pause about concluding too much about the supposed correlation between video gaming and aggression.

19   On obesity, see Dietz, W.H. "Television, Obesity, and Eating Disorders." *Adolescent Medicine: State of the Art Reviews* 4 (1993): 543–9. On school performance, see Morgan, M. "Television and School Performance." *Adolescent Medicine: State of the Art Reviews* 4 (1993): 607–22. On autism, see Aldman, Michael, Sean Nicholson, and Nodir Adilov. "Does Television Cause Autism?" 10 Dec. 2007 http://www.johnson.cornell.edu/faculty/profiles/Waldman/AUTISM-WALDMAN-NICHOLSON-ADILOV.pdf. Note that this is a

distinct issue from the possible overdiagnosis of autism, which many have suggested is at best the result of a radical change in the understanding of that condition. For *whatever* it is that is being diagnosed, whether it is truly autism or some more esoteric syndrome, is almost certainly being caused in part by excessive exposure to television.

20 Hume, David. *A Treatise of Human Nature*. London: Penguin, 1969. 521.

21 Anderson, Craig A. "Effects of Violent Video Games on Aggressive Behavior, Aggressive Cognition, Aggressive Affect, Physiological Arousal and Prosocial Behavior: A Meta-Analytic Review of the Scientific Literature." *Psychological Science* 12.5 (2001): 359.

22 Mill, John Stuart. *On Liberty*, in *On Liberty and Other Essays*. ed. John Gray. Oxford: Oxford University Press, 1991. 66; hereafter cited in text as *Liberty*. In light of these remarks, it is interesting to again consider the research that shows greater frontal lobe activity among players of violent video games. Given the role of the frontal lobes in rational planning, this at least suggests that, while FPS games might well make people more disposed toward minor aggression during bouts of play, these games might also contribute to the development of their abilities as active planners and choosers on something like the Millean model. See the discussion of strange patients with left pre-frontal lobe damage in Antonio Damasio. *Descartes' Error*. New York: HarperCollins, 1995.

23 Orwell, George. *1984*. New York: Penguin, 1961 and Huxley, Aldous. *Brave New World*. New York: Harper and Brothers, 1931.

24 See Niburg, Amy Kiste. *Seal of Approval, The History of the Comics Code*. Jackson: UPM, 1998. For a recent account covering the broader cultural import of comic books, see Hajdu, David. *The Ten Cent Plague: The Great Comic-Book Scare and How it Changed America*. New York: Farrar, Straus and Giroux, 2008. Anyone attuned to the contemporary moral panic over video games will get an uneasy sense of *deja vu* from reading the in-1954 massively influential Wertham, Frederic. *Seduction of the Innocent*. New York: Ameron Ltd., 1996.

25 Larry Flynt's supreme court victory in 1981 (which concerned a satirical comic in *Hustler* magazine) as well as the legal victories of producers of pornographic comics such as *Cherry Poptart* in the 1980s paved the way for wide distribution of non-pornographic comic books that could again appeal to adults. In particular, the legal defeat of the code by pornographers made possible the mid-1980s birth of the graphic novels in D.C.'s *Vertigo* series, highlighting such artists as Neil Gaiman and Alan Moore; their success then paved the way for the "Generation X" experimental and confessional writers such as Peter Bagge, Daniel Clowes, and Joe Mutt. Given the manifest and overwhelming artistic merits of many contemporary comic books and graphic novels, the 30-year dry spell (in addition to all of the lives destroyed) surely shows the overwhelming dangers of censorship.

26 For example, the initial release of *Grand Theft Auto: San Andreas* contained an Easter egg (hidden features in games that must be unlocked with some special code or pattern of behavior that would not occur to a player in the normal course of game-play) with an explicit sex scene (See Bray, Hiawatha. "Sex scene stirs up a fuss over Grand Theft Auto." *The Boston Globe*. 15 May 2008 http://www.boston.com/news/globe/living/articles/2005/07/09/sex_scene_stirs_up_a_fuss_over_grand_theft_auto/?page=1). When gamers discovered the Easter egg, the public outcry was furious, much louder than that occasioned by the nihilistic, graphic violence of the game itself. In newer releases and patched versions, the Easter egg is gone, but players of this vastly popular game can still watch their avatars shoot prostitutes in the head or beat them to death.

27 Hebert, Bob. *New York Times*, "Clueless in America." 22 Apr. 2008 http://www.nytimes.com/2008/04/22/opinion/22herbert.html?_r=1&ref=opinion &oref=slogin.

28 Representatives of the United States military at one point reportedly begged the show's producers to stop glorifying the torture of prisoners. See *Democracy Now!* "Is Torture on the Hit Fox TV Show '24' Encouraging Soldiers to Abuse Detainees?" 15 May 2008 http://www.democracynow.org/2007/2/22/ is_torture_on_hit_fox_tv.

29 In the first four years of the war on terror, more foreign detainees died in United States custody than the total number of American soldiers who died in North Vietnamese captivity during the entire Vietnam War.

30 Popescu, George. "Women in Video Games. From Barbie to Xena." in *Gender and the (Post) East/West Divide*. Eds. Mihaela Frunză and Theodora Eliza Văcărescu. 3 Apr. 2008 http://www.iiav.nl/epublications/2005/gendeRomania. pdf; hereafter, referred to in text as *Gender*.

31 Clover, Carol. *Men, Women and Chainsaws: Gender in the Modern Horror Film*. Princeton: Princeton University Press, 1992.

32 However, one must interpret the relevant form of "identification" to make this a plausible claim; the thesis still doesn't work for European horror films, where the initial killer is often female. See Totaro, Donato. *Offscreen*. "The Final Girl: A Few Thoughts on Feminism and Horror." 6 Aug. 2008 http://www.horschamp.qc.ca/new_offscreen/final_girl.html.

33 Such applications of Freudianism have lost their grip on the imaginations on the overwhelming majority of philosophers (and psychologists) ever since the publication of Grünbaum, Adolf. *The Foundations of Psychoanalysis: A Philosophical Critique*. Berkeley: University of California Press, 1985. Thus it is arguably more charitable to present Clover's argument as not resting on such weirdness.

34 For an analysis of the role of imagined violence that generates conclusions startlingly incompatible to those reached by Clover, see Jones, Gerard. *Killing Monsters: Why Children Need Fantasy, Super Heroes and Make Believe Violence*. New York: Basic Books, 2002.

35 In connection with this issue, see the discussion of cyberfeminism in Tsaliki, Liza. "Women and New Technologies." in *The Routledge Companion to Feminism and Postfeminism*. ed. Sarah Gamble. London: Routledge, 2001. 80–92.

36 This point is made forcefully in Coplan, Amy. "Feminist Final Girls: Why Horror Heroines are Real Women and Not Just 'Dicks in Drag.'" under review.

37 The contemporary debate about the portrayal of female avatars is extensively discussed by Kennedy, Helen, in "Lara Croft: Feminist Icon or Cyberbimbo? On the Limits of Textual Analysis." *Game Studies*. 6 Apr. 2008 http://www.gamestudies.org/0202/kennedy/.

38 See Thornham, Sue. "Second Wave Feminism." in *Feminism and Postfeminism*. ed. Sarah Gamble. London: Routledge, 1998. 29–42.

39 There is some evidence for this presented in Fisher, Helen. *Why We Love: The Nature and Chemistry of Romantic Love*. New York: Holt Paperbacks, 2004. Perhaps her most interesting example is the fact that the regions of the brain that process visual stimuli tend to be more active when men look at photos of their spouses than when women look at photos of theirs.

40 For examples of these sorts of exaggerated dimorphisms from *World of Warcraft*, see Rubenstein, Andrea. "Idealizing Fantasy Bodies." *Iris Gaming Network*. 10 May 2008 http://www.theirisnetwork.org/archives/12.

41 See Gamble, Sarah. "Postfeminism." in *Feminism and Postfeminism*. ed. Sarah Gamble. London: Routledge, 1998. 43–54.

42 Evolutionary biology and cognitive science conclusively refute blanket

assertions about the cultural contingency of beauty norms. There is overwhelming convergence by people from different ethnicities in judgments of relative beauty among women. These judgments have repeatedly been shown to track features relevant to selective fitness such as facial symmetry and waist-to-hip ratio. Moreover, these preferences positively correlate with how likely infants are to initially respond positively to adult women. See Etcoff, Nancy. *Survival of the Prettiest*. Norwell: Anchor, 2000. The proper role of such appeals to biology is a very difficult matter, though. Hume's warnings about the fallacy of deriving an "ought" from an "is" are especially important here: if all people have certain innate dispositions to nastiness (in their judgments of physical beauty or anywhere else), this does not mean that it is morally permissible to be nasty. On the other hand, another bit of philosophical common sense is that one can reasonably be thought to have an obligation only to the extent that one is capable (at least in principle) of fulfilling that obligation.

43   See Sartre, Jean-Paul. *Being and Nothingness*. Trans. Hazel E. Barnes. New York: Simon and Schuster, 1956.

44   Dadlez, E.M. *What's Hecuba to Him?: Fictional Events and Actual Emotions*. University Park: The Pennsylvania State University Press, 1997. 137.

45   See reference from note 42.

46   To see the potential danger of video games in this connection, note that when almost all commercial rap music began to ape the violently psychopathic misogyny and thuggery (as well as production techniques) of founding NWA member Dr. Dre's *The Chronic*, the alarmists who initially decried NWA's music suddenly seemed to have a point.

47   Feuerstein, Georg. *The Yoga-Sutra of Patañjali: A New Translation and Commentary*. Rochester: Inner Traditions, 1979. 7.

48   Boeringer, S.B. "Associations of Rape-Supportive Attitudes with Fraternal and Athletic Participation." *Violence Against Women* 5 (1999): 81–90.

49   Frintner, M.P., and L. Rubinson. "Acquaintance Rape: The Influence of Alcohol, Fraternity Membership, and Sports Team Membership." *Journal of Sex Education & Therapy* 19 (1993): 272–84.

50   See Aristotle. *Nicomachean Ethics*. Trans. Sir David Ross. Oxford: Oxford University Press, 1998. 36; hereafter cited in text as *Ethics*.

51   See Venkatesh, Sudhir. "Unjustifiable Carnage, Uneasy Alliances, and Lots of Self-Doubt: What *Grand Theft Auto IV* gets right about gangland and illegal economies," *Slate*. 11 May 2008 http://www.slate.com/id/2191012/.

4 Games and God's Goodness (World-Builder and Tycoon Games)

1   The real-world environments that allowed a Stalin or Mao to exercise power have not yet been replicated in these games with any success. Both Stalin and Mao constantly had to present themselves as moderates tilting the balance between two irreconcilable factions. Simple decision theory explains this fact of dictatorship. If a corporation is owned by three people, two with 40% of the stock each and one with 20%, the person with 20% is just as powerful as the other two. For each person must get one other person to vote with her in order to win any votes. So successful dictators must always create strife between two sides and then exert power by decisively acting in favor of one of them. See Montefiore, Simon. *Stalin: The Court of the Red Tsar*. New York: Vintage, 2005; Short, Phillip. *Mao: A Biography*. New York: Henry Holt, 1999.

2   Our task is slightly complicated by the fact that god games are always at least duotheist; considered solely in relation to the diegetic realm in question, *both* the player/avatar *and* the game's designers have certain characteristics traditionally associated with God. When we include games such as Left Behind

Games' *Left Behind: Eternal Forces* that purport to accurately portray the Christian God of the nondiegetic realm, we have, in effect, the *tritheism* of player/avatar, designer, and deity. Fortunately, no unclarity results just as long as one is clear about which of the three Gods is being referred to any given context.

3 Publishing rights for the game series were purchased by Take-Two from Atari in 2004.

4 The Creative Assembly designed the games. Electronic Arts published *Shogun: Total War* (2000), Activision published *Medieval Total War* (2002) and *Rome Total War* (2004), and Sega published *Medieval Total War II* (2006).

5 A clear and very helpful discussion of the relationships amongst these three properties may be found in Hartshorne, Charles. *Omnipotence and Other Theological Mistakes*. New York: State University of New York Press, 1984.

6 Cogburn, J. "Paradox Lost." *Canadian Journal of Philosophy* 34 (2004): 195–216.

7 The first rigorous western discussion of this issue is to be found in Boethius. *The Consolation of Philosophy*, Trans. Victor Watts. New York: Penguin, 1969. Boethius argues that God is an eternal being, in the sense that he (somehow or other) exists outside of time. Boethius thought that if one conceived of God in this way, one could believe both that God infallibly knows the future (which would be perceived by him as a sort of "eternal present") and that human beings have free will. This view was more recently popularized in Lewis, C.S. *Mere Christianity*. New York: Macmillan, 1952, and is viewed by many Christians as the part of the most orthodox solution to the philosophical problem of free will.

8 There are, of course, more sensible-sounding answers available within the Christian theological tradition. To get an overview of the Gospels informed by scholarship, see Mack, Burton. *Who Wrote the New Testament? The Making of the Christian Myth*. New York: HarperOne, 1996; Funk, Robert. *The Five Gospels: What Did Jesus Really Say? The Search for the Authentic Word of Jesus*. New York: HarperOne, 1996; The Jesus Seminar. *The Gospel of Jesus*. Santa Rosa: Polebridge Press, 1999.

9 Hill, Jim, and Rand Cheadle. *The Bible Tells Me So: Uses and Abuses of Holy Scripture*. New York: Doubleday, 1996.

10 We use the Bible merely because the authors' religious background gives them vastly greater familiarity with it. The issue confronts all religions with canonical texts. For some entertaining evidence that all scripture is problematic in these ways, see the controversial and lively discussions of the various texts in Hitchens, Christopher. *God is Not Great: How Religion Poisons Everything*. New York: Hachette, 2007.

11 It is worth noting, however, that nonfundamentalist Christian theologians should (and most would) regard the Projection Argument as perfectly sound. Within the Roman Catholic tradition, for example, it is often taught that the Bible's authority cannot be invoked independently of the tradition of orthodox interpretation that has evolved over the continuing history of the Church. Of course, this theological approach really just postpones the problem, since all of the issues that we have already raised here about the difficulty of interpreting the text itself will be bound to arise when it comes to interpreting the unclear and contradictory pronouncements of the Church itself. In fairness though, the Roman Catholic tradition involves a great deal of philosophical debate and welcomes far more diversity of doctrine than most non-Catholics or Catholic lay people realize.

12 "So God said to Noah. . . . You are to bring into the ark two of all living

creatures, male and female, to keep them alive with you. Two of every kind of bird, of every kind of animal and every kind of creature that moves along the ground will come to you to be kept alive.' " (*Genesis* 6) Compare this to "The Lord then said to Noah, 'Take with you seven of every kind of clean animal, a male and its mate, and two of every kind of unclean animal, a male and its mate, and also seven of every kind of bird, male and female, to keep the various kinds alive throughout the earth.' " (*Genesis* 7).

13   See *Exodus* 20–34; *Deuteronomy* 1–10, which disagree on the builder of the ark, where Moses carried the covenant and who created the second set of tablets.

14   See *Matthew* 26, *Mark* 14, *Luke* 7, and *John* 12, which disagree on when in the ministry the anointment took place, who owned the house, who anointed Jesus, how Jesus was anointed, and who objected.

15   See *Matthew* 28, *Mark* 16, *Luke* 24, and *John* 20, which disagree on whether there was an earthquake, who saw Jesus, and who was at the tomb.

16   In this context it is important to note that we have not even mentioned the empirical evidence against certain key stories in the Bible. The Egyptians and Romans kept records and it is barely conceivable that there would be no mention of all three "slaughters of the innocents." Also, the fact that some of the Gospels get the geography in and around Judea desperately wrong is evidence that they were written long after the Diaspora caused by the crushing Roman victory in the Judean War. We don't discuss such examples in the main body of the text because even though no rational, informed person would continue to hold the Bible true in these regards, it is still in some very, very weak sense *possible* that the scientific method has completely failed us (perhaps due to a Cartesian "evil demon" hypothesis being true). It is not even *possible* that an empirical contradiction, of the sort the Bible is littered with, could be true.

17   There are, of course, many other video games that have been developed by Christians, some of which can be interpreted fruitfully from a wider Christian perspective. Perhaps the best examples of this are the vastly more successful and theologically suggestive games *Myst* and *Riven*, the designers of which, Rand and Robyn Miller, are both Christians.

18   Plato. *Euthyphro*, in *Five Dialogues*. Trans. G.M.A. Grube. Indianapolis: Hackett Publishing Company Inc., 1981. 15–16.

19   It would be unfair not to remark at this point that a number of philosophers sympathetic to Divine Command theory have been sensitive to this accusation and have tried to respond to it in a principled, nonarbitrary way. Most plausible variants follow Thomas Aquinas in arguing that there is something in the nature of God such that he *could* not, for example, command wanton cruelty. It is questionable, though, whether the resulting theory really should be called "Divine Command theory." Rather, when worked out, such views present God as playing a different metaethical role. For example, say that God is by necessity Love. Then an act is right because someone is in the right relationship with God, which would consist merely in being genuinely loving. On this view, rightness and wrongness are metaphysically dependent upon God, but the issuance of commands by God—and therefore, arguably, religious belief itself, since one could have the right relationship with God without cognitive awareness of God's nature or existence—are metaphysically superfluous. One might argue that they are not epistemically superfluous, but then one must face the problems that we described in the previous section of this chapter. For a discussion of different variants of the theory, see Austin, Michael. "Divine command theory." Internet Encyclopedia of Philosophy. 21 March 2008 http://www.iep.utm.edu/d/divine-c.htm#SH4c.

20 Dostoyevsky, Fyodor. *The Brothers Karamazov*. Trans. David Magarshack. London: Penguin Books, 1958. 743.

21 Mill, John Stuart. *Utilitarianism*. Indianapolis: Hackett, 1979. 7.

22 For the relevant debates, see Greenberg, Karen, ed. *The Torture Debate in America*. Cambridge: Cambridge University Press, 2005.

23 Kant, Immanuel. *Foundations of the Metaphysics of Morals*, Trans. Lewis White Beck. New York: Bobbs Merrill, 1959. 39; hereafter cited in text as *Foundations*.

24 Some other nonreligious ethical theories that enjoy popular currency and are taught in many college philosophy and professional ethics courses include Virtue Theory, Particularism, Contractarianism, and Relativism. All of these views have been defended by major philosophers; for a much more detailed introduction to these topics, see Shafer-Landau, Russ, ed. *Ethical Theory: An Anthology*. Oxford: Wiley-Blackwell, 2007.

25 Rousseau, Jean-Jacques. *On The Social Contract*, in *The Basic Political Writings*. Trans. Donald A. Cress. Indianapolis: Hackett Publishing Company, 1988. 143–4.

26 Roberts, Wess. *Leadership Secrets of Attila the Hun*. New York: Warner Books, 1990.

27 These sorts of self-serious, intellectually pretentious books on "leadership" in business are satirized with wonderful precision in the unjustly neglected Kersten, E.L. *The Art of Demotivation—Manager's Edition: Transforming Your Least Valuable Asset—Your Employees*. Austin: Despair, Inc., 2005.

28 Successful military occupations have always involved some combination of three factors: (1) genocidal levels of killing at the outset, (2) collective reprisals, and (3) siding heavily with one indigenous ethnic group against another. One rarely hears about this aspect of the Allied occupation of Europe after World War II, since many popular historical treatments systematically ignore the strategic bombing of Japan and Germany, the forced relocation of millions of ethnic Germans following defeat, the multiyear famine, and half a century's depredations of Soviet occupation. See McDonogh, Giles. *After the Reich: The Brutal History of the Allied Occupation*. New York: Basic Books, 2007. Given the inevitably atrocious cost of empire, when is it worthwhile to interfere violently in another polity?

   By any rational measure, the people of Spain and Russia should have sided with the Napoleonic armies and against the nobles and priests who had reduced them to humiliating vassalage punctuated by starvation. But instead they followed their home-grown despots and killed those attempting to gift them with the Napoleonic Code, the adoption of which would almost certainly have vastly improved the lives of Spanish and Russian people right up to the present day. Led by the very priests and aristocrats who degraded and oppressed them, the peasants of Spain created a festering sore that began the undoing of Napoleon's ambitions, and the peasants of Russia finished the process. (See Broers, Michael. *Europe Under Napoleon: 1799–1815*. New York: Hodder Arnold, 1988; Asprey, Robert. *The Reign of Napoleon Bonaparte*. New York: Basic Books, 2002.) Had Napoleon managed to get his armies to uniformly adopt the three aforementioned policies of occupation, history might have turned out quite differently. But would it have been worth it? Or would this be a case of "burning the village in order to save it," as a tragic-faced American GI remarked to CBS reporter Morley Safer in August, 1965, just prior to using his Zippo lighter to burn down a thatch home, rendering a Vietnamese family utterly destitute in the process?

   Broadly Kantian ethical considerations strongly support a constitutional government such as that guaranteed by the Napoleonic Code. But at the same time, the Kantian would surely have rigidly principled reasons for disapproving of Napoleon's drive to conquer politically autonomous foreign nations. Similarly, some utilitarian considerations strongly support the defeat of the indigenous oppressors of nineteenth-century Russia and Spain. But, given the cost of empire, a pessimistically minded advocate of the Greatest Happiness Principle might have ended up preferring to leave the people of these countries alone in their ignorant, persecuted misery.

5 The Metaphysics of Interactive Art (Puzzle and Adventure Games)

1   This ambiguity is to some extent resolved at the end of the lovely game *Riven*, the second, more linear game in the *Myst* series, when the player floats off into the "starry void" after finishing his dealings with Atrus and Gehn. For a more extended discussion of the philosophical implications of this scene, see Chapter Seven.
2   Moore, G.E. *Principia Ethica*. Mineola: Dover Publications Inc., 2004; hereafter cited in text as *Principia*.
3   See Gendler, Tamar Szabo, and John Hawthorne, eds. *Conceivability and Possibility*. Oxford: Oxford University Press, 2002.
4   Of course, there are also contemporary defenders of this strongly relativistic thesis about responses to works of art. Perhaps the most famous such argument can be found in Sontag, Susan. *Against Interpretation and other Essays*. New York: Picador USA, 2001.
5   Wimsatt, W.K., Jr., and Monroe C. Beardsley. "The Affective Fallacy" in *The Verbal Icon*. Lexington: University of Kentucky Press, 1954. 21; hereafter cited in text as *Verbal*.
6   Hume, David. "Of the Standard of Taste." *Of the Standard of Taste and Other Essays*. New York: Bobbs–Merrill, 1965. 7; hereafter cited in text as *Standard*.
7   This sort of convergence of opinion alone can't *guarantee* objectivity, for a culture could very well converge on false judgments. Rather, in a *healthy* culture such convergence helps us to focus on the properties that determine positive aesthetic value. As long as the health of a culture can be characterized independently of the aesthetic judgments made by people in the culture there is no circularity here. However, to be fair, this is an extraordinarily difficult philosophical issue, and the view suggested here is controversial.
8   Fish, Stanley. "Interpreting the Variorum." *Is There a Text in This Class: The Authority of Interpretive Communities*. Cambridge, MA: Harvard University Press, 1980. 173.
9   Our eventual concessions to neo-Humeanism in the present chapter do not presuppose the plausibility of this rather radical-sounding pronouncement about the nature of "meaning" in general. For a clear and convincing refutation of positions like Fish's see Searle, John. "Literary Theory and its Discontents." *New Literary History* 25 (1994): 637–67.
10   Of course, one might avoid holding that interpretations individuate separate artworks by holding that the artworks just have inconsistent properties (Cooke, Brandon. "Art Critical Contradictions." under review, argues for such a position about deep interpretative disagreements concerning artworks). This view is called "dialetheism." For an argument about how such a view might preserve our intuitions concerning moral objectivity, see Cogburn, Jon. "The Philosophical Basis of What? The Anti-Realist Case for Dialetheism." *The Law of Non-Contradiction*. Eds. Priest, Graham, J.C. Beall, and Bradley Armour-Garb. Oxford: Oxford University Press, 2004.
11   Silcox, Mark, and Jon Cogburn. "Computability Theory and Literary Competence." *The British Journal of Aesthetics* 46 (2006): 369–86.

12 See especially "xTuring Machine Lab: Introduction to Turing Machines." 15 May 2008 http://math.hws.edu/TMCM/java/labs/xTuringMachineLab. html, which also contains a very nice discussion of how Turing machines work. Also see The Alan Turing Internet Scrapbook, "Turing Machines Implemented in JavaScript." 15 May 2008 http://www.turing.org.uk/turing/scrapbook/ tmjava.html, which is easy to use.

13 Our account of a Turing machine here varies in a couple of (trivial) ways from the description originally offered by Alan Turing himself. For the original, see Alan Turing, "On Computable Numbers, with an Application to the Entscheidungsproblem." *Proceedings of the London Mathematical Society* 42 (1936–37): 230–65. For an accessible account of Turing's work and its historical and philosophical genesis, see Davis, Martin. *The Universal Computer: The Road from Leibniz to Turing*. New York: W.W. Norton, 2000.

14 See the relevant discussion in Smith, Peter. *An Introduction to Gödel's Theorems*. Cambridge: Cambridge University Press, 2007.

15 Note that for more than one-place Turing machine programs such an algorithm would end up treating all places after the first place in the function as zero. For example, if we fed the Halting program the number corresponding to the addition function (not just of positive numbers as our Program 2 does, but also including zero) and five, it would determine that the program does halt for five and zero, since we did not put anything in for the second place in the function. The problem can be posed, and also proved unsolvable in the same manner, without this restriction.

16 For the mathematically-ambitious reader, here's a quick breakdown of how such a "diagonalization" argument works. If there is a halting program, then it is one of the programs enumerated in the enumeration corresponding to the Universal Turing Machine program. But then you can make a two-dimensional grid where the rows correspond to each different one-place Turing machine program (these are programs that compute one-place functions such as "plus three") in the universal enumeration and the columns correspond to inputs. From Turing's proof, one can show that if there is a halting program, one can fill the grid such that place m, n in the grid contains a 1 if machine m (in our enumeration corresponding to the universal Turing machine) halts for input n, and 0 if it does not. Now travel down the diagonal of our grid, defining a new function. For input n, return 1 if the diagonal value for n (the value of Turing machine number n for input n) is 0, return 0 if it is 1. This diagonal function will not be in our chart, because it is different from every function in the chart at the diagonal. But again, if there is a halting program, the function is Turingmachine executable. Call this function d. Now from d one can define a Turing machine program that agrees with d on everything d halts on (it returns 1 in every case) but that instead of halting on 0 goes into a loop where the tape head moves to the right indefinitely. But wait, this new program is not on the initial enumerated list of one-place Turing machine programs from the universal Turing machine! The new program differs in its halting behavior from every program in that initial list. But this is a contradiction, since the initial list contains every one-place Turing machine program. Therefore, by *reductio ad absurdum*, there is no such function, and the faulty assumption is that there exists a halting machine program.

17 Such a game need not be as boring as the one described earlier. For more colorful and potentially entertaining examples, see Stephenson, Neil. *The Diamond Age*. New York: Spectra, 2000 in which a computer programmer builds a series of interactive games to teach his daughter about the basic limitation theorems of computability theory.

18 For a more detailed version of this argument, see Cogburn, Jon, and Mark

Silcox. "Computing Machinery and Emergence: The Metaphysics and Aesthetics of Video Games" *Minds and Machines* 15 (2003). 73–89.

19   The claim that we're making here about the absence of interpretation in the appreciation of music probably does not really apply to "program" music—works, such as Stravinsky's *Rite of Spring* or Berlioz's *Symphonie Fantastique* that are written specifically to aid in the telling of stories, or to produce other nonmusical images or ideas in the mind of the listener.

6 Artificial and Human Intelligence (Single-Player RPGs)

1   Some terminology: when people refer to "traditional RPGs" they intend to either pick out the original text-based role playing games such as the earliest instantiations of *Ultima* or menu-based RPGs such as the early versions of *Final Fantasy*. With menu-based RPGs, the player selects from a finite list of possibilities and then watches the action unfold in the diegetic realm. Modern RPGs like *Oblivion* allow much greater control of the avatar's movement with a video game controller. We thank Chris Ray for explaining the history of these genres to us in terms of such interface issues.

2   For these reasons, it is no accident that game-master Steven Erikson and Ian Cameron Esslemont's fantastically articulated *D & D* game-world Malazan has yielded the most exciting set of fantasy novels to be published in years. Erikson's projected ten novel series (seven of which have been completed as of this writing) begins with Erikson, Steven. *Gardens of the Moon*. London: Bantam, 1999. The first in the overlapping series by Esslemont is Esslemont, Cameron. *Night of the Knives*. London: Bantam, 2007.

3   The hypothesis of the uncanny valley effect was first put forward by the roboticist Masahiro Mori in 1970. The scientific credibility of this theory about both robots and animated human simulacra is still the topic of heated debate. For an interesting experimental use of the hypothesis, see MacDorman, Karl F. and Hiroshi Ishiguro. "The Uncanny Advantage of Using Androids in Cognitive and Social Science Research." *Interaction Studies* 7 (2006): 297–337.

4   James, William. *Principles of Psychology Vol 1*. New York: Cosimo, 2007. 488.

5   It is debatable how radical all of this really is. Wheeler, Michael. *Reconstructing the Cognitive World*. Cambridge, MA: MIT, 2005. 2–53 (hereafter cited in text as *Reconstructing*) makes a very compelling case that Descartes argued for a recognizable precursor to the theory of mind we describe here. Of course, it still would not have happened without the development of formal logic, the digital computer, and the discoveries of the thinkers we discuss here. See Section 6.4.3.1 for a very brief history of these developments.

6   For a plethora of examples of CRUM successes in modeling diverse cognitive skills, see Thagard, Paul. *Mind: Introduction to Cognitive Science*, Second Edition. Cambridge, MA: MIT, 2005 as well as Thagard, Paul. *Mind Readings: Introductory Selections on Cognitive Science*. Cambridge, MA: MIT, 1998. For an excellent collection of essays defining, defending, and debating the intellectual foundations of artificial intelligence, see Haugeland, John. *Mind Design II: Philosophy, Psychology, and Artificial Intelligence*. Cambridge, MA: MIT, 1997.

7   When one takes a university level course in artificial intelligence, one typically learns to program logic-oriented tasks in LISP and PROLOG as well as learning-tasks in connectionist networks. In a particularly good class, students will study general architecture such as the LISP applications SOAR and ACT-R as well as famous programs, from the classic Generalized Problem Solver to more specific systems involving things like air travel, chess playing, machine language translation, statistical and rule governed information gathering from large corpora,

program checking, etc. By far the most accessible, authoritative, and comprehensive textbook is Norvig, Peter and Stuart Russell, *Artificial Intelligence: A Modern Approach*, Second Edition. New York: Prentice Hall, 2002. A fantastic and indispensable book that explains in detail (with actual working samples of code) all of the classic artificial intelligence applications is Norvig, Peter. *Paradigms in Artificial Intelligence Programming, Case Studies in Common Lisp*. New York: Morgan Kaufman, 1991. Norvig's book is also invaluable for its treatment of the logic-based programming language Prolog, which he shows how to implement in Lisp. Unfortunately, since federal money in the United States has dried up for this kind of research in favor of dumb networking and algorithm issues relevant only to speed and volume of communication capacity, artificial intelligence does not have the place in the curriculum that it deserves, and many students in the United States now get degrees in computer science without ever having studied it.

8   For further discussions, see Moor, James, ed. *The Turing Test: The Elusive Standard of Artificial Intelligence*. Dordrecht: Springer, 1989 and Stuart Schieber, ed. *The Turing Test: Verbal Behavior as the Hallmark of Intelligence*. Cambridge, MA: MIT, 2004.

9   Turing, Alan. "Computing Machinery and Intelligence," in *Mind Design II*, ed. John Haugeland. Cambridge, MA: MIT, 1997. 31.

10 This example is from Kripke's famous critique of Russell's descriptive theory of meaning in Kripke, Saul. *Naming and Necessity*. Cambridge: Cambridge University Press, 1980.

11 See *Stanford Encyclopedia of Philosophy*. "Propositions." 3 Jan. 2008 http://plato.stanford.edu/entries/propositions/ for a full discussion.

12 See Fodor, Jerry. *The Language of Thought*. Cambridge, MA: Harvard University Press, 2005; and especially *Stanford Encyclopedia of Philosophy*. "The Language of Thought." 11 June 2008 http://plato.stanford.edu/entries/language-thought/ for a full discussion.

13 One must always be very suspicious of claims about purported instances of "surprising similarity." The proper response is, "Similar compared to what?" Any two arbitrarily selected things are similar in innumerable ways, so of course all the world's languages are similar in surprising manners. In addition, extant human languages both evolved from common ancestors and must be such that human beings can communicate efficiently with them, so again, of course they are similar in interesting ways. Why this is supposed to have anything do with the language of thought or (perhaps more significantly) the structure of syntax has never been clear to the authors. For an extraordinarily accessible treatment that is sympathetic to the linguistic motivations behind the language of thought hypothesis, see Pinker, Steven. *The Language Instinct: How the Mind Creates Language*. New York: HarperCollins, 1995.

14 Fodor, Jerry. *Psychosemantics: The Problem of Meaning in the Philosophy of Mind*. Cambridge, MA: MIT, 1988. 23–4.

15 For example, the command to move the hexadecimal value 61 (97 decimal) into the processor register named "al", can be expressed in the machine code for an x86/IA-32 processor as "Binary: 10110000 01100001 (Hexadecimal: 0xb061)." This example is taken from *Wikipedia*. "Assembly Language." 3 Jan. 2008 http://en.wikipedia.org/wiki/Assembly_Language.

16 Assembly language expresses the command from the previous footnote in this manner: "mov al, #061h."

17 For a nice explanation of this revolutionary piece of software, see Wikipedia. "Maya." 25 April 2008 http://en.wikipedia.org/wiki/Maya_(software), and for the product itself see Autodesk. "Autodesk Maya." 25 April 2008 http://usa.autodesk.com/adsk/servlet/index?siteID=123112&id=7635018.

18   One can get free demos from *AllClear*, 25 April 2008 http://www.allclearonline.com/.

19   For a helpful discussion of why this possibility is inherent in all human languages, see Pinker, Steven. *The Language Instinct: How the Mind Creates Language*. New York: HarperCollins, 1995.

20   For an argument that the concept of "tacit knowledge" does not bear the explanatory weight placed upon it by Fodor and Chomsky, see Cogburn, Jon. "Inferentialism and Tacit Knowledge." *Behavior and Philosophy* 32 (2005): 503–24.

21   In subsequent decades, however, there were a number of clear successes in computational linguistics using approaches to syntax not sanctioned by Chomsky, and a general pattern of failure in work done under the rubric of Chomsky's postulated frameworks for the syntax of human languages. The unclarity and computational badness of his own transformational framework has led Chomsky to claim that he never held that generativity should be constrained by recursivity (and hence, what a computer can in principle do). Unfortunately, there is such overwhelming textual evidence against this claim that (along with others of Chomsky's own strident assertions about what he has always believed) it has come to strike many as almost pathologically sophistic. See Ney, J. A. "On Generativity: The History of a Notion that Never Was." *Historiographia Linguistica* 20 (1993): 441–54.

22   Although text adventure games like those produced by companies such as *Adventure International* and *Infocom* are no longer commercially viable, there is a large and thriving community of programmers, authors, and amateur artisans who still make these sorts of games and circulate them freely over the Internet, and the programming tools used to build them now are much more powerful and easier to use than any that were available in the 1980s. More information about this exciting underground art form and the community that supports it can be found in Grenade, Stephen. "Introducing Interactive Fiction." 19 April, 2008 http://brasslantern.org/beginners/introif.html.

23   Daniel Dennett's analysis of belief is consistent with this perspective. See Dennett, Daniel. *The Intentional Stance*. Cambridge, MA: MIT Press, 1989.

24   The influential post-Freudian analyst Jacques Lacan appears to make exactly this error in his famous remark that "the unconscious is structured like a language." See Lacan, Jacques. "The Insistence of the Letter in the Unconscious." in *Structuralism*, Ed. J. Ehrmann. Garden City, NY: Anchor Books, 1957. 103.

25   See the discussion of this phenomenon in Stich, Stephen. *From Folk Psychology to Cognitive Science, The Case Against Belief*. Cambridge, MA: MIT Press, 1985.

26   Wilson, Mark. "Predicate Meets Property." *Philosophical Review* 91 (1982): 549–89.

27   We cannot state strongly enough that this is *not* an issue for compositional semantics. Our ability to understand one another is just as stunning as the Chomskyan ability to differentiate grammatical from ungrammatical sentences, and part of the story about how it works must be along the lines first suggested by the work of the enormously influential logician (and real estate agent) Richard Montague. According to this approach, sentences are composed of phrases that are composed of words, and the compositional meanings of sentences are functions of the meanings of phrases which are a function of the meanings of words. Linguists working in the Montagovian tradition have developed truly universal theories of the inferential function of *non-referring* terms such as quantifiers (e.g., "every," "some," "more than," "six," "the"), modals (e.g., "can," "must"), productive morphological changes such as pluralization, and cross dependency (e.g., pronouns). Since Montague showed how it could be done, research into the compositional semantics of natural languages

has become one of the great success stories of twentieth-century science. For an excellent account of this development as well as relatively recent work, see Lappin, Shalom, ed. *The Handbook of Contemporary Semantic Theory.* London: Blackwell, 1997.

28 See Pustejovsky, James and Branimir Boguraey, eds. *Lexical Semantics: The Problem of Polysemy.* Oxford: Oxford University Press, 1996. For an interesting example involving a chain of synonyms leading from "black" to "white," see Borgmann, Dmitri. *Beyond Language: Adventures in Word and Thought.* New York: Charles Scribner's Sons, 1967.

29 See Wittgenstein, Ludwig. *Philosophical Investigations.* New York: Prentice Hall, 1999. Sections 65–6.

30 See Wikipedia. "Quaternions." 26 April 2008 http://en.wikipedia.org/wiki/Quaternion.

31 See Atkins, S. "Building a Lexicon: the Contribution of Lexicography." *International Journal of Lexicography* 4:3 (1991): 163–204; hereafter referred to in text as *Lexicography*.

32 In *Lexicography* Atkins shows how six different standard dictionaries each give distinct definitions of "acknowledge," "admire," "admit," "danger," "reel," and "safety." There is no systematicity to how the senses of these words are distinguished by each dictionary, and, indeed, within each dictionary. Atkins concludes that dictionaries should properly be understood not as stating "the meanings" of words either in the sense of actually distinguishing all the senses of a word from each other and from the senses of other words, or in the sense of stating what a competent speaker needs to know about the usage of a word in order to understand it. This has nothing to do with any intrinsic flaw in dictionaries, but is rather because word meaning simply does not work that way.

33 For a compelling demonstration of how extant philosophical "theories of reference" are unmade by this very point, see Stich, Stephen. *Deconstructing the Mind.* Oxford: Oxford University Press, 1998.

34 The most serious attempt at this within the game industry is the continuing development of a software application called *Storytron* by the revolutionary game theorist and designer Chris Crawford. See his description of what this application is supposed to accomplish at "Storytron Overview," 20 Jan. 2008 http://www.storytron.com/overview/ov_index.html.

35 In Putnam, Hilary. *Representation and Reality.* Cambridge, MA: MIT, 1991, Putnam makes an argument against the language of thought that can actually be strengthened by reference to Wilson and Stich's work. Putnam argues that if the language of thought really is a language, then it is beset by the same forms of indeterminacies (those now most clearly explained by Wilson and Stich) as natural language. But then it can't do the explanatory work that Fodor would have it do. While we heartily endorse this conclusion, we have made a prior point. Even if the referring expressions in the language of thought somehow magically had determinate content, the indeterminacy of natural language content alone makes it the case the language of thought cannot do the job that it is supposed to.

36 Things may be looking up for the machines, though. See Wikipedia. "Computer Chess." 7 Jan. 2008 http://en.wikipedia.org/wiki/Computer_chess#Advanced_chess.

37 See Dreyfus, Hubert *What Computers Still Can't Do.* 2nd ed. Cambridge, MA: MIT, 1972.

38 Dennett, Daniel. "Cognitive Wheels: The Frame Problem of AI." in Hookway, C. ed. *Minds, Machines, and Evolution.* Cambridge: Cambridge University Press, 1984. 129–51.

39 Partly, this is a function of the logical issues discussed in the next section. The

general question of whether a set of first-order logic sentences is consistent is one that is not decidable via a Von Neumann computable procedure. Since natural languages are expressively richer than first-order logic, this entails (by the Church-Turing Thesis) that there is no perfectly general algorithm to even *detect* inconsistency, much less correct for it in a rational manner.

40   The general problem instantiated here (the fact that the holistic nature of our beliefs entails that one can hold onto a cherished belief in light of *any* evidence and still remain logically consistent) was explicitly stated, and discussed, by A.J. Ayer, in *Language, Truth, and Logic*. New York: Dover, 1936. For some reason it is often referred to as the "Quine-Duhem Problem," or the "Duhem-Quine Thesis." But Duhem never put it forward (his belief that no empirical data would be able to decide whether matter was discrete or dense only concerned the physics of his day and had nothing to do with the perfectly general gap between logical consistency and rationality that Ayer exploits) and attributions of the thesis to Quine cite work written over a decade after Ayer's.

41   On this claim, see Megill, Jason and Jon Cogburn. "Easy's Getting Harder all the Time, Human Emotions and the Frame Problem." *Ratio* XVII 3 (2005): 306–16.

42   See also Thompson, Evan. *Mind in Life*. Cambridge, MA: Harvard University Press, 2007.

43   The formal language that these thinkers designed is usually referred to as the "predicate calculus." It is the historical predecessor of the languages that students learn in undergraduate formal logic courses in universities today. Two such instructive and helpful textbooks are Bergmann, Merrie, James Moor and Jack Nelson. *The Logic Book*. 4th ed. New York: McGraw Hill, 2004 and Lemmon, E.J. *Beginning Logic*. Indianapolis: Hackett, 1978.

44   The procedure that is nowadays referred to as "Gödel numbering" is relatively straightforward. Each unit of the formal language in question is assigned a unique number, and then properties of prime factorization are used to extend this into unique numbers for sentences and then sequences of sentences. For example, where $\lceil \alpha \rceil$ denotes the Gödel number for the grammatical unit α, the vocabulary of first-order arithmetic can be assigned the following numbers:

$$\lceil \forall \rceil = 1,$$
$$\lceil \exists \rceil = 3,$$
$$\lceil \neg \rceil = 5,$$
$$\lceil \to \rceil = 7,$$
$$\lceil \vee \rceil = 9,$$
$$\lceil \wedge \rceil = 11,$$
$$\lceil = \rceil = 13,$$
$$\lceil (\rceil = 15,$$
$$\lceil) \rceil = 17,$$
$$\lceil s \rceil = 19,$$
$$\lceil 0 \rceil = 21,$$
$$\lceil + \rceil = 23,$$
$$\lceil \times \rceil = 25,$$
$$\lceil x \rceil = 2, \lceil y \rceil = 4, \lceil z \rceil = 6, \lceil z_1 \rceil = 8, \lceil z_2 \rceil = 10, \lceil z_3 \rceil = 12 \ldots$$

Note that this leaves open all of the odd numbers greater than twenty-five.

Then to get the Gödel number of a string of symbols you first determine the number of symbols in the string. For example "$\neg \exists y (s0 = y)$" has nine symbols in it. Then, if the string has n symbols in it, you line up the first n prime numbers. Since our sample string has nine symbols on it, we line up the first nine prime numbers.

2, 3, 5, 7, 11, 13, 17, 19, 23

Then we raise each prime number to the Gödel number of the corresponding piece of vocabulary. For "$\neg \exists y(s0 = y)$" this gives us the following.

$2^{\ulcorner \neg \urcorner}, 3^{\ulcorner \exists \urcorner}, 5^{\ulcorner y \urcorner}, 7^{\ulcorner (\urcorner}, 11^{\ulcorner s \urcorner}, 13^{\ulcorner 0 \urcorner}, 17^{\ulcorner = \urcorner}, 19^{\ulcorner y \urcorner}, 23^{\ulcorner) \urcorner}$

When we plug in the assigned values from the chart above, we get:

$2^5, 3^3, 5^4, 7^{15}, 11^{19}, 13^{21}, 17^{13}, 19^4, 23^{17}$

Then, to get the Gödel number of "$\neg \exists y(s0 = y)$" we just multiply the numbers together.

$2^5 \times 3^3 \times 5^4 \times 7^{15} \times 11^{19} \times 13^{21} \times 17^{13} \times 19^4 \times 23^{17}$

Presenting this number in binary notation is left as an exercise to the reader (just kidding).

By this technique, *any* string of symbols from the vocabulary of first-order arithmetic, grammatical or not, will have a *unique* Gödel number. But then we can raise the question of whether the property of being a grammatical sentence in the language of first-order arithmetic is something that can be mechanically checked. Gödel showed this by demonstrating that the set of Gödel numbers corresponding to the set of grammatical sentences is primitive recursive. This just means that there is a primitive recursive function that returns "1" for the Gödel number of a sentence and "0" for the Gödel number of a string of symbols that is not a sentence.

For a more detailed presentation of some of the mathematics behind Godel's fascinating method for treating language and inference arithmetically, as well as the main results he and others have proven using these methods, see Smith, Peter. *An Introduction to Gödel's Theorems*. Cambridge: Cambridge University Press, 2007.

45 This task is vastly more difficult than people (including the overwhelming majority of linguistically ignorant philosophers of language) assume. To have a genuinely algorithmic translation between natural and formal languages, one must axiomatize the grammar of the natural language in the same way that Euclid (for example) provided a set of axioms for plane geometry. One must also map the relevant grammatical units onto one another in a rule-governed manner. Montague was the first to devise a way to accomplish these two tasks precisely because he was able to satisfy these two demands with a non-trivial fragment of English; all of contemporary computational linguistics stands on his shoulders. For a clear and relatively accessible presentation of Montague's methods, see Dowty, D., R. Wall, and S. Peters. *Introduction to Montague Semantics*. Dordrecht: D. Reidel, 1981. For a discussion of linguistically relevant forms of compositionality, see Cogburn, Jon and Roy Cook. "Inverted Space: Minimal Verificationism, Propositional Attitudes, and Compositionality." *Philosophia: Philosophical Quarterly of Israel* 32 (2005): 73–92.

46 For a succinct account of how Turing's notion was transformed, see Wikipedia. "Church-Turing Thesis." 7 Jan. 2008 http://en.wikipedia.org/wiki/Church%27s_thesis.

47 That is, a set of numbers is recursive in the neo-Gödelian sense if, and only if, it

is lambda definable in Church's sense, and that this obtains, if and only if, it is Turing machine computable.

Any more detailed explanation of these mathematical concepts here would be too elaborate for a book of this nature. However, for the mathematically ambitious, in Peter Smith's *An Introduction to Gödel's Theorems* one can find a fascinating discussion of the sense in which the mathematical function of primitive recursion has a deep correspondence to "for" loops (*Introduction*, 88–90), composition to nesting, and minimization to "do until" routines (*Introduction*, 266) in modern computer languages that will be familiar to most readers who have taken even a single course in programming.

48   Rosser, J.B. "An Informal Exposition of Proofs of Gödel's Theorem and Church's Theorem." *The Journal of Symbolic Logic* 4 (1939): 53–60.

49   The second kind of distinctively human talent just described might seem abstruse to those not familiar with formal languages, but it really is not. Consider the following two sentences: (a) There is something that is simultaneously triangular and not triangular, and (b) Frank's birthday cake is triangular. People can reliably tell that not only is the first sentence false, but there is no way that it could be true, even if we were to change the meaning of the non-logical predicate "triangular." On the other hand, Frank's mom could easily have made him a circular cake. The ability to formalize such sentences in logic allows us to pose the question of whether this ability to distinguish between logical truths, contradictions, and logically contingent sentences is something that can be programmed with 100% accuracy into a computer.

50   Chomsky himself has recently hinted that he now wishes to understand the concept of generativity in a way that is inconsistent with Church's Thesis. But the cost of this is prohibitive, and commentators on Chomsky's recent work have been mostly skeptical. The main problem is that the unclearness of exactly what generativity is supposed to be (if it is not limited in terms of what a computer can do) looks suspiciously similar to the unclarity in the various forms of syntax offered by new wave Chomskyan syntacticians (those still committed to Chomsky's so-called "Minimalism").

The problem with middle to later Chomskyan syntax from a perspective concerned with computational tractability is that for Chomskyans the notion of "inference" appealed to in CRUM of necessity becomes completely divorced from any engineering applications, which means digital computers no longer show that CRUM is true of at least *something*. Fortunately, while adherents see the Minimalist framework as benefiting from the Great Man's own philosophical commitments (e.g., that there is in some sense only one language that is known innately by humans prior to learning a natural variant, that evolution can't account for this, that simplicity in science works in a peculiar way, and that natural language syntax must be generated by transformational machinery from shared deep structure), rival non-transformational computationally friendly syntactic frameworks are vastly more clear and have greater empirical coverage. This is the case even though the plurality of academic syntacticians still follow the later Chomsky.

In linguistics proper, though, severe disgruntlement has been building for a long time. For example, Geoffrey Pullum's famous note in 1989 about Government and Binding Theory (Pullum, Geoffrey. "Formal Linguistics Meets the Boojum." *Natural Language and Linguistic Theory* 7 (1989): 137–43) gave humorous expression to the fears and disgust of linguists who still strive for the clarity manifest in Chomsky's earliest work. Non-Chomskyan syntacticians (e.g., Johnson, David and Shalom Lappin. *Local Constraints and Economy*. Stanford: Center for the Study of Language and Information, 1998) conclude that computationally unfriendly grammar does not gain its unclarity from the deepness of its explanation. Rather, a shallow philosophical program (Chomsky's beliefs about innateness and simplicity as well as how these must constrain the architecture of syntax) has been wedded to a muddy methodology to yield a theory that is completely intractable from a computational standpoint.

The point is that new wave Chomskyan syntax should not lead us to reject Church's Thesis; there are still no compelling cases of genuinely effective procedures that fail to be recursive. Linguists who examine Minimalism from this perspective (e.g., Asudeh, Ash & Ida Toivonen. "Systematic imperfections." 8 Jan. 2008 http://www.ling.canterbury.ac.nz/personal/toivonen/pdf/asudeh-toivonen-RA.pdf) find it to be *prima facie* inconsistent on a number of points, and to the extent that consistent versions of it can be presented, find the central transformational conceit ("move") to be superfluous, and the resulting theories to be in any case non-compositional, needlessly complex, and unconstrained. Minimalism itself begins to look like bad philosophy. On Chomsky's nativism in this context see Cowie, Fiona. *What's Within: Nativism Reconsidered.* Oxford, Oxford University Press, 1999. On Chomsky's philosophically and scientifically bizarre use of the notion of "simplicity" to motivate his theories, see Johnson and Lappin's book as well as the increasingly influential Cullicover, Peter and Ray Jackendoff. *Simpler Syntax.* Oxford: Oxford University Press, 2005.

51 We hope that our remarks in the current chapter are not taken as an endorsement of the current relative paucity of research funding for CRUM. Unfortunately, philosophical critiques of artificial intelligence have been widely interpreted as supporting the abandonment of AI altogether. If the authors of this book are correct that the core of computer science is the study of the human–computer interface, then it follows that there should be vastly more attempts by academic computer scientists to apply CRUM-ish applications to industry. At the very worst, it will not be possible to fully develop a successor theory of mind until we are much, much clearer about CRUM's limitations.

52 See Batterman, Robert. *The Devil in the Details: Asymptotic Reasoning in Explanation, Reduction, and Emergence.* New York: Oxford University Press, 2006 for an account of how reduction in the limit is the primary way that successor theories explain the successes of previous theories in the sciences. Note that the United States National Air and Space Administration used classical physics to put people on the moon. Even though classical dynamics and mechanics are false and have been replaced by post-classical quantum theory and relativity, the acceptable margins of error combined with mathematical complexity make it impossible to use anything but classical physics in the overwhelming majority of technical contexts. This is why perhaps most academic applied mathematics involves problems that arise in classical physics.

53 Perhaps the most commercially successful CRUM program so far is the Cyc ontology, which grew out of Doug Lenant's work in academic AI. Endeavors such as this are being shamefully underfunded in United States research universities. While it is a consequence of our arguments that, just as classical physics could not explain the behavior of Mercury, Cyc-like approaches on their own will not ultimately yield human-like AI, it is still the case that Cyc and its descendents should constitute a major part of research into the human–computer interface. If video games incorporated a Cyc-like ontology, and used it both to compositionally model game states and to govern the behavior of NPCs, whole new vistas of intelligent gaming would be in front of us. We thank Jon Curtis, Cyc Senior Project Manager and Senior Ontologist, for providing a tour of the Cyc facilities and explaining their commercial applications and cutting edge research. See Cycorp, Inc. 22 Jan. 2008 http://www.cyc.com/cyc for detailed information and free downloads.

54   This possibility is depicted with astonishing prescience in William Gibson's lovely novel *All Tomorrow's Parties*. New York: Berkley Books, 1999.

7 Epilogue: Video Games and the Meaning of Life

1   Plato. *Republic*. Trans. G.M.A. Grube. Indianapolis: Hackett Publishing Company, Inc., 1992. 71–75.

2   Nietzsche, Friedrich. *Thus Spake Zarathustra*. New York: Algora Publishing, 2003; hereafter cited in text as *Zarathustra*.

3   For a list of "archetypal" college professors, see Jon Cogburn's Blog, "Updated List of (Jungian Arche-) Types of Irritating Professors." 3 Dec. 2007 http://drjon.typepad.com/jon_cogburns_blog/2007/11/updated-list-of.html.

4   For a fuller, more nuanced discussion of the sense in which these unconscious notions can be said to be "the same" from person to person, see Jung, C.J. "Psychological Types," *The Basic Writings of C.J Jung*. Ed. V.S. de Laszlo. New York: The Modern Library, 1959.

5   The principal cause for this phenomenon in the game industry has been the enormous popularity of the writings of Joseph Campbell (see especially Campbell, Joseph. *The Hero with a Thousand Faces*. Princeton: Princeton University Press, 1972), an enthusiastic Jungian who has written several books about the influence of mythic archetypes on literature and human thought.

6   Jung, C.J. "The Relations Between the Ego and the Unconscious." *The Basic Writings of C.J Jung*. Ed. V.S. de Laszlo. New York: The Modern Library, 1959. 136; hereafter cited in text as *Relations*.

7   Hacking, Ian. *Rewriting the Soul: Multiple Personality and the Sciences of Memory*. Princeton: Princeton University Press, 1995; hereafter cited in text as *Rewriting*.

8   For a quite different argument in the service of a similar claim see Horwitz Allan, and Jerome Wakefield. *The Loss of Sadness: How Psychiatry Transformed Normal Sorrow Into Depressive Disorder*. New York: Oxford University Press, 2007. One related problem is that American insurance companies will not pay for happiness-inspiring drugs unless they are treating diagnosable illnesses. So the understandable desire to get the pills to people who clearly need them can lead to re-describing sadness itself as an illness.

9   Vogler, Christopher. *The Writer's Journey: Mythic Structure for Storytellers and Screenwriters*. Studio City, CA: Michael Wiese Productions, 1992. 16; hereafter cited in text as *Writer's*.

10   Actually, the term from Aristotle's *Ethics* that usually gets translated as "happiness" is a rather mysterious one. The Greek word *eudaimonia* literally means something more like "being well-looked-after by a demon/nature spirit/guardian angel."

11   This comes across most clearly in Aristotle. *On Interpretation*. Trans. H.P. Cooke. Oxford: Loeb Classical Library, 2002. Chapter 9.

12   Some of the best "Myst clones" that were released during this period were The Adventure Company's *The Crystal Key*, Sierra's *Lighthouse: The Dark Being*, and Viacom New Media's *Are You Afraid of the Dark?: The Tale of Orpheo's Curse*.

13   Actually, this paraphrase of Heidegger represents an oversimplification in at least one important way. Heidegger himself rarely uses the term "human" at all in *Being and Time*. The expression that he employs in all of the passages that we describe here as being about the "human" condition is "Da-sein." Translated literally from the German, this expression means "being there." Heidegger's writing style is extraordinarily ambiguous, and scholars are divided over the question of why Heidegger uses just this term and what its connotations are.

But Heidegger himself provides an important clue when he says that a proper understanding of Da-sein will add to our understanding of "the methodology of the human sciences" (*Being* 33).

14 Sartre, Jean-Paul. "Existentialism and Humanism." *Jean-Paul Sartre: Basic Writings*, Ed. Stephen Priest. New York: Routledge, 2000. 43.

15 Sartre, Jean-Paul. *Being and Nothingness*. trans. Hazel E. Barnes. New York: Simon and Schuster, 1956. 98–9.

16 In Sartre's greatest novel, *Nausea*, the main character engages in a fascinating philosophical meditation on this topic while walking through a room filled with portraits of dead soldiers, politicians, and civic leaders. See Sartre, Jean-Paul. *Nausea*. trans. Lloyd Alexander. New York: New Directions Books, 1938. 112–29.

17 It is perhaps worth mentioning here that Rand and Robyn Miller, the pair of brothers who were the lead designers of *Myst* and *Riven*, are in fact devout Christians. Most philosophically inclined Christians have had a more optimistic view of human life—or of the life hereafter at any rate—than existentialist philosophers such as Sartre and Heidegger. But there is nothing straight-forwardly incompatible about these two ways of thinking.

18 For a playable version, go to Al Hensel. "Conway's Game of Life." 4 Dec. 2007 http://www.ibiblio.org/lifepatterns/.

19 Al Hensel's website (cited in the previous endnote) has links to papers dis-cussing the relevant mathematical properties and their putative philosophical significance.

20 Darwin, Charles. "The Origin of Species." *The Origin of Species and The Descent of Man*. London: Encyclopedia Britannica, Inc., 1952. 63.

21 Dennett, Daniel. *Darwin's Dangerous Idea: Evolution and the Meanings of Life*. New York: Simon and Schuster, 1995. 21; hereafter in text cited as *Darwin's*.

22 This ambitious thesis of *biological determinism* has, in fact, been seriously defended by a few social scientists. The most famous articulation of it can be found in Wilson, Edward. *Sociobiology: The New Synthesis, Twenty-fifth Anniversary Edition*. New York: Belknap Press, 2000. According to this provocative and influential book, all of the social sciences are really just *branches* of evolutionary biology.

23 See Darwin's extensive and fascinating discussion of the phenomenon of "Sex-ual Selection" in *The Descent of Man*, in *The Origin of Species and The Descent of Man*. London: Encyclopedia Britannica, Inc., 1952, Parts 2 and 3.

24 Perhaps the most well-known philosophical examination of the significance of leisure to our conception of what is valuable in human life can be found in Pieper, Josef. *Leisure: The Basis of Culture*. Indianapolis: The Liberty Fund, 1999.

25 Historians of the ancient world have often remarked upon this connection, without having had much to say about its significance. See, for example, Lonsdale, Stephen H. *Dance and Ritual Play in Greek Religion*. Baltimore, MD: The Johns Hopkins University Press, 2000.

Bibliography

al-Ghazali, Abu Hamid Muhammed. *The Incoherence of the Philosophers*. Trans. Michael E. Marmura. Provo, UT: Brigham Young, 2002.

Alhoff, Fritz., Ed. *The Philosophy of Wine: A Symposium on Thinking and Drinking*. London: Wiley-Blackwell, 2007.

Andersen, J.L., and P. Aagaard. "Myosin Heavy Chain IIX Overshoot in Human Skeletal Muscle." *Muscle and Nerve* 23.7 (2000): 1095–1104.

Anderson, Craig, and Karen E. Dill. "Video Games and Aggressive Thoughts, Feelings and Behavior in the Laboratory and in Life." *Journal of Personality and Social Psychology* 78 (2000): 772–790.

Aristotle. *Poetics*. Trans. Kenneth A. Telford. South Bend, IN: H. Regnery, 1961.

——. *Nicomachean Ethics*. Trans. David Ross. Oxford: Oxford University Press, 1998.

——. *On Interpretation*. Trans. H.P. Cooke. Oxford: Loeb Classical Library, 2002.

Asprey, Robert. *The Reign of Napoleon Bonaparte*. New York: Basic Books, 2002.

Atkins, S. "Building a Lexicon: The Contribution of Lexicography." *International Journal of Lexicography* 4.3 (1991): 163–204.

Ayer, A.J. *Language, Proof, and Logic*. New York: Dover, 1936.

——. *The Foundations of Empirical Knowledge*. London: Macmilllan, 1958.

Barton, Carlin. *The Sorrows of the Ancient Romans*. Princeton, NJ: Princeton University Press, 1993.

Batterman, Robert. *The Devil in the Details: Asymptotic Reasoning in Explanation, Reduction, and Emergence*. Oxford: Oxford University Press, 2006.

Benacerraf, Paul, and Hilary Putnam., Eds. *The Philosophy of Mathematics*. Cambridge: Cambridge University Press, 1983.

Berg, A. Scott. *Max Perkins: Editor of Genius*. New York: Penguin, 1997.

Bergmann, Merrie, James Moor, and Jack Nelson. *The Logic Book*. 4th ed. New York: McGraw Hill, 2004.

Berkeley, George. *Principles of Human Knowledge and Three Dialogues Between Hylas and Philonous*. London: Penguin Classics, 2004.

Berman, Morris. *The Reenchantment of the World*. New York: Bantam Books, 1984.

Boeringer, S.B. "Associations of Rape-Supportive Attitudes with Fraternal and Athletic Participation." *Violence Against Women* 5 (1999): 81–90.

Boethius. *The Consolation of Philosophy*. Trans. Victor Watts. New York: Penguin, 1969.

Boolos, George, John Burgess, and Richard Jeffrey. *Computability and Logic*. 5th ed. Cambridge: Cambridge University Press, 2007.

Borgmann, Dmitri. *Beyond Language: Adventures in Word and Thought*. New York: Charles Scribner's Sons, 1967.

Broers, Michael. *Europe Under Napoleon: 1799–1815*. New York: Hodder Arnold, 1988.

Campbell, Joseph. *The Hero with a Thousand Faces*. Princeton, NJ: Princeton University Press, 1972.

Canfield, Jack, and Mark Victor Hansen. *A 2nd Helping of Chicken Soup for the Soul*. Deerfield Beach, FL: Health Communications, 1995.

Carrol, Noel. *The Philosophy of Horror: Or, Paradoxes of the Heart*. London: Routledge, 1990.

Chalmers, David. *The Conscious Mind: In Search of a Fundamental Theory*. Oxford: Oxford University Press, 1996.

Clark, Andy. *Being There: Putting Brain, Body, World Together Again*. Boston, MA: MIT, 1997.

——. *Natural Born Cyborgs: Minds, Technologies, and the Future of Human Intelligence*. Oxford: Oxford University Press, 2003.

Clark, Andy, and David Chalmers. "The Extended Mind." *Analysis* 58 (1998): 10–23.

Clover, Carol. *Men, Women and Chainsaws: Gender in the Modern Horror Film*. Princeton, NJ: Princeton University Press, 1992.

Coffa, Alberto. *The Semantic Tradition from Kant to Carnap*. Cambridge: Cambridge University Press, 1991.

Cogburn, Jon. "Deconstructing Dummett's Anti-Realism: A New Argument Against Church's Thesis." *The Logica Yearbook* (2002).

——. "Manifest Invalidity: Neil Tennant's New Argument for Intuitionism." *Synthese* 134.3 (2003): 353–362.

——. "Paradox Lost." *Canadian Journal of Philosophy* 34 (2004): 195–216.

——. "The Philosophical Basis of What? The Anti-Realist Case for Dialetheism." *The Law of Non-Contradiction*. Eds. Graham Priest, J.C. Beall, and Bradley Armour-Garb. Oxford: Oxford University Press, 2004.

——. "Inferentialism and Tacit Knowledge." *Behavior and Philosophy* 32 (2005): 503–24.

——. "Tonking a Theory of Content: An Inferentialist Rejoinder." *Logic and Logical Philosophy* 13 (2005): 31–36.

——. "Notes from the Ungerground." Under review.

Cogburn, Jon, and Roy Cook. "Inverted Space: Minimal Verificationism, Propositional Attitudes, and Compositionality." *Philosophia: Philosophical Quarterly of Israel* 32 (2005): 73–92.

Cogburn, Jon, and Jason Megill. "Are Turing Machines Platonists? Inferentialism and the Computational Theory of Mind." Under review.

Cogburn, Jon, and Mark Silcox. "Computing Machinery and Emergence: The Metaphysics and Aesthetics of Video Games." *Minds and Machines* 15 (2005): 73–89.

Cohen, L. Bernard. *The Birth of a New Physics*. New York: L.L. Norton, 1985.

Cook, Roy, and Jon Cogburn. "What Negation is Not: Intuitionism and '0=1'." *Analysis*, 60.1 (2000): 5–12.

Cooke, Brandon. "Imagining Art." *British Journal of Aesthetics* 47 (2007): 29–45.

——. "Art Critical Contradictions." Under review.

Coplan, Amy. "Feminist Final Girls: Why Horror Heroines are Real Women and Not Just 'Dicks in Drag'." Under review.

Cowie, Fiona. *What's Within: Nativism Reconsidered*. Oxford: Oxford University Press, 1999.

Craig, William. "On Áxiomatizability Within a System." *Journal of Symbolic Logic* 18 (1953): 30–32.

Culler, Jonathan. "Literary Competence." *Reader-Response Criticism: From Formalism to Post-Structuralism*. Ed. Jane Tompkins. Baltimore: Johns Hopkins University Press, 1980.

Cullicover, Peter, and Ray Jackendoff. *Simpler Syntax*. Oxford: Oxford University Press, 2005.

Dadlez, E.M. *What's Hecuba to Him?: Fictional Events and Actual Emotions*. University Park, PA: Pennsylvania State University Press, 1997.

Damasio, Antonio. *Descartes' Error*. New York: HarperCollins, 1995.

Darwin, Charles. *The Origin of Species. The Origin of Species and the Descent of Man*. London: Encyclopedia Britannica, 1952.

Dasgupta, Surendranath. *A History of Indian Philosophy: Volumes 1–5*. Delhi: Motilal Banarsidass, 2004.

Davidson, D., and G. Harman., Eds. *The Logic of Grammar*. Encino, CA: Dickenson, 1975.

Davis, Martin. *The Universal Computer*. New York: W.W. Norton, 2000.

Dennett, Daniel. "Cognitive Wheels: The Frame Problem of AI." *Minds, Machines, and Evolution*. Ed. C. Hookway. Cambridge: Cambridge University Press, 1984. 129–151.

——. *The Intentional Stance*. Cambridge, MA: MIT, 1989.

——. *Consciousness Explained*. New York: Back Bay Books, 1991.

——. *Darwin's Dangerous Idea: Evolution and the Meanings of Life*. New York: Simon and Schuster, 1995.

Descartes, René. *Meditations on First Philosophy*. Trans. John Cottingham. Cambridge: Cambridge University Press, 1986.

——. *The Philosophical Writings of Descartes, Volume I*. Trans. John Cottingham, Robert Stoothoff, and Dugald Murdoch. Cambridge: Cambridge University Press, 1985.

Dietz, W.H. "Television, Obesity, and Eating Disorders." *Adolescent Medicine: State of the Art Reviews* 4 (1993): 543–549.

Dostoyevsky, Fyodor. *The Brothers Karamazov*. Trans. David Magarshack. London: Penguin Books, 1958.

Dowty, D., R. Wall, and S. Peters. *Introduction to Montague Semantics*. Dordrecht: D. Reidel, 1981.

Dreyfus, Hubert. *What Computers Still Can't Do*. Cambridge, MA: MIT, 1972.

Erikson, Steven. *Gardens of the Moon*. London: Bantam, 1999.

Esslemont, Cameron. *Night of the Knives*. London: Bantam, 2007.

Etcoff, Nancy. *Survival of the Prettiest*. Norwell, MA: Anchor, 2000.

Falzon, Christopher. *Philosophy Goes to the Movies*. London: Routledge, 2007.

Feuerstein, Georg. *The Yoga-Sutra of Patañjali: A New Translation and Commentary*. Rochester, NY: Inner Traditions, 1979.

Fish, Stanley. "Interpreting the Variorum." *Is There a Text in This Class: The Authority of Interpretive Communities*. Cambridge, MA: Harvard University Press, 1980.

Fisher, Helen. *Why We Love: The Nature and Chemistry of Romantic Love.* New York: Holt Paperbacks, 2004.

Fodor, Jerry. *Psychosemantics: The Problem of Meaning in the Philosophy of Mind.* Cambridge, MA: MIT, 1988.

——. *The Language of Thought.* Cambridge, MA: Harvard University Press, 2005.

Fodor, Jerry, and Z. Pylyshyn. "How Direct is Visual Perception? Some Reflections on Gibson's 'Ecological Approach'." *Cognition* 9 (1981): 139–196.

Frege, Gottlob. *The Frege Reader.* Ed. Michael Beaney. Oxford: Blackwell, 1997.

Friedman, Michael. *Reconsidering Logical Positivism.* Cambridge: Cambridge University Press, 1991.

Frintner, M.P., and L. Rubinson. "Acquaintance Rape: The Influence of Alcohol, Fraternity Membership, and Sports Team Membership." *Journal of Sex Education & Therapy* 19 (1993): 272–284.

Funk, Robert. *The Five Gospels: What Did Jesus Really Say? The Search for the Authentic Word of Jesus.* New York: Harper One, 1996.

Gamble, Sarah. "Postfeminism." *Feminism and Postfeminism.* Ed. Sarah Gamble. London: Routledge, 1998. 43–54.

Gardner, Howard. *The Mind's New Science: A History of the Cognitive Revolution.* New York: Basic Books, 1987.

Gendler, Tamar Szabo, and John Hawthorne., Eds. *Conceivability and Possibility.* Oxford: Oxford University Press, 2002.

Gentile, Douglas. *Media Violence and Children.* Westport, CT: Praeger, 2003.

Gibson, James. *The Ecological Approach to Visual Perception.* Hillsdale, NJ: Lawrence Erlbaum, 1979.

Gibson, William. *All Tomorrow's Parties.* New York: Berkley Books, 1999.

Goldsmith, John. *Ideology in Linguistic Theory: Noam Chomsky and the Deep Structure Debates.* London: Routledge, 1996.

Goodman, Nelson. *Languages of Art.* Indianapolis, IN: Hackett, 1976.

Greenberg, Karen., Ed. *The Torture Debate in America.* Cambridge: Cambridge University Press, 2005.

Grenade, Stephen. "Introducing Interactive Fiction." 19 Apr. 2008 http://brasslantern.org/beginners/introif.html.

Grice, Paul. *Studies in the Way of Words.* Cambridge, MA: Harvard University Press, 1985.

Grimes, J. "On the Failure to Detect Changes in Scenes across Saccades." *Perception: Vancouver Studies in Cognitive Science, Vol. 2.* Ed. K. Akins. Oxford: Oxford University Press, 1996.

Grünbaum, Adolf. *The Foundations of Psychoanalysis: A Philosophical Critique.* Berkeley, CA: University of California Press, 1985.

Hacking, Ian. *Rewriting the Soul: Multiple Personality and the Sciences of Memory.* Princeton, NJ: Princeton University Press, 1995.

Hajdu, David. *The Ten Cent Plague: The Great Comic-Book Scare and How it Changed America.* New York: Farrar, Straus and Giroux, 2008.

Hanh, Thich Nhat. *Living Buddha, Living Christ.* New York: Riverhead Books, 1995.

Harrington, Anne. *The Cure Within: A History of Mind-Body Medicine.* New York: W.W. Norton, 2008.

Harris, Randy Allen. *The Linguistics Wars.* Oxford: Oxford University Press, 1993.

Hartshorne, Charles. *Omnipotence and Other Theological Mistakes*. New York: State University of New York Press, 1984.

Haugeland, John. *Mind Design II: Philosophy, Psychology, and Artificial Intelligence*. Cambridge, MA: MIT, 1997.

Heidegger, Martin. *Being and Time: A Translation of* Sein und Zeit. Trans. Joan Stambaugh. Albany, NY: State University of New York Press, 1996.

Hill, Jim, and Rand Cheadle. *The Bible Tells Me So: Uses and Abuses of Holy Scripture*. New York: Doubleday, 1996.

Hitchens, Christopher. *God is Not Great: How Religion Poisons Everything*. New York: Hachette, 2007.

Hobbes, Thomas. *Leviathan*. Eds. Richard E. Flathman and David Johnston. New York: W.W. Norton, 1997.

Hofstadter, Douglas. *Gödel, Escher, Bach: An Eternal Golden Braid*. New York: Basic Books, 1979.

——— . *I Am A Strange Loop*. New York: Basic Books, 2007.

Hornby, Nick. *Songbook*. New York: Penguin, 2003.

Horwitz, Allan, and Jerome Wakefield. *The Loss of Sadness: How Psychiatry Transformed Normal Sorrow Into Depressive Disorder*. New York: Oxford University Press, 2007.

Hume, David. "Of Personal Identity." *Personal Identity*. Ed. John Perry. Los Angeles, CA: University of California Press, 1975.

——— . "Of the Standard of Taste." *Of the Standard of Taste and Other Essays*. New York: Bobbs-Merrill, 1965.

James, William. *Principles of Psychology, Vol 1*. New York: Cosimo, 2007.

Jesus Seminar, The. *The Gospel of Jesus*. Santa Rosa, CA: Polebridge, 1999.

Johnson, David, and Shalom Lappin. *Local Constraints and Economy*. Stanford, CA: Center for the Study of Language and Information, 1998.

Jones, Gerard. *Killing Monsters: Why Children Need Fantasy, Super Heroes and Make Believe Violence*. New York: Basic Books, 2002.

Judson, Olivia. *Dr. Tatiana's Sex Advice To All Creation: The Definitive Guide to the Evolutionary Biology of Sex*. New York: Holt Paperbacks, 2003.

Jung, C.J. "Psychological Types." *The Basic Writings of C.J Jung*. Ed. V.S. de Laszlo. New York: The Modern Library, 1959.

——— . "The Relations Between the Ego and the Unconscious." *The Basic Writings of C.J Jung*. Ed. V.S. de Laszlo. New York: The Modern Library, 1959.

Kalderon, M., Ed. *Fictionalism in Metaphysics*. Oxford: Clarendon, 2005.

Kant, Immanuel. *Critique of Judgement*. Trans. J.H. Bernard. New York: Hafner, 1951.

——— . *Foundations of the Metaphysics of Morals*. Trans. Lewis White Beck. New York: Bobbs Merrill, 1959.

——— . *Critique of Pure Reason*. Trans. Norman Kemp Smith. New York: St. Martin's Press, 1975.

Keefe, Rosanna. *Theories of Vagueness*. Cambridge: Cambridge University Press, 2000.

Kennedy, Helen. "Lara Croft: Feminist Icon or Cyberbimbo? On the Limits of Textual Analysis." *Game Studies*. 6 Apr. 2008 http://www.gamestudies.org/0202/kennedy/.

Kirsten, E.L. *The Art of Demotivation—Manager's Edition: Transforming Your Least Valuable Asset—Your Employees*. Austin, TX: Despair, 2005.

Klinesmith, Jennifer, Tim Kasser, and Francis T. McAndrew, "Guns, Testosterone and Aggression: An Experimental Test of a Mediational Hypothesis." *Psychological Science* 17 (2006): 568–571.

Kneale, William, and Martha Kneale. *The Development of Logic.* Oxford: Oxford University Press, 1962.

Kohler, I. "The Formation and Transformation of the Perceptual World." *Psychological Issues* 3.4 (1964): 1–173.

Kripke, Saul. *Naming and Necessity.* Cambridge: Cambridge University Press, 1980.

Lacan, Jacques. "The Insistence of the Letter in the Unconscious." *Structuralism.* Ed. J. Ehrmann. Garden City, NY: Anchor Books, 1957.

Lappin, Shalom., Ed. *The Handbook of Contemporary Semantic Theory.* London: Blackwell, 1997.

Laurel, Brenda. *Computers as Theatre.* Indianapolis, IN: Addison-Wesley Professional, 1982.

Lemmon, E.J. *Beginning Logic.* Indianapolis, IN: Hackett, 1978.

Lewis, C.S. *Mere Christianity.* New York: Macmillan, 1952.

Longinus. *On the Sublime. Classical Literary Criticism.* Trans. T.S. Dorsch. Middlesex: Penguin Books, 1965.

Lonsdale, Stephen. *Dance and Ritual Play in Greek Religion.* Baltimore, MD: The Johns Hopkins University Press, 2000.

Lovecraft, H.P. *Tales.* New York: Library of America, 2005.

MacDorman, Karl F., and Hiroshi Ishiguro. "The Uncanny Advantage of Using Androids in Cognitive and Social Science Research." *Interaction Studies* 7 (2006): 297–337.

Mack, Burton. *Who Wrote the New Testament? The Making of the Christian Myth.* New York: HarperOne, 1996.

Marx, Karl, and Friedrich Engels. *The German Ideology, Including Theses on Feuerbach.* Amherst, MA: Prometheus Books, 1998.

Mascaró, Juan. Trans. *The Bhagavad Gita.* London: Penguin Books, 1962.

Mathiak, Klaus and René Weber. "Toward Brain Correlates of Natural Behavior: fMRI during Violent Video Games." *Human Brain Mapping* 26 (2006): 948–956.

McDonogh, Giles. *After the Reich: The Brutal History of the Allied Occupation.* New York: Basic Books, 2007.

Megill, Jason, and Jon Cogburn. "Easy's Getting Harder all the Time: Human Emotions and the Frame Problem." *Ratio* XVII 3 (2005): 306–316.

Mill, John Stuart. "On Liberty". *On Liberty and Other Essays.* Ed. John Gray. Oxford: Oxford University Press, 1991.

——— . *Utilitarianism.* Indianapolis, IN: Hackett, 1979.

Montefiore, Simon. *Stalin: The Court of the Red Tsar.* New York: Vintage, 2005.

Moore, G.E. *Principia Ethica.* Mineola, NY: Dover, 2004.

Moor, James., Ed. *The Turing Test: The Elusive Standard of Artificial Intelligence.* Dordrecht: Springer, 1989.

Morgan, M. "Television and School Performance." *Adolescent Medicine: State of the Art Reviews* 4 (1993): 607–622.

Murdoch, Iris. *The Fire and the Sun.* London: Viking, 1991.

Murray, Janet. *Hamlet on the Holodeck: The Future of Narrative in Cybserspace.* Cambridge, MA: MIT, 1998.

Nagel, Ernest, and James Newman. *Gödel's Proof.* New York: New York Press, 1960.

Nagel, Thomas. "What Is It Like To Be A Bat?" *Philosophical Review* 83 (1974): 435–451.

Ney, J.A. "On Generativity: The History of a Notion that Never Was." *Historiographia Linguistica* 20 (1993): 441–454.

Niburg, Amy Kiste. *Seal of Approval, The History of the Comics Code*. Jackson: UPM, 1998.

Nietzsche, Friedrich. *Thus Spake Zarathustra*. New York: Algora, 2003.

Noë, Alva. *Action in Perception*. Cambridge, MA: MIT, 2004.

Norvig, Peter. *Paradigms in Artificial Intelligence Programming, Case Studies in Common Lisp*. New York: Morgan Kaufman, 1991.

Norvig, Peter, and Stuart Russell. *Artificial Intelligence: A Modern Approach*. 2nd ed. New York: Prentice Hall, 2002.

Parfit, Derek. "Personal Identity." *Personal Identity*. Ed. John Perry. Los Angeles, CA: University of California Press, 1975.

Parmenides. "The Way of Truth." *Early Greek Philosophy*. Ed. Jonathan Barnes. London: Penguin Books, 1987.

Pieper, Josef. *Leisure: The Basis of Culture*. Indianapolis, IN: The Liberty Fund, 1999.

Pinker, Steven. *The Language Instinct: How the Mind Creates Language*. New York: HarperCollins, 1995.

Plato. *Euthyphro. Five Dialogues*. Trans. G.M.A. Grube. Indianapolis, IN: Hackett, 1981.

——. "Meno". *Five Dialogues*. Trans. G.M.A. Grube. Indianapolis, IN: Hackett, 1981.

——. *Republic*. Trans. G.M.A. Grube. Indianapolis, IN: Hackett, 1983.

——. *Sophist*. Trans. Nicholas White. Indianapolis, IN: Hackett, 1993.

Politis, Vasilis. *Routledge Philosophy Guidebook to Aristotle and the Metaphysics*. New York: Routledge, 2004.

Popescu, George. "Women in Video Games. From Barbie to Xena." *Gender and the (Post) East/West Divide*. Ed. Mihaela Frunză and Theodora Eliza Văcărescu. 3 April 2008 http://www.iiav.nl/epublications/2005/gendeRomania.pdf.

Pullum, Geoffrey. "Formal Linguistics Meets the Boojum." *Natural Language and Linguistic Theory* 7 (1989): 137–143.

Pustejovsky, James, and Branimir Boguraey., Eds. *Lexical Semantics: The Problem of Polysemy*. Oxford: Oxford University Press, 1996.

Putnam, Hilary. *Representation and Reality*. Cambridge, MA: MIT, 1991.

Roberts, Wess. *Leadership Secrets of Attila the Hun*. New York: Warner Books, 1990.

Rosenberg, Jay. "Spontaneity Unchained: An Essay in Darwinian Epistemology." *Idealismus als Theorie der Representation?* Ed. Ralph Schumacher. Berlin: Mentis Verlag, 2001. 181–209.

Rosser, J.B. "An Informal Exposition of Proofs of Gödel's Theorem and Church's Theorem." *The Journal of Symbolic Logic* 4 (1939): 53–60.

Rousseau, Jean-Jacques. *On The Social Contract. The Basic Political Writings*. Trans. Donald A. Cress. Indianapolis, IN: Hackett, 1980.

Rushall, B. S., and L.G. Lippman. "The Role of Imagery in Physical Performance." *International Journal for Sport Psychology* 29 (1997): 57–72.

Ruskin, John. *The Elements of Drawing*. New York: Dover, 1971.

Russell, Bertrand. *An Inquiry into Meaning and Truth*. London: George Allen and Unwin Limited, 1940.

———. *The Problems of Philosophy.* Oxford: Oxford University Press, 1983.

———. *Marriage and Morals.* London: Routledge, 1985.

———. *In Praise of Idleness and Other Essays.* London: Routledge, 2004.

Ryle, Gilbert. *The Concept of Mind.* London: Penguin Books, 1990.

Sartre, Jean-Paul. *Being and Nothingness.* Trans. Hazel E. Barnes. New York: Simon and Schuster, 1956.

———. "Existentialism and Humanism." *Jean-Paul Sartre: Basic Writings.* Ed. Stephen Priest. New York: Routledge, 2000.

———. *Nausea.* Trans. Lloyd Alexander. New York: New Directions Books, 1938.

Schieber, Stuart., Ed. *The Turing Test: Verbal Behavior as the Hallmark of Intelligence.* Cambridge, MA: MIT, 2004.

Seager, William. *Theories of Consciousness.* London: Routledge, 1999.

Searle, John. 1994. "Literary Theory and its Discontents." *New Literary History* 25 (1994): 637–667.

Sellars, Wilfrid. "Philosophy and the Scientific Image of Man." *Frontiers of Science and Philosophy.* Ed. Robert Colodny. Pittsburgh: University of Pittsburgh Press, 1962.

Shafer-Landau, Russ., Ed. *Ethical Theory: An Anthology.* Oxford: Wiley-Blackwell, 2007.

Shapiro, Stewart. *Philosophy of Mathematics: Structure and Ontology.* Oxford: Oxford University Press, 2000.

Short, Phillip. *Mao: A Biography.* New York: Henry Holt, 1999.

Silcox, Mark, and Jon Cogburn. "Computability Theory and Literary Competence." *The British Journal of Aesthetics* 46 (2006): 369–386.

Sirridge, Mary. "J.R. Tolkien and Fairy Tale Truth." *British Journal of Aesthetics* 15.1 (1975): 81–92.

Smith, Peter. *An Introduction to Gödel's Theorems.* Cambridge: Cambridge University Press, 2007.

Smolin, Lee. *The Trouble with Physics: The Rise of String Theory, the Fall of Science, and What Comes Next.* New York: Mariner Books, 2007.

Solomon, Robert, and Kathleen Higgins., Eds. *The Philosophy of (Erotic) Love.* Kansas City, MO: University of Kansas, 1991.

Sontag, Susan. *Against Interpretation and Other Essays.* New York: Picador USA, 2001.

Sparshott, Francis. "The Riddle of *Katharsis.*" *Centre and Labyrinth: Essays in Honour of Northrop Frye.* Ed. Eleanor Cook. Toronto, ON: University of Toronto Press, 1993.

Stephenson, Neil. *The Diamond Age.* New York: Spectra, 2000.

Stich, Stephen. *From Folk Psychology to Cognitive Science, The Case Against Belief.* Cambridge, MA: MIT, 1985.

———. *Deconstructing the Mind.* Oxford, Oxford University Press, 1998.

Suzuki, D.Z. *Mysticism Christian and Buddhist.* London: The Buddhist Society, 2002.

Tennant, Neil. "On Paradox Without Self Reference." *Analysis* 55.3 (1995): 199–207.

Thompson, Evan. *Mind in Life.* Cambridge, MA: Harvard University Press, 2007.

Thornham, Sue. "Second Wave Feminism." *Feminism and Postfeminism.* Ed. Sarah Gamble. London: Routledge, 1998. 29–42.

Totaro, Donato. "The Final Girl: A Few Thoughts on Feminism and Horror." *Off-screen*. 6 Aug. 2008 http://www.horschamp.qc.ca/new_offscreen/final_girl.html.

Tsaliki, Liza. "Women and New Technologies." *The Routledge Companion to Feminism and Postfeminism*. Ed. Sarah Gamble. London: Routledge, 2001. 80–92.

Turing, Alan. "On Computable Numbers, with an Application to the Entscheidungs-problem." *Proceedings of the London Mathematical Society* 42 (1936–37): 230–265.

——. "Computing Machinery and Intelligence." *Mind Design II*. Ed. John Haugeland. Cambridge, MA: MIT, 1997. 29–56.

Van Heijenoort, Jean. *From Frege to Gödel: A Sourcebook in Mathematical Logic*. Cambridge, MA: Harvard University Press, 2002.

Vinge, Vernor. *A Fire Upon the Deep*. New York: Tom Doherty Associates, 1992.

Vogler, Christopher. *The Writer's Journey: Mythic Structure for Storytellers and Screenwriters*. Studio City, CA: Michael Wiese Productions, 1992.

Wedgwood, C.V. *The Thirty Years War*. New York: The New York Review of Books, 2005.

Wertham, Frederic. *Seduction of the Innocent*. New York: Ameron, 1996.

Wheeler, Michael. *Reconstructing the Cognitive World*. Cambridge, MA: MIT, 2005.

Whitehead, Alfred, and Bertrand Russell. *Principia Mathematica*. 2nd ed. Cambridge: Cambridge University Press, 1950.

Wilson, Edward. *Sociobiology: The New Synthesis, Twenty-fifth Anniversary Edition*. New York, Belknap, 2000.

Wilson, Mark. "Predicate Meets Property." *Philosophical Review* 91 (1982): 549–589.

——. *Wandering Significance: An Essay on Conceptual Behavior*. Oxford: Oxford University Press, 2006.

Wimsatt Jr., W.K., and Monroe C. Beardsley. "The Affective Fallacy." *The Verbal Icon*. Lexington, KY: University of Kentucky Press, 1954.

Wittgenstein, Ludwig. *Tractatus Logico-Philosophicus*. Trans. C.K. Ogden. New York: Routledge, 1999.

——. *Philosophical Investigations*. New York: Prentice Hall, 1999.

Woit, Peter. *Not Even Wrong: The Failure of String Theory and the Search for Unity*. New York: Basic Books: 2006.

Wolfe, Jeremy, et al. *Sensation and Perception*. Sunderland: Sinauer Associates, 2005.

Wolf, Mark J. P. "Morals, Ethics, and Video Games." *The Video Game Explosion: A History from PONG to Playstation and Beyond*. Ed. Mark J. P. Wolf. Westport, CT: Greenwood, 2008. 283–291.

Wood, Mary. *Categorial Grammars*. London: Routledge, 1993.

Wright, Crispin. *Truth and Objectivity*. Cambridge, MA: Harvard University Press, 1992.

——. *Saving the Differences: Essays on Themes from Truth and Objectivity*. Cambridge, MA: Harvard University Press, 2003.

Wright, Crispin, and Bob Hale., Eds. *A Companion to the Philosophy of Language*. London: Blackwell, 1999.

Zigler, Zig. *See You at the Top*. Gretna: Pelican, 1975.

Index

Aagard, P. 45
acquaintance, knowledge by 114
action 116–17; framelessness of 127–30;
    opportunities for 39–40
action RPGs 109–11, 118, 120, 124–5
actors 137–8
adventure games 91–108, 124–5
aesthetic distance 57–8
aesthetics 91–108; interacting narratives
    91–3, 107; response-based 93–6;
    standard of taste 96–107
affordances 160
Age of Empires 73, 75
Aidyn Chronicles 93, 135
Alexander the Great 87
AllClear 118
Alzheimer's disease 12, 46
analytic philosophy xiii, 135
Anarchy Online 3
Andersen, J.L. 45
Anderson, Craig A. 58, 59–60, 61, 163
'angry fruit salad' 38
angst 148, 149
Anti-Personality Disorder 59
appearance/reality distinction 22–5
Aquinas, Thomas 168
archetypes 138–9
*Are You Afraid of the Dark? The Tale of
    Orpheo's Curse* 180
argument from different minds 26, 38–9
argument from fallibility 80–1
Aristotle 51–2, 55–6, 57, 123, 143–5,
    153–4
arithmetic, non-enumerability of 132–3
art 53–4, 91–108; aesthetic distance
    57–8; affective response 108;
    audience reception 93–6; standard of
    taste 96–107
artificial intelligence (AI) 109–34

artist-centric aesthetic properties
    99–100
Asheron's Call 6
assemblers 118
assembly languages 117–18
Atkins, S. 175
audience 93–6
audience-centric aesthetic properties
    99–100
autonomy argument 141, 143
avatar 3, 55
Axis and Allies 3
Ayer, A.J. 28–9, 158–9, 176

Bagge, Peter 164
Baghavad Gita 23
Baldur's Gate 109, 135
Baldur's Gate: Dark Alliance 65, 97
'Barbie' characters 65, 66
Batterman, Robert 179
Battlefield 52
Battlefield 1942 55, 64–5, 70
Battlefield Vietnam 63–4, 68
Beardsley, Monroe 96
beauty norms 68, 165–6
Beethoven, Ludwig van 98
belief: linguaform account 113–16;
    underdetermination of content 121–7
benign homuncularism 116–17,
    118–19
Bentham, Jeremy xi, 84
Berkeley, George 33–4, 44
Bible, The 78–81, 167–8
biological determinism 154, 181
Bioshock 93
Black and White 88, 89
Boeringer, S.B. 71
Boethius 167
Breakout! 91

Broken Sword 92, 99–100
Bush, George 2

Caesar, Julius 87
Call of Duty 30, 52, 63
Campbell, Joseph 180
Catechumen 63
categorical imperative 85–6, 90
Catherine the Great 87
Cave, Nick 70
censorship 52, 62; ESRB 52–3, 58, 62,
    63, 65, 162
Chalmers, David 12–13, 14, 46
children 60
Chomsky, Noam 119–21, 174, 178–9
Chrono Trigger 124
Church, Alonzo 131, 132
Church-Turing thesis 132
Church's thesis 132, 178–9
Civilization 73, 74–5, 82, 87, 88, 149
Clancy, Tom 64, 93
Clark, Andy 12–13, 14, 46
classical physics 134, 179
Clover, Carol J. 66–7
Clowes, Daniel 164
Clue 3
Cogburn, Emily Beck 162–3
cognitive interface 111
collective unconscious 138
colors 37–8
combinatorial syntax 113–14
comic books 62, 164
Command and Conquer 82
competence 120–1, 133
compilers 118
compositional expressions 124
compositional semantics 113–14, 174–5
computational paradox 112–13, 119,
    120, 121
Computational-Representational
    Understanding of Mind (CRUM)
    112–34, 179; competence 120–1,
    133; Fodorean mind as design team
    117–19; framelessness of action
    127–30; generativity 119, 133, 174,
    178; language of thought and benign
    homuncularism 116–17; limits of
    mechanized inference 130–3;
    linguaform account of belief and
    meaning 113–16; underdetermination
    of content 121–7
Conan the Barbarian 87
Constantine 50
content, underdetermination of 121–7

contradictions 80–1
Conway, John Horton 149–53, 154
Counterstrike 51
Crawford, Chris 175
Crichton, Michael 64
Crysis 52
Crystal Key, The 98, 180
Custer's Revenge 162
Cyc ontology 179

Dadlez, E.M. 69
Dance Dance Revolution 44
Darwin, Charles 151–3
David Copperfield (Dickens) 98
Day of Defeat 64
Death Race 162
decision theory 166
Deeper Blue 127–8
Deer Hunter 30
Dennett, Daniel 128–9, 153, 154
deontology 85–6, 88–9, 90
Descartes, René 8–9, 23, 158
description, knowledge by 114–15
design of video games 37, 134; ethical
    dilemmas and 83–90; Fodorean mind
    as design team 117–19
Destroy all Humans! 63
detachment 57–8
Diablo 93, 143
diagonalization 106, 171
dictators 73, 166
dictionaries 126, 175
diegetic world 26, 74, 109
different minds, argument from 26,
    38–9
Dill, Karen E. 59–60, 163
divine command theory 81–3, 168
Donkey Kong 65
Doom 23, 51, 63, 91, 97
Dostoyevsky, Fyodor 83–4
Double Dragon 65
Dragon Warrior 124
Dre, Dr 166
Dreyfus, Hubert 128
Duhem-Quine thesis 176
Dungeons and Dragons (*D & D*) 3, 4,
    14, 109
Dungeon Siege 118, 142
duotheism 166

Earth and Beyond 138
Easter eggs 164
Edwards, Alayne 1, 15, 139
Edwards, Chris 1, 15, 139

Elder Scrolls 109, 110, 112, 118, 135–6
Elder Scrolls Construction Set 118
Eliot, T.S. 108
Empire Earth 87, 149
emulation argument 52–5, 58
enactivism 21; empirical considerations in favor of the enactive theory 43–8; Noë's enactive theory of perception 38–42
Entertainment Software Ratings Board (ESRB) 52–3, 58, 62, 63, 65, 162
epics 92
epistemological skepticism 96
Equilibrium 62
Erikson, Steven 142, 172
Esslemont, Ian Cameron 172
ethical dilemmas 82–3; and game design 83–90; playability of 87–90
ethical norms 63–70
ethical systems 73–90; divine command theory 81–3, 168; games as practical theology 74–6; scriptural ethics 76–81
Euthyphro dilemma 82–3
Eve Online 138
Everquest 3, 138
evolution 123, 151–3
existentialism 146–9, 155
eXistenZ 22
extended mind thesis 13–14, 15–16, 46
extension 9
external world problem 33–8; empirical problem 33; philosophical problem 33–6
Extreme Paintball 97
eye of the mind 27, 31, 32–3, 117

F-properties (factual color properties) 40–2, 160
Facebook 15
fallibility, argument from 80–1
female characters 65–8; normalizing the outrageous 68–70
feminism 66–8
Feuerstein, Georg 71
fictional self 2–6
fictionalism 157; naïve 5–6, 141
films 22, 23, 33, 54, 111; final girl 66–7
Final Fantasy 145–6, 172
final girl 66–7
first-order logic 132–3, 175–6, 178
first-person shooters (FPSs) 39, 50–72
Fish, Stanley 99
Fisher, Helen 165
flexible adaptive behavior 112–13, 121

Flynt, Larry 164
focal point 29, 159
focusing 29–30, 33
Fodor, Jerry 116–17; Fodorean mind and game design 117–19
Foucault, Michel 141
frame problem 127–30
fraternity membership 71
Frederick the Great 87
free will 145
freedom 60–3, 148
Frege, Gottlob 131
Freudian psychoanalysis 122
frontal lobes 59, 164
function, human 143–6, 147, 153–4

Gaiman, Neil 142, 164
game master (GM) 4–5, 110
Game of Life 149–53, 154
Gandhi, Mahatma 89
Gears of War 39, 56, 57, 58, 63
general strategy 107, 108
generativity 119, 133, 174, 178
Ghost Recon 64
Gibson, James 160
Gibson, William 180
Glaucon 53
God 75–6, 90; divine command theory 81–3, 168
god games 73–90
Godfather, The 64
Gödel, Kurt 131, 132
Gödel numbering 131, 176–7
Gorgias 156
Gospel of Thomas 78
grammar 119, 120–1
Gran Turismo 39
Grand Theft Auto 50, 54–5, 70, 72, 91
Grand Theft Auto: San Andreas 164
graphical user interface 127
'great' leaders 87
greatest happiness principle 84–5, 86, 88–9
Grim Fandango 92, 97, 146
Guitar Hero 44, 45

Hacking, Ian 140–1
Half Life 51, 62
halting problem 105–7, 132–3, 171
Halo 63
happiness 143–4; greatest happiness principle 84–5, 86, 88–9
harm, avoidance of 84
Harry Potter 92, 138

haute couture 155
Hebert, Neal 157
hedonism xi-xii
Heidegger, Martin 33, 39–40, 147–8, 149, 180–1
Hensel, Al 181
'hero's journey' narrative 142–3
heuristics programming 128–9
Hexen 97
Hitchhiker's Guide to the Galaxy, A 120
Hitler, Adolf 87
Hobbes, Thomas xi
Hofstadter, Douglas 14, 157–8
Homer 53–4, 65, 92
Homeworld 97
homuncularism, benign 116–17, 118–19
homunculus: player and 31–3; player as 26–33
homunculus fallacy 31–2, 117
Hooligans 56, 72
Huizinga, Johan xi
human function 143–6, 147, 153–4
Hume, David 10, 60–1, 96–8
hunting, recreational 155
Huxley, Aldous 62

idealism 34–5
ideally competent speaker 120–1
identity criteria 1–2, 7–9
Iliad (Homer) 53–4, 65, 92
imitation 137
inconsistencies 80–1
individuation 139
inference 35–6, 129; limits of mechanized inference 130–3
interactive narratives 91–3, 107
interface: cognitive 111; graphical user interface 127; kinesthetic 17, 18; sensory 17, 111; visual 29–30; world-builder games 74–5
interpretation of scriptures 78–80
inverting eyeglasses 46–8

Jade Empire 135
James, William 111
Johnson, Samuel 126
Joust 98
Jung, C.J. 138–9, 142

Kant, Immanuel 85–6, 141
Kasparov, Gary 127–8
katharsis 55–6, 70
katharsis argument 55–8, 59–60

Kids in the Hall 40
kinesthetic interface 17, 18
King, Martin Luther, Jr 89
King's Quest 98
Kinoshita, Yoshiyuki 158
Knights of the Old Republic 92
knowledge by acquaintance 114
knowledge by description 114–15
knowledge of relations 36–8
Kohler, I. 46–7
Kveum, Stetson 156

Lacan, Jacques 174
language of thought 115, 173, 175; and benign homuncularism 116–17
'Lara Croft' 66, 67–8
law of non-contradiction 8
Leadership Secrets of Attila the Hun (Roberts) 87
Left Behind: External Forces 76–7, 81
left-to-right inverting eyeglasses 46–8
leisure 154–5
Lenant, Doug 179
level editors 118
lexical semantics 124–7
liar paradox xi, 156
liberty 60–3, 148
Lighthouse: The Dark Being 180
linguaform account of belief and meaning 113–16
literary competence 99
logic, first-order 132–3, 175–6, 178
Louis the Fourteenth 87
'Lucy' characters 65–6

machine code 117–18
machine language 117–18
macros 118
Madden Football 23, 30
Malazan 172
Mao Zedong 166
Mario Tennis 27
Martin, George R.R. 142
massively multiplayer online role playing games (MMORPGs) 3–4, 138
Mass Effect 93
Match.com 15
Matrix, The 22, 23, 62, 161
Max Payne 52, 57, 58, 69
Maya 118, 127
meaning: linguaform account of 113–16; word meaning 124–7

meaning of life 135–55; Aristotelian view 143–6, 153–4; existentialism 146–9, 155; *Game of Life* 149–53, 154; the games we choose 153–5; philosophical critique of role playing 137–43
mechanized inference, limits of 130–3
Medieval Total War 87
meditation 43, 161
menu-based RPGs 172
Messiah 62
metameric pairs 37–8, 159–60
Microsoft X Box 17, 18, 19, 42
military occupations 169
Mill, John Stuart xi, 61–2, 84
Miller, Rand 168, 181
Miller, Robyn 168, 181
Mind Forever Voyaging, A 22, 120
mind-independence argument 94–5
Monkey Island 146
Monopoly 3
monotheism 75–6
Montague, Richard 131, 174–5, 177
Moore, Alan 164
Moore, G.E. 94–5
moral character 50–72; empirical considerations 58–60; emulation argument 52–5, 58; ethical norms 63–70; *katharsis* argument 55–8, 59–60; liberty 60–3
Mori, Masahiro 172
Mortal Kombat 52, 55, 66
multiple personality disorder (MPD) 139, 140–1
multi-user dungeons 125
muscle memory 44–6
Mutt, Joe 164
MySpace 15
Myst 92–3, 107, 146–7

naïve fictionalism 5–6, 141
Napoleon 169–70
narrative structure 142–3
natural-language parsers 120, 174
natural selection 123, 151–3
Need for Speed Underground 65
neo-Humeanism 98–9
Nero 50
Neverwinter Nights 109
Nietzsche, Friedrich 137
Nintendo 64 xii
Nintendo Wii 17–22, 42, 48–9
Noë, Alva 29, 31, 37–8, 47; enactive theory of perception 38–42

non-contradiction, law of 8
non-player characters (NPCs) 4–5, 82, 110, 112
norms, ethical 63–70
Norvig, Peter 173
novelty 142
numbers 125–6, 131–2; Gödel numbers 131, 176–7
NWA 70, 166

objectivity argument 95–6
Oblivion 109, 110, 111, 112, 129, 172
Odyssey (Homer) 92
omnibenevolence 75–6, 83
omnipotence 75–6
omniscience 75–6
Orwell, George 62
Outlaw Golf 27
Outlaws! 63
outrageous, normalization of the 68–70

P-properties (perspectival properties) 40–2, 160
Pac-Man 91
pack mind 14, 158
paradox of the stone 76
Paranoia 3
Parfit, Derek 10–11
Parmenides 7–8
particular providence 90
paternalism 61–2
perception 17–49; and action 116; empirical considerations in favor of enactive theory 43–8; enactive theory of 21, 38–42; phenomenalism 20, 22–33, 43–4; problem of the external world 33–8
performance/competence distinction 120–1, 133
persona 138–9
personal identity 1–16; fictional self 2–6; spatially vague self 13–14; temporally vague self 6–13
Peter the Great 87
phenomenalism 20, 22–33, 43–4; and player as homunculus 26–33; and realism 27–30
Philip of Macedon 87
photorealism 23
Pitfall! 98
Plato 23, 82, 137, 162; violence in the arts 51–2, 53–4, 55, 58, 65
Playstation 17, 18, 42
Polar Express, The 111

polygons 37
PONG xii
Popescu, George 65
positive thinking 43–4, 161
possibilities 147
Postal 72
POW golfer myth 43, 161
practical knowledge 42
practical theology 74–6
Pratchett, Terry 142
predicate calculus 176
Primavera, La (Botticelli) 98
principle of utility 84–5, 86, 88–9
prior restraint 162
privileged perceptions 28–9
projection argument 78–80
propositional knowledge 40
propositions 115
psychological underdetermination
    problem 122–4
Pullum, Geoffrey 178
push-pin xi, 156
push-pull effect 38
Putnam, Hilary 175

Quine-Duhem problem 176

rational element 145
reader response school 99
readiness-to-hand 39–40
real-time world builder games 75
real-world robotics 130
realism 23, 48–9; ESRB rating system
    and 52–3; phenomenalism and 27–30;
    quest for greater realism and
    playability of ethical dilemmas 87–90;
    uncanny valley effect 110–11, 129,
    134, 172
recreational hunting 155
Red Dead Revolver 63
referential parts of speech 124
relativism 28, 159
relations, knowledge of 36–8
representational semantics 113–14
Resident Evil 57–8
Resistance: Fall of Man 161
response-based aesthetics 93–6
Return to Castle Wolfenstein 64
reversing lenses 46–8
Riven 148, 170
role playing games (RPGs) 1–6, 14–16,
    109–11, 124–5, 135–6; action RPGs
    109–11, 118, 120, 124–5;
    philosophical critique of role playing

137–43; role playing by the rules
    141–3
Roman Catholicism 167
Roman gladiators 50
Rome Total War 64, 75, 82, 88
Rome Total War: Barbarian Invasion 88
Rosser, J.B. 131–2
Rousseau, Jean-Jacques 87, 141
rules, role playing by the 141–3
Russell, Bertrand 23–6, 34–8, 131, 158;
    argument about knowledge of
    relations 36–8; linguaform account of
    belief and meaning 113–16; problems
    of philosophy argument 25–6, 35–6,
    40
Russia 169

Sartre, Jean-Paul 147–8, 181
scientific realism 35
scriptural ethics 76–81
Second Life 1, 15, 51, 67, 138, 139
self *see* personal identity
Sellars, Wilfrid 159
semantic underdetermination problem
    124–7
sensation 24
sense data 24, 28–9, 32–3, 34–5, 35–8;
    arguments for 25–6; language 115–16
sensory interface 17, 111
Serious Sam 56
Settlers, The 149
sexism 65–70
sexual dimorphism 67–8
Shakespeare, William 70, 93
Sheik, The 64
Ship, The 51
Shogun Total War 75
Siege Editor 118
Silent Scope 44
SimCity 73
similarity argument 11–12
Simlog 44–5
Sims, The 65–6, 89–90
Sims Online, The 15, 138
sleep 154
Smith, Peter 178
snapshot conception of vision 31
Snopes.com 43
social-networking websites 15
Socrates 53, 65, 82, 137
Soldier of Fortune 50–1, 55
Sony Playstation 17, 18, 42
Sophocles 55
Soul Plane 64

Space Bunnies Must Die! 97
Spain 169
Sparshott, Francis 162
spatially vague self 13–14
Splinter Cell: Chaos Theory 64
Stalin, Joseph 87, 166
Stephenson, Neil 171
Storytron 175
surface spectral reflectances (SSRs) 37–8, 159–60
Suzuki, D.Z. 48

tabletop RPGs 3–5, 14, 109–10
taste, standard of 96–107
temporally vague self 6–13
Tetris 13
text adventure games 120, 174
Thirteen 63
Thirteenth Floor, The 22
Thomas, Gospel of 78
thought 9; language of *see* language of thought
Tiger Woods PGA Tour '08 27
time 154–5
Tolkien, J.R.R. 142
Tomb Raider 66, 67, 68, 69
Top Secret 3
Top Spin 27
Total War 64, 75, 88
traditional RPGs 172
translation thesis 115–16, 126, 130
Traveler 3
tritheism 167
Tropico 73
truthiness 43–4
Turing, Alan 105, 113, 131, 132
Turing computable functions 103–5
Turing enumerability 104–5
Turing machines 100–7, 131, 171
'Turing test' 113
Turing's thesis 131
turn-based world builder games 74–5, 76
24 65, 165

Ultima 172
uncanny valley effect 110–11, 129, 134, 172

underdetermination of content 121–7; psychological 122–4; semantic 124–7
unhealthy psychic states 139
Universal Turing Machine 106
Unreal Tournament 51
utilitarianism 84–5, 86, 88–9

vague self 6–14, 15–16; spatially vague self 13–14; temporally vague self 6–13
Vietnam POW golfer myth 43, 161
Vinge, Vernor 14, 158
violence 50–63, 70–1, 71–2; empirical considerations 58–60; emulation argument 52–5, 58; *katharsis* argument 55–8, 59–60; liberty 60–3
visual interface 29–30
visualization 43–4
Vogler, Christopher 142
voluntarism 146
Von Neumann, John 131
Von Neumann computable procedures 132–3

walkthroughs 99–100
Wheeler, Michael 121, 130, 172
Whitehead, Alfred North 131
Wii 17–22, 42, 48–9
Wii Fit 17
Wii Sport 27; *Boxing* 18, 19, 21; *Golf* 19, 22, 43
Wilson, Edward 181
Wilson, Mark 124, 125
Wimsatt, W.K. 96
Wittgenstein, Ludwig xi, 125
Wolfenstein 3D 59–60, 63
women *see* female characters
word meaning 124–7
world builder games 73–90
World of Warcraft 3, 4, 14, 125, 135

X Box 17, 18, 19, 42
'Xena' characters 66
Xena: Warrior Princess 66
xenophobia 63–5

zero-player game 149–53
Zork 98, 120